Dr. Charles Va...
670 Wright Street
... MI 49250

W9-BZF-923

THE SUPPLY SIDE

Debating
Current Economic
Policies

Thomas R. Swartz
Frank J. Bonello
Andrew F. Kozak

University of Notre Dame

Dushkin Publishing Group, Inc.
Guilford, Connecticut 06437
ISBN: 0-87967-476-8

This book is dedicated to three outstanding teachers -

JOSEPH F. FLUBACHER LEONARD D. MALIET

LAWRENCE L. WATERS

and to seven expensive, but outstanding, kids -

MARY ELIZABETH   REBECCA JOURDAN
KAREN ANN   JOHN ANTHONY
JENNIFER LYNN   DAVID JOSEPH
            ANNE MARIE

STAFF

Jeremy Brenner   Managing Editor
Brenda Filley   Production Manager
Charles Vitelli   Designer
Libra VonOgden   Typesetting Coordinator
LuAnn Zukowsky   Copy Editor

Copyright ©1983 by the Dushkin Publishing Group, Inc., Guilford, CT. All rights reserved. No part of this book may be reproduced, stored or otherwise transmitted by any means—mechanical, electronic or otherwise—without written permission from the publisher.

Library of Congress Catalogue Card Number: 83-070925

Manufactured in the United States of America

First Edition; First Printing

Table of Contents

CREDITS

Chapter Two

Page 14. Reprinted by permission of *Harvard Business Review*. "The Moral Crisis in American Capitalism," by Robert Wuthnow, March/April 1982. Copyright ®1982 by the President and Fellows of Harvard College; all rights reserved.

Page 20. "Historical Origins of Supply-side Economics," by Robert Keleher, *Economic Review*, January 1982. Reprinted by permission of the Federal Reserve Bank of Atlanta.

Page 27. From, "Supply-side Economics: What Chance for Success?" by Aris Protopapadakis, *Business Review*, May/June 1981. Reprinted by permission of the Federal Reserve Bank of Philadelphia.

Page 32. From, "Return of the Economic Royalists," by Stephan Rousseas, *Challenge*, January/February 1982. Copyright ®1982. Reprinted by permission of M.E. Sharpe, Inc. Armonk, NY.

Page 36. From, "Waiting for Lenny," by Michael Kinsley. Copyright ®1982 by *Harper's* Magazine. Reprinted from the March 1982 issue by special permission.

Page 42. From, "Spring Fervor," TRB from Washington, *New Republic*, May 1982. Reprinted by permission of the *New Republic*. ®1982, the New Republic, Inc.

Page 44. From, "The Philosophy of Reaganism," by Emma Rothschild. Reprinted with permission of the *New York Review of Books*. Copyright ®1982 NYREV, Inc.

Page 47. From, *Economic Report of the President, 1982*.

Chapter Three

Page 51. From, "Taxes, Revenues, and the 'Laffer Curve,'" by Jude Wanniski, the *Public Interest*, Winter 1980. Reprinted by permission of the author. Copyright ®1978 by Jude Wanniski.

Page 59. From, *Program for Economic Recovery* and the *Economic Report of the President, 1982*.

Page 63. From, "The Social Consensus and the Conservative Onslaught," by John Kenneth Galbraith, *Millenium Journal of International Studies*, Spring 1981. Reprinted by permission of the author.

Page 69. From, "The Philosophy of Reaganism," by Emma Rothschild. Reprinted with permission of the *New York Review of Books*. Copyright ®1982 NYREV, Inc.

Page 73. From, "Reagan's Doubtful Game Plan," by Alfred Eichner, *Challenge*, May/June 1981. Reprinted by permission of M.E. Sharpe, Inc., Armonk, NY.

Page 75. From, *Economic Report of the President, 1982*.

Page 77. From, "Weidenbaum Analyzes Benefit-Cost Analysis," *Across the Board*, February 1982. Reprinted by permission of the Conference Board.

Page 83. From, "OSHA Hits Brown Lung Rules," *Dollars and Sense*, May/June 1982. Excerpted by permission of the Economic Affairs Bureau, Inc.

Page 88. From, "Poison at the EPA," *New Republic*, March 24, 1982. Copyright ®1982. Reprinted by permission of the New Republic, Inc.

Chapter Four

Page 93. From, *A Program for Economic Recovery*, 1981 and *Economic Report of the President, 1982*.

Page 101. From, "An Analysis of Modern-Day Unemployment: The Minimum Wage," by John F. Cogan. Delivered at the Hoover Institution January 11, 1982.

Page 105. From, "Government and the Rich," by Yale Brozen, *National Review*, July 9, 1982. Reprinted by permission of National Review, Inc. Copyright ®1982.

Page 109. From, "Welfare Dependency: Fact or Myth?" by Richard Coe, *Challenge*, September/October 1982. Copyright ®1982. Reprinted by permission of M.E. Sharpe, Inc., Armonk, NY.

Page 117. From, "Keeping Labor Lean and Hungry," by Francis F. Priven and Richard A. Cloward, *Nation*, November 1981. Copyright ® 1981. Reprinted by permission of the Nation.

Page 122. From, "The Price of Freedom: Defense Is Our Best Social Program," by Commander James P. Mullins, U.S.A.F. Delivered to the Iron Gate Chapter, Air Force Association, June 9, 1982.

Chapter Five

Page 134. From, "Taxes and Government Spending," Republican Party Platform, July 19, 1980. Copyright 1980. Reprinted by permission of Congressional Quarterly, Inc.

Page 137. From, "The 1982 Tax Bill: Toward Economic Recovery," by Ronald Reagan, August 16, 1982.

Page 140. From, "Do Deficits Matter?" by Lora Collins, *Across the Board*, April 1982. Reprinted by permission of the Conference Board, Inc. Copyright ®1982. All rights reserved.

Page 145. From, "How Not to Balance the Federal Budget," by William Nordhaus, *New York Times*, September 5, 1982. Copyright ®1982 by the New York Times. All rights reserved.

Page 149. From, "Where Volcker and Reagan Differ," by David Eastburn, *Forbes*, March 13, 1982. Copyright ®1982 by David Eastburn. Reprinted by permission of the author.

Page 151. From, "Monetarism Under Fire," *Dun's Business Review*, May 1982. Copyright ®1982. Reprinted by permission of Dun and Bradstreet, Inc.

Page 155. From, "Reaganism Is Working," by Beryl Sprinkel, *Challenge* July/August 1982. Copyright ®1982. Reprinted by permission of M.E. Sharpe, Inc., Armonk, NY.

Page 160. Reprinted from the August 24, 1981 issue of *Business Week* by special permission. Copyright ®1981 by McGraw-Hill, Inc., New York, New York. All rights reserved.

Page 165. From, "Gold Standard," *Economic Report of the President*, Council of Economic Advisors, 1982.

Chapter Six

Page 170. From, "The Roots of the American Public Philosophy," by William Schambra, *Public Interest*, Spring 1982. Copyright ®1982. Reprinted by permission of National Affairs, Inc.

Page 179. From, "Federalism," *OMB Major Themes and Additional Budget Debate, Fiscal Year 1983*. Office of Management and Budget, 1982.

Page 185. From, "The Idea of the Nation," by Samuel H. Beer, *New Republic*, July 19 & 26, 1982. Copyright ®1982. Reprinted by permission of the New Republic, Inc.

Page 194. From, "The War on the Poor," by Nick Kotz, *New Republic*, March 24, 1982. Copyright ®1982. Reprinted by permission of the New Republic, Inc.

Chapter Seven

Page 202. From, "Thatcherism," by David Hale, *Across the Board*, December 1981. Copyright ®1981. Reprinted by permission of the Conference Board, Inc.

Page 210. From, "Mrs. Thatcher's First Year," by James Bishop, *Illustrated London News*, May 1980. Copyright ®1980. Reprinted by permission of the Illustrated London News and Sketch, Ltd., London England.

Page 218. From, "A Report on Margaret Thatcher's Progress—by Hayek and Friedman," by David Dimbleby, *Across the Board*, July/August 1981. Reprinted by permission of the Conference Board, Inc. and the *Listener*, London, England.

Page 223. From, "Mrs. Thatcher's Economic Policy in Practice," by Terry Ward, *Journal of Post Keynesian Economics*, Summer 1982. Reprinted by permission of the Journal of Post Keynesian Economics. Copyright ®1982. All rights reserved.

Page 231. From, "Supply-Side Economics: Growth versus Income Distribution," by Kenneth Jameson, *Challenge*, November/December 1980. Copyright ®1980. Reprinted by permission of M.E. Sharpe, Inc. Armonk, NY.

Preface

The election of Ronald Reagan to the presidency of the United States in November 1980 marked a dramatic shift to the right in political power. His election also marked an equally dramatic shift to the right in economic policy. This new economic policy focused upon actions designed to impact the supply side of the economy in the hope that the economy's ability to produce goods and services would greatly increase. During his first year in office, President Reagan and his administration worked diligently to make this new economic policy a reality. This diligence was rewarded. Nearly every major element of his program became the "law of the land" with the passage of the Omnibus Budget Reconciliation Act and the Economic Recovery Tax Act in 1981.

What was the logic underlying this sharp redirection in economic policy? Why was it, and why has it remained, so bitterly opposed? These questions are addressed in this book. We have chosen to let the participants in this economic debate speak for themselves. Ronald Reagan, his Council of Economic Advisors, and other members of his administration propose, explain, and defend this new economic policy. The liberal critics and occasional conservative who raise their voices in opposition are also represented. We think we have included the principal components of this debate. We leave it to you the reader to assess these positions. Carefully examine the logic they employ. Try to keep in perspective the passionate pleas of both sides. But do work your way through this book: The policies that are discussed may alter the very character of public policy for the remainder of this century.

This book, like most books, would not have been written were it not for the encouragement and help of friends and co-workers. Our Dean, Robert E. Burns, set the project in motion by sending T.R. Swartz off to London so that he could look at Thatcherism first-hand. Our chairperson, Charles K. Wilber, provided a little release time and a bit of summer research support. And our editorial advisor at the Dushkin Publishing Group, Jeremy Brenner, cleared all the remaining obstacles and made it possible for us to complete the manuscript in record time. Lastly, we must mention our secretarial help, Ms. Cheryl Reed and Ms. Sandra Tengblad, who typed repeated drafts of this work and never complained about our tortured handwriting.

T.R.S.
F.J.B.
A.F.K.

Introduction

"Most of the Change We Think We See in Life Is Due to Truths Being in and out of Favor"
Robert Frost
Black Cottage (1914)

Like Robert Frost's "truths," supply-side economics in the 1980s represents "economic truths" that have been "in and out of favor." Economists, lawyers, shopkeepers and even presidents have rediscovered these truths. They have re-found a set of solutions to solve the most pressing problem that this society or any society must face: *scarcity.* Whatever its merit or lack of merit, supply-side economics, with its unique view of the world and its apparent widespread acceptance, promises to change the way policy planners address this problem. This is a change that will affect each and every one of us. This is a change that deserves our most careful attention.

Even though supply-side economics, as practiced by the Reagan administration, may continue to encounter some hard times in the implementation and exercise of its policies, supply-side theoreticians and practitioners have been successful in moving the economics profession to the right. This, in turn, has laid the foundation to move U.S. domestic policy to the right. Ten years ago newspaper reporters, magazine columnists and television commentators tended to ignore the conservative supply-side perspective. These makers of public opinion focused upon Keynesian demand-management solutions. Today, many of these same individuals embrace the economic prescriptions of the supply-siders. Even the "nonbelievers" who continue to reject these prescriptions feel obliged to at least mention them as possible alternatives. Given this intense public exposure, does anyone question the impact these "economic truths" will have on public policy for the remainder of this century?

But what is supply-side economics? What changes will it bring to our lives? Who will benefit from these changes? Who will lose? These are some of the important questions that are debated in this book. The readings that you will encounter have been carefully chosen to offer a fair, honest and, we hope, balanced view of supply-side economics. We have attempted to examine and critique the major issues found in supply-side economics from the perspective of its supporters and its critics. Thus, we hope you don't find us telling you in this book what is "right." We hope you do, however, find the basis to determine what is "right" for you.

What Is Supply-Side Economics?

Supply-side economics is one branch of conservative economics. Indeed, the supply-side economists of the 1980s like to think of themselves as the modern day standard-bearers of Adam Smith's 18th century classical economics. As we note on the pages of this book, other groups of conservative economists also lay claim to this high honor. But putting aside the differences that are found among conservative economists for the moment, there are many points on which they agree. Not the least is the *primacy of the individual.* Society, we are reminded, is the sum of its individuals. Individuals should be free to act and, in the process of acting freely, they should determine the answers to the three questions that arise from the existence of scarcity:

a) What should society produce?
b) How should society produce it?
c) Who should get what society produces?

For the conservative economist, it is the free choice of the individual which drives the economic system. Thus supply-side economics represents a rejection of the 20th century philosophy that promotes collective choice (governmental action) as the means of achieving a just society. Since collective choice as the means to this important end is rejected, the size and the influence of the government sector must be reduced while the size and the influence of individual decision-making is expanded. Thus, in the phraseology of the supply-siders, "the economy is returned to the people."

In more formal economic terms, this increased dependence upon individual decision-making represents a revival of traditional microeconomic choice theory—the use of good old supply and demand. This amazingly simple but incredibly useful theoretical apparatus is returned to a place of honor in the evaluation of the pros and cons of various private and public programs. This represents a dramatic shift away from practices which have become popular since the New Deal days of the Roosevelt administration. During that 50-year span when conservative economics was "out of favor," individual choices were suppressed in attempts to generate sophisticated macroeconomic models—models which focused upon aggregate income flows such as total investment, the growth of Gross National Product, or the extent of personal saving. In practical terms, for the student of economics, the reawakening of this sleeping giant will mean more attention must be paid to the microeconomic lessons taught by Alfred Marshall in his 1890 *Principles of Economics* (the book which first presented a unified supply and demand analysis) and less attention paid to the macroeconomic lessons taught by John M. Keynes in his 1935 *General Theory* (the book which first challenged classical economics and laid the foundation for government action to control aggregate demand).

Within this microeconomic context, the supply-siders' assault against the Keynesian "demand manipulators" is summarized in a rather simple axiom:

You get more of something by taxing it less;
You get less of something by regulating it more.

What the supply-siders are saying is that government in its role as a tax collector and/or regulator interferes with the operation of the private market. These interferences, whether they are the result of tax/subsidy schemes or the by-product of government regulation, distort and change the natural market results, and in the process these programs introduce *disincentive effects* into the economic system. Because of the widespread "tinkering" of the Federal government in the postwar years, these disincentive effects are found in every nook and cranny within the economic system. However, they are most obvious and most costly when they raise their ugly heads in the labor market arena or in the savings/investment sector of the economy.

A few examples might serve to highlight the concerns of the supply-siders. For the moment, consider the disincentives that are found in our labor markets. The supply-siders would argue that if you are worried about "absenteeism," "excessive tardiness," "goofing-off on the job," "dropping out," "low skills/no skills," etc., the solution is there for the taking: *tax the workers' income less.* That is, if your policy objective is to increase the output of workers, the workers must receive adequate reward for their work effort. This can be easily accomplished by reducing the tax liability associated with that work effort. This increased reward will have a double incentive effect: the workers' after-tax income increases, causing the workers to increase their work effort, and the cost of leisure increases, which will also cause the workers to increase their work effort.[1]

Now let's change the arena and assume that your policy objective is to increase the amount of investment in the community, with the hope that this increased investment will lead to future economic growth. Again, tax reductions are the appropriate policy for the supply-side advocate. A lower tax rate for investment income should result in more investment activity. Again, you build in an incentive to have people save and invest—much like our example of taxes on work effort. However, there is yet another way to look at this incentive effect: reducing taxes on the income earned from investments means that a whole new group of investments are now profitable. As these now-profitable investments are undertaken, society's capacity to produce goods and services, earn income, and enjoy an increased standard of living is expanded.

Even in these simple examples it is easy to see how a tax reduction can lower the economic cost of a desirable activity (work, investment) and, as a by-product, increase the cost of an undesirable activity (idleness, hoarding). Increasing the cost of an undesirable activity can also be done directly through taxation. For example, if your policy goal is to directly attack idleness, supply-side advocates would ask you to examine the economic incentives associated with unemployment compensation and numerous welfare programs. The current programs effectively decrease the cost of idleness.

Thus, following supply-side logic, if you wish to foster work incentives, the public sector should reduce or eliminate these subsidies for non-work. Simply put, this would increase the cost of not working and, after an adjustment period, this microeconomic policy would lead to an increase in work effort.

How practical are these arguments? Have they been tried before? If they have been implemented before, what were the consequences? These are important issues which are addressed by this book.

Key Issues in Supply-Side Economics

In order to achieve the important objective of balance with regard to the questions raised by the supply-siders, it is often necessary to compare and contrast the supply-side

1 This latter point may not be immediately obvious to the uninitiated student of economics. But consider a worker who is offered a chance to work an hour of overtime on a Friday afternoon and earn $10. If there were no tax on his work effort and he turned down the overtime to go have a beer with his friends, that one single hour of leisure would cost him $10. That's rather expensive leisure. Now consider the more realistic case where his work effort is subject to taxes. If his tax rate was 25 percent, what after-tax income does this worker have to forgo to go have a beer with his friends? You've got it: $7.50. That's still an expensive beer, but it's not as expensive as $10. What is the cost of that one hour of leisure when his tax rate is 30, 40, or 50 percent? The higher the tax rate, the lower the cost of leisure, and the more leisure is substituted for work effort.

economic policies with those which are offered by the post-World War II liberal establishment. This does not mean that there is now a consensus among the various conservative groups as to the appropriateness of individual policy recommendations. Where and how the supply-siders part ways with their fellow conservatives in North America is also highlighted in this book. One last comparison is necessary. This is a comparison of the U.S. experience under the leadership of President Reagan with those experiments of supply-side economics currently underway in other parts of the world— most notably in England under Prime Minister Margaret Thatcher and in Chile under the leadership of General Augusto Pinochet. Although these experiences with supply-side economics do not always attract widespread news coverage in the North American press, they represent experiments which are of longer standing than the relatively short-lived North American policies.

Capitalism

In order to fully appreciate the debate over supply-side economics, one must understand the basic mechanisms of a capitalist economy. Chapter 1 reveals the logical underpinnings of a capitalist economy while also pointing out the distinct features of a market system which separate it from other economic systems. In addition, it also elucidates the conservative/liberal argument over the proper role for government in a free market economy. Is there too much government involvement? Too little? Is government involvement a necessary evil to insure an equitable economic system? These and other related issues are also addressed in this first chapter.

The Foundations

Chapter 2 outlines the importance and significance of the historical circumstances surrounding the modern day development of supply-side economics. In particular, Chapter 2 traces the rise of 18th century libertarianism and demonstrates how this philosophic tradition of individualism was manifested 200 years later in the practical political/economic policies of the North American supply-siders. The readings in this section outline the history of supply-side economics and trace the development from the early work of philosophers such as David Hume and economists like Adam Smith, David Ricardo and J.B. Say. It moves through the "dark days of Keynesianism" and concludes with the triumphant return of supply-side economics that is associated with the election of Ronald Reagan. In short, Chapter 2 examines the historical connections between philosophy, economics and social/political policy.

The Mechanics of the North American Supply-Side Experiment

In Chapters 3, 4, 5 and 6 the book then turns to a detailed discussion of supply-side economic policy and theory. Each major policy area and its theoretical foundations are carefully analyzed:

  (i) tax policy/government regulation;
 (ii) domestic social programs and military expenditures;
(iii) budget deficits and monetary policy; and
(iv) decentralization through a "New Federalism."

The supply-side advocates find government action in these areas to be directly related to the sluggish performance of the U.S. economy throughout the decade of the 1970s. They anticipate that the reforms inspired by supply-side economics will eliminate this sluggishness by dramatically increasing productivity. Opposition, of course, is loud and clear. Some maintain that this is nothing more than "voo-doo economics"—that is, the prescriptions written by the supply-siders will only work for "true believers" since there is no substance to the economics underlying the policies. A number of other critics assert that some impact on economic output and growth will result from these policies but that this will come at a very high cost to those who can least afford it: the poor. That is, many see the cost of implementing supply-side economics as a loss of equity in the system. This "trade-off between equity and efficiency" thus attracts much attention in this critical section of the book.

Also of particular importance in this section is the discussion of budgets and budget deficits. One efficient way to evaluate the impact of the policies that have been implemented by the supply-siders in the U.S. is to examine the budget proposals that were adopted. This is undertaken in Chapters 4 and 5. This analysis provides the reader with a glimpse of the future. What role will government play? What is expected from business, private individuals and charitable organizations? These are major concerns that are debated in these chapters.

In addition to these questions, Chapter 5 raises a related fundamental issue: Will these budgets result in deficits? If so, what impact will these deficits have on the health of the overall economy and on its parts—business firms and family members? And just as important, what is the proper monetary policy in the face of deficits? There is probably no other issue associated with supply-side economics which is more misunderstood than the question of budget deficits. We hope that in this chapter you will find some answers to the questions that seem to be raised everyday by the news media.

International Experiences with Supply-Side Economics

Too often we are led to believe that it is only the U.S. that is intent upon reforming the liberal-based Keynesian public policy. This is a misleading perception. The Tory government in England, led by Prime Minister Margaret Thatcher is one of the most forceful advocates of supply-side policies. Although the British experiment differs in significant ways from the North American version, they share many basic characteristics. How do they differ? How are they alike? What has been the effect of these policies in another developed economy? The final chapter of this book will examine international experience with supply-side, and draw some conclusions for our own outlook.

Some Concluding Comments

We think this book presents a balanced view of supply-side economics. We think it provides a basis to understand better the important theoretical and practical implications of this phenomenon that is sweeping not only the U.S. but governments in the Western world.

Whatever you as an individual think of supply-side economics—whether you think it is "good" or "bad"—the fact of the matter is that it is going to be around for some time to come. It is not a flash in the pan. It is not a truth destined to soon be "out of favor" and forgotten. The basic tenets of this policy have been too widely accepted to suffer such a fate or to be dismissed as a fad. Regardless of its short-run achievements or lack of achievements, we can be certain that at least parts of this integrated set of theories and policies will remain. For this reason alone, this book which presents the views of the supporters and the critics of supply-side economics is of value. It provides the reader with a tool to discern whether or not supply-side economics is a "revolution in our own time."

Since we live in a democracy, we have the privilege and the responsibility of shaping our destiny; we must learn of this "revolution." We as voters must decide whether this is "good" or "bad." We mustn't let this important decision be left to whim or fancy. It is too important.

CHAPTER 1

Capitalism and Supply-Side Economics

Introduction

If asked to describe in a single word the type of political and economic policies that are endorsed by President Reagan and his administration, most would probably characterize them as "conservative." If these same persons were pushed and asked to define "conservative" they would probably indicate that it is the belief that the role of government in modern society, particularly in the economic realm, should be reduced and seriously limited.

These responses would, of course, be accurate. The policies of the Reagan administration are conservative policies. They represent an attempt to limit the role of government in accordance with that familiar conservative philosophy: "the government which governs least, governs best." But it must be remembered that this conservative philosophy is not universally accepted. It is challenged, and challenged rigorously. Much of this opposition comes from the "liberal" community. In contrast to the conservatives, liberals maintain that government action can be taken, indeed must be taken, to remedy the abuses and inequities that arise in a social order which relies exclusively or predominantly on individual action. Rather than viewing government as a coercive force that usurps individual freedoms and smothers individual initiatives, liberals see government action as a necessary force which promotes a more just and humane society. This, then, is the gist of the conservative-liberal debate in its broadest terms.

What is less obvious is why this particular brand of conservative economics, called supply-side economics, is so warmly embraced by the conservatives and attacked so vociferously by liberals. To understand this requires both an appreciation of capitalism as an economic system and an appreciation of the specifics of supply-side economics.

Capitalism

All societies from the most primitive societies found in certain parts of East Africa and Australia to the technologically advanced societies of Eastern and Western Europe must develop an economic system to deal with the reality of that fundamental economic problem of *scarcity*. Consumption priorities must be set. Production schedules and techniques must be decided upon. And that critical question of the distribution of output must be settled. There are many ways to address these three issues of *"what," "how,"* and *"for whom to produce."* In North America, Western Europe, Japan and certain parts of the developing world, society has decided to answer these questions with *markets*, that is, by developing an economic system that we call *capitalism*.

Two features combine to give capitalism its unique character, which clearly distinguishes it from alternative economic systems. The first is that the factors of production—natural resources, capital equipment and even one's own labor power—are privately owned. Capitalism thus extends the notion of personal property rights to include the goods and services that are the outputs of productive activity as well as the inputs of productive activity. The second critical feature of capitalism is that the means of production are privately controlled. The owner of a factory is free to use that factory in any way he or she wishes, to produce what they wish in whatever way they wish to produce it.

The presence of individual ownership and individual control provides the residents of capitalist countries with a great deal of economic freedom. But even though certain individuals are benefitted by capitalism, the question remains: does it work to the benefit of the larger society? The advocates of capitalism answer with an emphatic yes. Their positive response is based upon the notion of "a harmony of interests in society." That is, individuals driven by their self-interest will produce those things most wanted by society, they will produce them in the most efficient fashion, and they will distribute those things to those who are most willing to buy them. In other words, self-interested individual action results in the production of those goods and services that society wants the most at the least possible cost. Thus, capitalism is an efficient/equitable economic system. No one person or elite group of persons determines what will be produced, how it will be produced or who will get it. Everyone in society has a direct input into the determination of these basic economic questions. Again, most importantly, this system which maximizes society's total gain is also totally consistent with the attempt of individuals to maximize their private gain.

Nonetheless, the possibility of gross abuse and exploitation of individuals poses a distinct problem for any society which fosters such unfettered individualism. For example, suppose that the producer, while producing what society wants, charges an excessively high price or pays labor an excessively low wage. What in capitalism, where self-interest is the prime motivator, prevents the producers from exploiting other individuals? The free market advocate certainly would not turn to government with its price ceilings or minimum wages. Rather, the champions of capitalism maintain that competition from other producers will discipline those who would abuse their position. If a product is produced by a single firm and that firm charges an exorbitant price, then the act of charging that exorbitant price will result in an excessive or above normal profit. Other firms which produce other products and earn only normal profits will become aware of this situation. It is in their self-interest to transfer the factors of production that they own and control to the production of this over-priced good. This will increase the supply of that product and, under most circumstances, this will in turn lead to a decrease in price as the new firms compete with the old firm. With the fall in price the excess profits will evaporate. In short, for the conservative, competition is the answer to the possible abuses and excesses which unbridled self-interest might create.

Considering the fact that individual freedom is the bulwark of conservative philosophical thought, it is not surprising that an economic system which idealizes individual self-interest, private ownership and control would be the choice of conservatives. Combining this philosophical and economic perspective inevitably results in the perception that any action of the state is primarily coercive in nature and an intrusion on the rights of individuals. As conservatives see it, the state should not be in the position of dictating to the individuals in society. The state should not impose political beliefs, mandate religious behavior, or arrogate decision-making power in the economic sphere. Individuals can fulfill their true human potential only by actions taken thoughtfully and freely. In accordance with this framework, capitalism offers to eliminate, or at least to reduce to an absolute minimum, state involvement in economic affairs. For conservatives, economic freedom is to capitalism what political freedom is to democracy. Thus conservatives view themselves as the only true supporters of democracy, since many argue that political freedom is not sustainable without economic freedom.

This is not to say that modern capitalist society must be completely without government involvement in the economic arena. Even conservatives with extreme views recognize some legitimate economic functions of government. For example, the state must see to the provision of an orderly supply of money; the state must provide for the provision of certain public goods such as national defense, a highway system and other forms of social overhead capital (bridges, dams, harbors); and the state must establish a legal code and establish a mechanism to enforce these laws. In those rare instances of "natural monopolies," where competition is not possible, the state must provide regulation to ensure against abuses. The state must also provide for those who, through no fault of their own, may be unable to provide for themselves. Finally, in order to provide these services, some level of taxation must be imposed by the state. The difficulty is where and how to draw the line between what is a proper government function and what is an improper government function. This is a question which separates extreme conservatives from their more moderate colleagues and conservatives from liberals. Take, for example, the social consumption of public goods. A public good is a good whose benefits are enjoyed by one individual without reducing or restricting the benefits which are enjoyed by others. Such goods are unlikely to be produced by a pure capitalist society because a potential consumer will be unwilling to buy the good. Instead the individual will wait for his or her neighbor to buy it and obtain the benefits of the good through the neighbor's consumption. Everyone, conservatives and liberals alike, see national defense as a public good, although they may disagree on how much national defense we need. But the real problems arise when we ask what else constitutes a public good. Should the government be responsible for a clean environment? Should it own and manage our postal service? Are we satisfied with our education system? Is that education system weak because it is run by the government? Therefore, we can see that even if conservatives and liberals agree that some functions of government are legitimate in a capitalist economy, there is much disagreement on the degree to which government should be involved and the specifics of its involvement. Conservatives call for a limited governmental role. Where government action is necessary, this role should be consistent with capitalism's market-oriented focus (a voucher system for education, the marketing of property rights for pollution control, a volunteer army). Liberals, on the other hand, see violations of equity and long-run costs involved with employing some of these market devices, and consequently they argue for greater direct government action and the use of policies which do not necessarily mirror the market mechanism.

At this juncture we should note yet another related issue which separates conservatives from liberals. Liberals are quick to concede that capitalism offers many advantages, especially in the areas of individual freedom and economic efficiency. Indeed, most liberals are quite market-oriented themselves. However, they believe that the price paid for this freedom and efficiency is at times too high. This price is the presence of significant degrees of inequality in the distribution of income and wealth. The rules of the capitalist game require that those who make large contributions to economic well being be compensated with large rewards. The problem, as liberals see it, is that once having achieved a position of wealth, an individual may be able to maintain and even enhance his or her position without any further economic effort. That is, once wealth is acquired it can be used to buy the best in education, in medical care, in legal advice (in justice?), and in economic expertise. Clearly from this perspective individuals do not start off on an equal footing and the distance between rich and poor, even if both are experiencing an improvement in their economic conditions, is likely to increase over time. Because of this characteristic of capitalism, liberals believe that government actions must go beyond providing some minimal level of well being for people unable to care for themselves. Rather, government must pursue a policy designed to provide equal opportunity for all by actively redistributing income and wealth to compensate for the inherent tendency of capitalism to generate a concentration of economic power. The conservative reply to this is that such redistributive action by government not only restricts economic freedom, it reduces economic incentives and, as a result, the driving force which improves the well being of both rich and poor may be lost. This disagreement over equity and efficiency is fundamental to the arguments between conservatives and liberals and, as will be shown, to their positions on supply-side economics.

Supply-Side Economics

It must be remembered that supply-side economics is not "the" conservative economics; it is one brand of conservative economics. It does, however, share the same historic tradition and the same basic concerns of the more traditional conservative economics. That is, conservative economics is generally directed toward limiting or reducing the economic role of government and, in those areas where government action is necessary, to use policies which are most consistent with the maintenance of economic freedom. Indeed, after years of New Deals, New Frontiers, and Great Societies, conservatives have rebelled. Most now argue that it is no longer a question of limiting the growth of government involvement, but rather it is a question of reducing the economic role of government. They believe that if the conservative ideal is to the right and the liberal view to the left, then liberal actions have pushed the economy too far to the left. Therefore, by reducing the government's involvement in the economy, the economy will move to the right and come closer to the conservative ideal. This, in turn, will restore a greater degree of economic freedom and reinstill economic incentives.

The North American experiment with supply-side economics is a case in point. Although President Reagan has been able to distance himself from his political rivals on the right by emphasizing his support for the new supply-side economics, in reality many of the specific Reagan economic policies are standard conservative prescriptions. One such policy, long advocated by the conservative camp, calls for a reduction in the rate of growth in Federal government spending. This is quite consistent with the general conservative position. Reductions in government spending, even if the reductions are only in relative terms and not in an absolute sense, will reduce the extent of government involvement in the economy. Here two points should be noted. First, it must be remembered that the Reagan administration has called for a reduction in the rate of growth in Federal government spending, not a reduction in the number of dollars spent by the Federal government. Second, within the total aggregate of Federal government spending, some categories of spending will experience actual dollar cuts, some will remain constant, others will grow moderately and a few categories will grow quite rapidly. These changes in the composition of spending are also consistent with the general spirit of conservatism. As we have noted, the provision of national defense is seen as a legitimate concern of government and this category of spending is slated for rapid increases—while social programs such as unemployment compensation, Aid to Families with Dependent Children and food stamps, which are viewed by conservatives as impediments to individual incentives to work, are spending categories which are scheduled to be reduced.

A second key element of the Reagan economic program is described as a "far-reaching program of regulatory relief." Once again, this is a strategy which is most obviously in accord with the traditional conservative view. Actually this general policy objective is composed of a variety of specific actions. These include an attempt to: (i) relax environmental and safety standards; (ii) use a more rigorous application of cost-benefit analysis in the evaluation of regulatory activity; (iii) employ market-type regulatory devices (pollution charges or taxes) rather than the establishment of minimum standards of performance; and (iv) foster and allow business mergers. Again, each of these specific actions result in a reduction in the involvement of government in the economy.

A third policy element, and the policy which is perhaps the most uniquely supply-side in nature, is the administration's attempts to reduce taxes. Reductions in taxes are consistent with the conservative view in two distinct ways. First, taxes divert resources away from families and firms and toward the public sector. This reduces economic freedom. Since economic freedom is held in very high regard by conservatives, they are avid supporters of tax reduction. Second, many conservatives maintain that the real benefit to reductions in taxes is that it will force an even greater cut in government spending and this, in turn, will lead to a lesser role for government in the economy.

Although conservatives generally support tax reductions, it is the way in which the Reagan tax reduction is structured that gives it its unique supply-side flavor. Rather than reduce the average tax rate by increasing personal exemptions, providing tax rebates, or allowing for a larger amount of tax-free income, the Reagan tax reform reduces marginal tax rates[1] on personal income. That is, this tax reduction plan is structured in a way that is intended to increase incentives to work. It is asserted that, by reducing marginal tax rates, the strongest possible incentive effects would be generated and that these incentives would encourage people to both work longer and harder and to invest more and more often.

The fourth element in the Reagan economic program is the "New Federalism." This program involves a realignment of responsibilities between the Federal government, on the one hand, and state and local governmental units on the other. Overall it is seen by the Reagan administration as a reduction in the scope of the Federal government with increased responsibilities for state and local governments, particularly in the area of public welfare. The policy is again consistent with basic conservative philosophy. As it has been stressed, conservative economists maintain that the market should be replicated wherever possible. When the market can't be replicated, attempts should be made to come as close as possible to market conditions. Thus, when government activity is necessary, that government activity should be undertaken as close to individual consumers/voters as possible. Free market advocates argue that at the Federal level it is more difficult for individuals to exercise control over governmental activities, while at the local level citizens can more clearly see what government is doing, more clearly evaluate the effectiveness of governmental actions, and, in general, act more like a functioning market by making government actions conform more closely to the needs of the individuals in a particular area. This last point is also consistent with the conservative emphasis on efficiency. A program or policy made at the Federal level is unlikely to fit the exact needs of all the diverse areas of the country. By initiating these programs and developing those policies at the local level, they will better service the needs of the people.

---

1   The marginal tax rate is the rate applied to particular increments or brackets of income.—Eds.

The fifth and final element of the Reagan program can be traced to the monetarist faction of the conservative camp. This policy is designed to assure a slower and more stable growth in the money supply. This policy is most consistent with conservatism since it makes government, or more specifically the monetary authority, a passive rather than an active economic force. Moreover, given this passive governmental role, private sectors will have greater weight in shaping important monetary and financial variables such as interest rates and the allocation of credit.

These, then, are the five major themes of the North American experiment with supply-side economics. The five components can all be considered a part of a supply-side strategy because they are all designed to improve the productive or "supply" side of the economy. As such, and because they are designed to return economic power to the private sector—thereby increasing economic freedom—these five components are all consistent with the traditional conservative economic philosophy.

But just as there continues to be disagreement about the desirability of a pure capitalist society (and, therefore, on the extent to which government should be involved with the economy), there is disagreement regarding the specific policies promulgated by the modern day supply-siders in North America. There is first the practical objection raised by the liberals: a reduction in the role of the government means a return to old inequities, a sacrifice of compassion. In addition to this general objection there are a number of very specific criticisms which come from a variety of sources. One group criticizes U.S. monetary proposals because it may mean high interest rates and prolonged bouts of unemployment for large numbers of individuals. Other groups object to the changes in government spending which result in severe cuts in social programs and a rapid rise in defense spending. Critics of the regulatory reform proposals point out that the progress made in environmental protection and worker safety will be reversed, and the new attitude toward business mergers will result in less competition. As for the tax reductions, two specific charges are heard most frequently. First, some maintain that the incentive effects of the reductions in marginal tax rates are likely to be very weak. Second, others assert that the structure of the tax rate reductions is weighted too heavily in favor of the rich. The complaints regarding the New Federalism include the charge that it is merely another way of achieving a dismantling of social programs. Lastly, if the attention paid to it by the media is a measure, there is a widespread concern with budget deficits. Many argue that the Reagan administration's actions have been poorly timed and that this poor timing has generated or at least contributed to the very large Federal government budget deficits that are currently experienced.

Thus there is no deficiency of controversy concerning supply-side economics. Both supporters and detractors are equally loud in voicing their concern.

CHAPTER 2

Philosophical, Historical and Economic Foundations of Supply-Side Economics

Those who are not truly committed to supply-side economics or to another variant of "economic conservatism," typically take the marketplace for granted. These non-believers treat the market as one more convenient way to allocate or distribute the goods and services that are produced in the productive sector of the economy. For these individuals, this allocation mechanism is judged to be "good" if it allocates resources efficiently and equitably, "bad" if it allocates resources inefficiently and inequitably.

But markets are more than just a means by which resources are allocated. Rather, markets allow individuals to express their economic freedom in much the same way as democracy allows individuals to express their political freedom. Thus, the conservative economist argues that if personal freedom is to be maintained, markets must be preserved. Unlike planned economies, market economies are driven by the power of individual decisions. Only in this system is an individual allowed to shape his or her own destiny. Indeed, these individual decisions, those of consumers and those of producers, make up the "Invisible Hand" that drives our economic system for the benefit of the whole of society.

The importance of markets as part of an integrated system that fosters the development of individual freedom is well articulated by Robert Wuthnow in his essay entitled "The Moral Crisis in American Capitalism." Wuthnow, author of the *Consciousness Revolution*, traces the logical connections between capitalism and democracy. He argues that the market "provided one of the few arenas in modern society in which people have an opportunity to participate directly in public life." Indeed, for Wuthnow the market is that place where "one can discharge . . . his or her moral responsibilities to society."

DEMOCRACY AND CAPITALISM

Robert Wuthnow, *Harvard Business Review,* March/April 1982

Periods of economic uncertainty inevitably provoke questions about the vitality of America's economic system. Today, of course, inflation, unemployment, and lagging productivity inspire debate about the efficiency of the market system itself. But for Americans, at least, a market-based economy means something more than just the exchange of goods and services at prices determined by levels of supply and demand. True, the market system as Americans understand it differs from economies dependent on barter or central planning, but this is the market in just its narrow economic sense. In American culture, the market carries additional significance.

Whether we acknowledge it consciously or not, the market influences our basic values, helps shape our suppositions about reality, and figures centrally in our tacit assumptions about daily life. We invest the market with moral importance and associate it with many of our most deeply held beliefs.

In fact, the market system is so inextricably woven into our view of the world that any threat to the market endangers not only our standard of living but, more important, the very fabric of our society.

Some observers argue that such a period of danger is already upon us. In a speech delivered at Harvard University shortly after his arrival in the United States, Aleksandr Solzhenitsyn, widely known for his revealing criticisms of Soviet society, claimed that the American system indeed suffers from a pervasive sickness—a sickness that even extends to a fundamental uncertainty about the institutions of capitalism. Noting the lack of public commitment, responsibility, and loyalty to the absolute values on which America was founded, Solzhenitsyn challenged us to renew our sense of moral obligation.

The Morality of the Marketplace

. . . Textbook economics holds that the marketplace is nothing more than a means for transacting business. This view is wrong. The marketplace provides one of the few arenas in modern society in which people have an opportunity to participate directly in public life. Indeed, with the possible exception of voting, market activities constitute the major form of such participation. Buying and selling, working and consuming link individuals to one another and to the collective goals of their society. In the market, therefore, one can discharge—or avoid—his or her moral responsibilities to society.

A Historical View

The founders of modern economic theory clearly recognized the moral character of the marketplace. Adam Smith, the great eighteenth-century spokesman for laissez-faire economics, was as interested in moral philosophy as in economic theory. To Smith, the freely functioning market was an instrument of human betterment, for as buyers and sellers pursued their private interests, an "invisible hand" guaranteed that prosperity would accrue to them all.

What was good for the pin maker was, in Smith's view, good for England. After all, the pin maker contributed to the good of society by making pins. If he withdrew from the market, hoarded his pins, or took an extended vacation, he not only damaged his personal interests as a businessman but failed to keep the public trust as well. His moral obligation, therefore, was to participate in the market.

The eighteenth century also thought the marketplace a buttress to moral virtues in that it placed a check on the individual's most dangerous passions.

By rationally pursuing one's own economic interest, one channeled unruly natural passions into socially desirable activities. Outside the market, these passions readily led to avarice, lust, fanaticism, and caprice; within it, they led to discipline and virtue. As Montesquieu once observed, "Commerce . . . polishes and softens barbarian ways."

Arguments like these also had political connotations. In the turbulent context of the eighteenth century, men of property and principle believed a strong market economy offered the best protection against the designs of the powerful, for by making social relations more predictable, it promoted both domestic and international peace. Yet the market was delicate, like a fine clock, and had to be treated with respect and devotion. By acting responsibly in the marketplace, a citizen discharged a moral duty.

How much these philosophical arguments actually swayed the merchants and industrialists of the time remains, of course, a matter for conjecture. At a minimum, historical evidence suggests that they were not the arguments of academicians alone. As Albert O. Hirschman has shown, eighteenth-century publications—and even eighteenth-century laws—were filled with debate about the moral quality of the market and about its responsibility for individual and social well-being.

By the nineteenth century, the market system had come to be such a familiar feature of social organization that it scarcely required an explicit moral defense. It was simply a fact of life.

In the United States, for example, the market system was widely regarded as a source of individual freedom and dignity. The famous McGuffey readers, on which more than 150 million Americans were reared, extolled the virtues of the marketplace as a means of building moral character. Similarly, in the popular rags-to-riches stories of the period, only by struggling in the marketplace did the individual discover his talents and contribute to the good of his fellow man. To the readers of Horatio Alger, the market never appeared to be a strictly economic device; it was, first and foremost, an engine for shaping moral character. . . .

Capitalism & Freedom

The dynamics of self-esteem, therefore, provide one set of assumptions on which the legitimacy of American capitalism rests; the relation between capitalism and freedom constitutes a second. Linking an institution to the highest values of a society is an obvious way of legitimating that institution. No wonder, then, that some apologists for the free market have exploited the notion of freedom in order to oppose government intervention in the economy and to extol the virtues of private enterprise. Others go further. According to Milton Friedman, for example, the free market provides the only sure protection for freedom of speech, freedom of religion, and freedom of thought.

But asserting a relation between capitalism and freedom is of little value unless that relation is thoroughly understood. Freedom assists in the day-to-day legitimation of the market system not so much by linking economic activity with abstract political philosophy as by reinforcing the sense of moral worth that individuals derive from the marketplace. This understanding of freedom is a recent development.

The Early Idea of Freedom

In societies lacking a fully developed market economy, freedom has generally been thought an attribute of groups. In traditional India, for example, the individual believed himself free insofar as he occupied a clearly defined rank within the hierarchical structure of the caste system. According to Louis Dumont, a French anthropologist who has devoted many years to the study of Indian culture, the Western concept of freedom as individual autonomy was virtually unknown in India until recent times. Even in societies where trade was well developed—among the Polynesian Islanders, for example, or in the Greek city-states—freedom was not associated with the individual merchant or trader but with the people collectively.

To the American colonists, freedom still lacked a focus on the individual. What they valued most was freedom from external political domination—in effect, the freedom to worship as they chose, to create fitting standards of government, and to build institutions appropriate to the New World. But these were all collective enterprises. The Puritan settlers of the seventeenth and eighteenth centuries were not the Protestant individualists of the nineteenth century. To the Puritans, freedom from external constraint meant not license but conformity to internal restraint.

Freedom in a Market Society

As the market economy grew to prominence during the nineteenth century, the idea of freedom became increasingly associated with individuals, not collective institutions. For Americans it was the rugged individualist on the frontier—the heroic woodsman, the pioneer, and the self-sufficient farmer—who then best symbolized freedom. And it was the market, not communal groups, that provided these newly autonomous individuals with an outlet for their produce and with the materials they needed for survival.

But self-sufficiency and autonomy, as definitions of freedom, were by themselves inadequate before the growing social complexity that accompanied the rise of large-scale industry. Contrary to what many observers have said, the growth of complex industrial bureaucracies did not erode the concept of freedom so much as give it a different meaning. No longer were free individuals able to think of themselves as purely separate creatures, like grains of sand on the seashore. Instead, freedom came to mean knowing one's place in the organization of society—that is, knowing what one's function was in relation to other individuals and groups.

The British anthropologist Mary Douglas likens this modern idea of freedom to a grid in which each cell is occupied by an individual who stands in specific, formal relation to the other occupants of the grid. In his study of prisons, factories, and military units, the French historian Michel Foucault takes this concept one step further by arguing that the similarity between cells and the modern view of the individual is more than just analogy. According to Foucault, the market economy actually created cells—cubicles, offices, places on assembly lines–that in turn shaped a notion of the person based not on self-sufficiency but on functional responsibility to some large organization or system.

True, in highly regimented settings like military units and assembly lines, the individual's functions are closely prescribed. As a market economy evolves, however, the opportunities for individual discretion increase, and it is in these acts of discretion that individual freedom is most vividly manifest. In setting priorities, in choosing among possible courses of action, in selecting jobs or career paths, and in making decisions as consumers, individuals dramatize their freedom.

The Right to Choose
In the contemporary marketplace, therefore, freedom means essentially the right to choose. But why is this type of freedom valued? To be sure, the freedom to explore personal talents and desires expresses fundamental beliefs about the value and dignity of the individual. But this is only part of the story—and perhaps not even the most important part, since many people readily sacrifice their individuality in favor of conformity to collective norms.

What the right to choose does, even if that right is often relinquished, is to make it possible for individuals to be held responsible for their actions. Responsibility for an action can, after all be imputed to an individual only if he or she could have chosen to do otherwise. If a sergeant orders me to march, for example, I can take little credit for my "decision" to march. But if I voluntarily purchase and maintain a home, the responsibility for that decision is mine alone.

Now, if the market works to sustain my loyalty by nurturing an image of myself as a good and decent person, it must not only provide me with opportunities to discharge moral obligations, it must also demonstrate to me that I am free to discharge them and can therefore be held responsible for them. The legitimacy of the market system depends heavily on its capacity to provide this sense of freedom.

Because the modern concept of freedom is largely subjective, it is difficult to determine in any absolute sense whether the market system actually reinforces freedom. No standard, easily measurable criteria like GNP or disposable income are available. The only relevant evidence is the feeling involved in making choices among the various products, services, and opportunities provided by the market.

But this kind of evidence is sufficient. As individuals make choices in their jobs and as consumers, they are likely to experience their freedom more vividly than in any Fourth of July celebration. This dramatically "experienced" freedom is real enough that it easily pushes into the background abstract questions about the freedom of those who cannot or who choose not to participate in the marketplace. Such questions are, of course, important, but their theoretical concern does not—and cannot—in practice disprove the mutual legitimation of marketplace and personal freedom. . . .

The market system provides an arena in which some of the moral obligations incurred by members of society can be fulfilled. This is so because the capacity to make choices in the marketplace reveals a deep relation between capitalism and personal freedom. A belief in objective economic laws, then, limits this freedom and thereby defines realistically those areas to which moral responsibility applies. Together these assumptions provide individuals with a measure of security against doubt—doubt that what they are doing is right and doubt that the system as a whole is worthwhile.

Historians suggest that the market system gradually acquired these meanings during the eighteenth and nineteenth centuries. As the market economy incorporated ever more of the adult population into the production of goods and services for commercial exchange, it came to be an important determinant of how individuals felt about themselves. Indeed, some historians—Polanyi, for example—argue that by the end of the nineteenth century the market had become the single most important institution in the life of industrialized societies. . . .

Finally, the notion of objective economic laws, which have long been taken for granted as part of reality, is also undergoing a subtle process of revision. The growing use of fiscal planning by government agencies and the private sector alike undercuts the belief that economic realities are simply "there" in the nature of things. As planning agencies assume responsibility for the economy, society will increasingly hold them—and not some neutral law—morally accountable for the failings of the system. . . .   **focus**

Thus, Wuthnow asserts that markets and democracy go hand-in-hand. Both are expressions of individual freedom. Both allow the development of human dignity. Both assume that people should be directly and intimately involved in decisions that affect them as individuals and as members of a larger society.

Given the linkage between the political institution of democracy and the economic institution of capitalism, it is only natural to suspect that these two institutions have sprung from the same historic roots. This issue is examined by Federal Reserve Bank of Atlanta economist, Robert E. Keleher. Keleher maintains that what we know in 1982 as supply-side economics can be traced directly to the thoughts of many great thinkers of the past, among them: the Scottish philosopher David Hume, the French economists known as the Physiocrats, the author of Say's Law,[1] J.B. Say, and, of course, the giants of the classical school of economics—Adam Smith, David Ricardo and John Stuart Mill.

Keleher finds that the economic distortions which stimulated these great minds to discover the intricacies of market economics—"high tax rates, a high degree of government regulation, and sluggish economic growth"—were also present in the 1960s and the 1970s and stimulated the rediscovery of market economics which we know today as supply-side economics.

1   Say's law holds that supply creates its own demand.—Eds.

SUPPLY SIDE: A THEORY FROM NOWHERE?

Robert E. Keleher, *Economic Review,* January 1982

A good many commentators view supply-side economics as a novel response to the demand-side policies that have been employed by various administrations over the past 20 years or so. They often characterize supply-side economics as both a novel theory and as most likely the latest fad among economists. Supply-side economics, after all, has been referred to as voodoo economics, snake-oil economics, as well as tooth-fairy economics. It has been called ill-conceived. One former Carter economic advisor referred to 1981 as the "Year of the Quack." Another former advisor to a previous Democratic administration referred to the supply-side tax program as "the most irresponsible fiscal action in modern times."

These characterizations—many of which were made by well-trained economists—display a short-sighted view of economic history. Supply-side economics is neither novel nor a fad. In fact, it constitutes a re-emergence of classical economics and the classical economic principles of public finance. In particular, the supply-side view represents a return to the dominant orthodox strain of macro public finance analysis which originated with the attacks of Hume, the Physiocrats, Smith, and others on mercantilism. Specifically, each and every one of the fundamental elements was stated over and over again by the classical economists.

The Mercantilists

In order to understand the message of the classical economists, we need to understand the circumstances under which they wrote. The period prior to 1750, for example, can be characterized as one dominated by mercantilist economic policies—primarily various forms of governmental intervention and control of the economy. This intervention took the form of strict regulation of markets and guilds, quotas, licensing for export and import trade, royal industries, public works, paternalism, the subsidization of certain industries, grants of monopoly charters and patents, and colonial restrictions. Special interest groups could obtain governmental favors such as price fixing and even exclusion of competitors. High tariffs and other taxes (such as transportation tolls, church taxes, and excise taxes) were rampant.

Moreover, mercantilists viewed wealth as a zero-sum game. Wealth to the mercantilist was something gained at the expense of someone else. As a consequence, mercantilists were more concerned with the transfer as opposed to the creation of wealth. In short, the mercantilist period was characterized by high tax rates, a high degree of government regulation, and sluggish economic growth.

High tax rates, a high degree of government regulation, and sluggish economic growth—does this sound familiar? Recently, several commentators have equated Reaganomics with turning-back-the-clock. Yet, it was policies of government regulation and high tax rates that were associated with the low growth and low standards of living commonplace before the period of laissez faire.

The Classical Economists

It was in this mercantilist environment that the writings of David Hume, the Physiocrats, and Adam Smith took root and flourished. Responding to high tax rates and government intervention, they began to piece together the basic elements of what is now known as supply-side economics. The Physiocrats, for example, acknowledged a relationship between tax rates and output. They indicated that if the state and church were to appropriate more than one third of the income of the landed proprietors, net product would decline. David Hume recognized this relationship as well as the tax rate/tax revenue relationship especially for tariffs.

Adam Smith, however, was the first economist who put it all together. Smith, building on the writings of the Physiocrats and Hume as well as on philosophers such as Locke and Montesquieu, presented a tax related scheme that fully incorporated all of the supply-side principles cited above. Rather than being concerned with the transfer of wealth as were the mercantilists, Smith was most concerned with the production or creation of wealth. To Smith, wealth consisted of real goods and services rather than the stock of gold, and a nation was rich or poor according to its annual production of goods and services.[1] Smith's focus on aggregate supply formed the basis of his primary theme, namely, the nature and causes of wealth and economic growth. This is evident in the full title of his classic, *An Inquiry into the Nature and Causes of the Wealth of Nations*. Indeed, this pervasive concern for economic growth dominated every aspect of classical economics.[2]

Smith argued that in order to increase economic growth, emphasis needed to be placed upon increasing aggregate supply and production rather than on increasing the monetary gold stock (the mercantilist prescription). According to Smith, increases in aggregate supply necessarily implied increases in the supply of labor and capital. In the *Wealth of Nations,* he stressed the importance of incentives in eliciting increases in labor and capital. Smith explicitly stated that wage increases would *always* increase the supply of labor. Taxes on wages, he said, were "absurd and destructive," and high taxes would "obstruct the industry of people" as well as promote tax avoidance activities such as smuggling.

Smith also showed that taxes on capital and profits would discourage saving-investing activity and promote an outmigration of capital and, hence, adversely affect economic growth. In sum, Smith recognized that changes in tax rates had important effects on incentives and affected the choices between work and nonwork, saving and consumption, and market and nonmarket activity.

Finally, Smith also clearly recognized the essentials of the relationship between taxes and output described above. One passage in the *Wealth of Nations* merits particular attention in that Smith explicitly states his intentions:

> "That the mercantile system (and its high rates of taxation) has not been very favorable to the revenue of the great body of the people, to the annual produce of the land and labour of the country, I have endeavored to show in . . . this inquiry. It seems not to have been more favorable to the revenue of the sovereign, so far at least as that revenue depends upon the duties of customs."[3]

Smith also clearly and repeatedly stated the Laffer view that when tax rates are high, tax revenues and tax rates can move in opposite directions. He continually asserted, for example, that high tariffs discouraged import consumption, promoted smuggling, and worked to diminish government revenue. More moderate tax rates, Smith contended, would provide larger tax revenues. *In sum, Smith endorsed all of the essential elements of supply-side economics outlined above.*

Smith's endorsement of a fully consistent supply-side view was important not only in and of itself but because he was so influential. Virtually all economists of later generations were familiar with his writings and, hence, were influenced by Smith to some degree.[4]

Say's Law

Among those so influenced were two economists, J. B. Say and James Mill. Say and Mill further refined some of Smith's views. In particular, they refined the primacy of aggregate supply into what became known as Say's Law. The central theme of Say's Law is that production and aggregate supply create wealth and economic growth. In other words, there cannot be more real income unless people produce more. The idea underlying Say's Law is quite simple: people produce in order to consume. Workers' or businessmen's buying power consists of their supplying power. Supply or production, then, is the wherewithal or means for demand and the origin of demand lies in production.

The goal of policy, according to Say's Law, should be to foster production and aggregate supply rather than consumption and aggregate demand. If aggregate supply is promoted, demand will take care of itself. Say himself stated this well:

> "The encouragement of mere consumption is no benefit to commerce; for the difficulty lies in supplying the means, not in stimulating the desire of consumption; and we have seen, that production alone, furnishes those means. Thus, *is the aim of good government to stimulate production, of bad government to encourage consumption.* . . . It is impossible to deny the conclusion, that the best taxes . . . are least injurious to reproduction."[5]

As a corollary to fostering aggregate supply, emphasis should be given to the encouragement of factor supplies. This emphasis on aggregate supply, according to Say's Law, is the fundamental ingredient to the creation of wealth and consequently economic growth.

Say's Law was strongly supported by James Mill, David Ricardo, John Stuart Mill, and many others. Supporters of Say's Law all recognized the important role of incentives in fostering the supply of labor, saving, and investment. Both Say and Mill, for example, indicated that increases in wages would *always* work to increase the supply of labor. Given their pervasive concern for economic growth, these economists supported tax policies which fostered work effort, savings, and investment, and hence, aggregate supply and production. Supporters of Say's Law recognized that high tax rates would work to destroy the incentives to work, save, and invest and therefore would adversely affect economic growth. John Stuart Mill, for example, stressed that high tax rates would "discourage industry by insufficiency of reward." High tax rates, Mill maintained, would diminish the motive to save and cause both capital and labor to migrate. According to Mill, when tax rates have reached this level, they should be reduced so as to stimulate the supply of labor, capital, and, hence, aggregate supply.

In sum, supporters of Say's Law endorsed all the key elements of supply-side economics outlined above. Say's Law constituted the essence of the supply-side view and formed the basis of much classical thinking on public finance. The fundamentals of supply-side economics, therefore, became well established with the development and elaboration of Say's Law and its implications. Because of its general acceptance, the emphasis on the primacy of aggregate supply and economic growth dominated economic thinking until about World War I.

Contributions to this view made by later economists consisted largely of more lucid clarifications or more elegant restatements of the same principles.

Some Restatements

In clarifying the relationship between tax rates and output, some of these later writers emphasized that high tax rates encouraged people to avoid taxes. They argued that high tax rates adversely affect production and output not only because of shifts from production into leisure (and from savings into consumption), but by encouraging shifts from taxable activity into nontaxable (and often unproductive) activity. This nontaxable activity included illegal activities, such as smuggling, fraud, and evasion, but also included legal activities such as the migration of factors of production. These classical writers repeated over and over again that one sure way to recognize when tax rates are excessive is to identify when a great deal of tax avoidance activity is taking place.

These writers also restated the relationship between tax rates and tax revenues. They declared over and over again that when tax rates were confined to moderate limits, they produced more tax revenue than when rates were excessive. When tax rates increased beyond moderate levels, tax revenues decreased not only because of decreased production but also because of shifts to tax avoidance activities. Some classical authors were so confident that tax revenues would increase with reduced tax rates that they advocated tax cuts in the face of fiscal deficits.[6] An example of a practical application of this was the administration of British Prime Minister William Gladstone who advocated cutting taxes in order to *reduce* the deficit.

Various writers in the mid-to-late nineteenth century continued to support these views and thus perpetuated supply-side economics. One prominent supply-side supporter was John Stuart Mill. It is well known that all through the second half of the 19th century Mill's *Principles of Political Economy* was the undisputed bible of economists. . . . As late as 1900, Mill's work was still the basic textbook in elementary courses in both British and American Universities.[7] This long, unchallenged dominance of Mill's work not only enhanced the prominence of Say's Law but extended credence to the supply-side view in general so that this view remained largely unchallenged by economists until the interwar period.

In addition to being supported by the profession's leading thinkers (like Mill), supply-side theory came to be well accepted by most economists and indeed was regarded as the dominant view of fiscal policy by public finance economists within the academic community. Any review of the period's public finance literature reveals a strong supply-side orientation. Public finance economists of the day placed most emphasis on the following principle: the best tax system is the one which interferes least with economic growth. Thus, the growth aspects of taxation were more important to these writers than any other concern of taxation. Some of the authors of this period actually made explicit empirical estimates of the point at which they believed taxation became exorbitant. One author, for example, indicated that when the sum of state, local, and federal taxation exceeds 12 or 13 percent of private incomes, it brings about a slowdown in economic growth.[8]

In sum, the public finance economists of the late nineteenth and early twentieth centuries fully endorsed the supply-side view. During this period, supply-side economics was the orthodox view among economists and, indeed, dominated macroeconomics so thoroughly that it was virtually never challenged.[9]

The Demise of the Supply-Side View

Events in the interwar period ended the century-long dominance of the supply-side view. Along with the demise of the supply-side view came the rejection of Say's Law. Fiscal considerations such as income distribution and stabilization came to replace economic growth as principal concerns of fiscal policy.

Much of the reason for the dramatic shift in emphasis in fiscal policy relates to the circumstances of the period. First, there was a dramatic collapse of the money supply and of aggregate demand. Since this produced large amounts of idle capacity and unemployment, there was no need to encourage aggregate supply, i.e., excess supplies of labor and capital were readily available. Rather, the proper policy prescription was to stimulate aggregate demand.

Second, because of the banking collapse, monetary policy was seen as entirely impotent. Because of this supposed inability to stimulate demand via traditional channels of monetary policy, it was thought that the stimulation of aggregate demand had to come from fiscal policy. Hence, the primary emphasis of fiscal policy shifted from fostering aggregate supply to stimulating aggregate demand. More generally, emphasis shifted from supply-oriented, long-run economic growth policies to short-run, demand-oriented policies concerned with stabilizing the business cycle, i.e., a shift from growth to stabilization. Paralleling the emergence of this new stabilization function of fiscal policy was a call to use taxation and spending policies to bring about a "more proper" distribution of income. Instead of aiming primarily to produce growth, then, fiscal policy became a tool to stabilize the economy and redistribute incomes.

The public finance textbooks of the 1930s and 1940s contain ample evidence of this shift in emphasis and the subordination of supply-side views. But the shift occurred not only in textbooks. It also appeared in the substantial increase in the relative size of the public sector vis-a-vis the private sector and in the growth in government spending for "social" purposes. This increased size of government, of course, necessitated increases in tax rates. Since taxation's effects on aggregate supply had been subordinated, however, there was little discussion of the effects of higher tax rates on the supply of labor and capital as well as on output and economic growth.

High tax rates were seen as not necessarily bad. Indeed, it was often contended that high tax rates had little if any adverse effects on the supply of labor. Some economists of this period even asserted that tax rate increases would increase work effort. Moreover, since saving was seen as a leakage from the income-expenditure flow, the "new economics" came to view increases in saving as adversely affecting economic activity. According to this view, output was determined by aggregate demand and not by saving or other factor supplies.

The Re-emergence of Supply-Side Economics

Recently there has been a re-emergence of supply-side views, sparked by economic circumstances all too familiar to everyone: (1) high and rising tax rates, (2) increased government regulation and intervention into the economy, (3) increasing amounts of tax-avoidance activities, and (4) lower rates of economic growth. Indeed, the circumstances of recent years have begun to resemble those conditions of the mercantilist era which induced the classical economists to reject mercantilist economic policies. Like the classical economists centuries earlier, some economists have come to recognize the adverse effects that high tax rates and government intervention can have on incentives, factor supplies, and economic growth. This has led to a re-emergence of supply-side (classical) principles of public finance. Although dormant, then, the supply-side view was not dead.

Footnotes

1   Thomas Sowell, "Adam Smith in Theory and Practice." *Adam Smith and Modern Political Economy*, edited by Gerald P. O'Driscoll, Jr., Iowa State University Press, Ames, Iowa, p. 5.
2   Ibid., p. 13.
3   Adam Smith, *An Inquiry Into the Nature and Causes of the Wealth of Nations*, edited by Edwin Cannan, University of Chicago Press, Chicago, 1976, ii, p. 438.
4   Incidentally, it is interesting to note that the same writers who influenced Smith—namely writers of the classical liberal tradition such as Locke, Montesquieu, and Hume—also influenced the founding fathers of the United States. Many of the above-cited essential features of supply-side economics, for example, can be found in the *Federalist Papers*. In No. 35 of the *Federalist Papers*, Hamilton contends that:
      "There is no part of the administration of government that requires extensive information and a thorough knowledge of the principles of political economy so much as the business of taxation. The man who understands those principles best will be least likely to resort to oppressive expedients, or to sacrifice any particular class of citizens to the procurement of revenue. It might be demonstrated that the most productive system of finance will always be the least burdensome."
Similarly, in No. 21, Hamilton describes the relationship between tax rates and tax revenues which is now referred to as the Laffer curve. Elements of supply-side economics, then, were recognized by the founding fathers as well as by Smith.
5   Jean-Baptiste Say, *A Treatise on Political Economy*, Book III, pp. 92, 196. (emphasis added)
6   See, for example, D. P. O'Brien, J. R. McCulloch: *A Study in Classical Economics*, p. 263.
7   Mark Blaug, *Economic Theory in Retrospect*, p. 180.
8   Paul Leroy-Beaulieu, "On Taxation in General" (1906), *Classics in the Theory of Public Finance*, edited by Richard Musgrave and Alan Peacock, p. 164.
9   W. H. Hutt, *A Rehabilitation of Say's Law*, p. 2.

Keleher's view of history, particularly of history repeating itself, is also voiced by Aris Protopapadakis of the Wharton School of Finance and Commerce. Protopapadakis reflects on the prosperity of the 1960s and finds that the promise of that decade of high growth and low inflation has gone unfulfilled for many in today's economy. It is this disappointment with the results of "demand-side" policies that has led to a resurgence of interest in the classical prescriptions which were dominant before the Great Depression.

THE RETURN OF CLASSICAL ECONOMICS

Aris Protopapadakis, *Business Review,* May/June 1981

The economic success of the 1960s gave way to unfulfilled expectations in the 1970s. The U.S. economy failed to deliver the price stability and the generally high growth of real income that had come to be expected. Perceiving this as the failure of Keynesian economic policies, some economists have advocated tax cuts and reductions in government regulations as the solution to the economic malaise that threatens to dominate the 1980s. These supply-side prescriptions represent a resurfacing of economic thinking dominant before the Great Depression.

Demand Management vs Supply-Side Economics

Supply-side economics is firmly rooted in classical economic theory. Until the Great Depression, economists believed that government could increase the level of output only by implementing policies that increase financial incentives to produce. But economists were unable to reconcile the high and persistent unemployment of the Great Depression with the teachings of classical economic theory. They eventually came to conclude that a slowdown of the growth of output was evidence that labor and capital were not being fully utilized because they were *involuntarily* idle, so that increasing financial rewards to production would not increase output or reduce unemployment. The policy prescriptions of classical economics were viewed as bankrupt and demand management was born.

Demand Management
Economic policy since World War II has been dominated by demand management policies. Demand management (often referred to as Keynesian economics) is the attempt to increase output by increasing demand for it, through government policies. There are two fundamental premises of demand management. One is that the level of economic activity can be affected in predictable and persistent ways by fiscal and monetary policies. The other is that the economy often experiences underutilization of labor (unemployment) and capital as a result of the failure of markets to work

satisfactorily. Since these underutilized resources could be put to work if more demand were forthcoming, Keynesians argue that it is up to the government to design policies aimed at increasing aggregate demand.

The two traditional tools of demand management are monetary and fiscal policy. To expand aggregate demand through monetary policy, the Federal Reserve increases the growth rate of the money supply above its longer term trend. This temporarily decreases the cost of borrowing to firms, which spurs investment and increases consumption demand as consumers try to spend the excess money. To expand aggregate demand through fiscal policy, the government can increase expenditures or reduce taxes. Demand increases directly, as government buys more goods and services or leaves more disposable income with consumers, part of which they choose to spend.

These traditional economic policies appeared to work reasonably well until the late 1960s. Since that time, it has become increasingly clear that the economy does not consistently respond in the way Keynesian economists predict; indeed, sometimes the response seems opposite to what they expect, as during periods when inflation and unemployment have risen simultaneously. This suggests that low productivity growth and high inflation might persist in spite of—some say because of—demand management policies.

The Supply-Side View
The main claim of supply-side economics is that aggregate economic behavior will respond measurably to changes in financial incentives, and in particular to those incentives that are affected by the economic policies of the government. Why? Because all the goods and services in the economy are produced by people. People are hired by firms or are self-employed; in either case they use tools, machines, computers, and communication systems to produce those goods and services. In a decentralized economic system the number and kinds of tools, machines, computers built, and how much each person works are a result of individual decisions in response to financial incentives in the markets. The cost of borrowing to finance investment, wages earned from employment, and the tax rates on income are three examples of financial incentives. As any of these incentives is changed, individuals may change their decisions about what kinds of jobs they want and how hard they want to work, while firms may change their investment and employment plans.

Recent economic research has shown some reasons why the level of output is not likely to respond to demand management policies in predictable ways. It argues that increased production requires the perception of higher rewards for working and investing—that output does not respond automatically to higher demand. If no additional incentives to produce are generated, increased demand is more likely to lead to higher prices than to more output. Proponents of supply-side policies therefore argue that the obvious remedy to stagnating growth is to concentrate economic policies on restoring the incentives to work and save, since it would be the only reliable way to increase aggregate output and productivity.

The principal supply-side policies that are currently advocated are reductions in tax rates on labor and capital income. Supply-siders claim that lower tax rates on wages, interest, dividends, and corporate income will increase output by increasing the incentives to work, increasing the supply of labor, and by increasing the incentives to save and invest. They also argue that the rapid increase in tax rates since the 1964 taxcut is largely responsible for the fall in the growth rate of productivity because it has diminished incentives to work and save. Thus, decreasing taxes will restore these incentives and cause an expansion of output.   focus

Let us now review what we learned. First, we have been told that supply-side economics springs from the 18th and 19th century philosophic/economic writings of a school of economists known as the classical economists. Second we know that classical economics is consistent, indeed quite complementary, to the libertarian philosophy of individualism which underpins our democratic institutions. Lastly, all three authors—Wuthnow, Keleher and Protopapadakis—suggest that although classical economics has been out of favor since the Great Depression of the 1930s, recent events—most notably high taxes, excessive government regulation, and the resulting slow economic growth accompanied by low levels of productivity—have led to a renewed interest in a variation of classical economics: *supply-side economics.*

However, some questions still remain. Before we turn to critiques of the philosophic/economic foundations of supply-side economics these questions should be addressed: (i) Why did classical economics fail in the 1930s? (ii) What replaced classical economics from the 1930s until the 1980s? and (iii) Why is there a renewed interest in classical economics today?

These questions are really quite closely related. In order to examine them, let's employ our old friends supply and demand. Assume, as the popular press does, that classical economics (supply-side economics) is supply-oriented and that its rival Keynesian economics (the alternative set of economic propositions which came into vogue after the economic collapse of the 1930s) is demand-oriented. Now assume that every economic society wishes to maintain stable prices and high levels of employment which will result in a correspondingly high level of output, which we call Gross National Product (GNP).

Now consider the economic circumstances of the 1930s and the 1980s. After the stock market crash of 1929, consumer and business optimism was at an all-time low. Business prices and business output were falling; indeed, business output fell by 50 percent. As a result plants were closed, railroad cars sat idle, and millions of North American workers were unemployed. In the face of this economic disaster, it was unlikely that a policy designed to increase the supply of business output would work. That is, it was probably unreasonable to expect business firms to invest in new plants and new equipment which were designed to produce more output when 50 percent of their existing capacity was idle and there was so little hope for economic recovery in the immediate future. It may be true that both monetary policy and fiscal policy during this period was ill-advised. However, the fact remains that although an increase in aggregate supply would have saved the day, business firms were not prepared to take such large gambles.

Keynesian Economics

Out of this chaos emerged Keynesian economics. Again, in over-simplified terms, Keynesianism was directed toward demand management. It rejected the supply-side solution on the grounds that you *can't* force business firms to increase supply. In the alternative, it argued that you *can* force an increase in demand. That is, the Federal government can print money and spend it, thus directly increasing demand, or the Federal government can reduce taxes in the private sector and/or give individuals and business firms direct subsidies. These tax reductions and subsidy programs make it possible for the private sector to spend more and thus increase demand.

This can be depicted visually. Consider Figure 1 and Figure 2. These two diagrams represent the supply-side solution and the Keynesian solution to the problems that plagued our economy during the 1930s. Remember that this period was marked by very low prices (P_L), or what we call deflation, and very low output (GNP_L) which resulted in considerable amounts of unemployment. This latter problem, very high levels of unemployment, was the major concern of policy makers. Note, both supply-side policies and Keynesian policies theoretically could solve this problem. Supply-siders would have you increase aggregate supply to S' (recall the unreasonableness of this expectation given the immense amount of idle capacity that already existed). If this shift in the supply curve could be accomplished, output and employment would increase (GNP_H) and prices would fall (P_L'). (The falling prices—hyperdeflation—would be a small price to pay for the improved employment picture.) Keynesians, on the other hand, would have you increase aggregate demand to D' (see Figure 2). This shift in the demand curve—which could be induced by increased government spending, reduced taxes, and/or the use of subsidies directed toward individuals and business—would increase output (GNP_H) and increase prices (P_S). Thus, in this case Keynesian policy solves the employment problem and the deflation problem.

This answers our first two questions. Supply-side, classical economics failed in the 1930s because you couldn't induce business firms to invest when they already had enormous amounts of excess capacity. Keynesianism replaced the supply-side policies. Keynesians maintained that unlike supply curves, demand curves can be manipulated.

But what about our third question? If Keynesianism was so successful in the 1930s—or at least it moved the economy in the right direction—why has it "fallen from grace" in the 1980s? The answer to this question is found in Figures 3 and 4, which indicate that in the 1980s the economy was plagued by *two* problems: unemployment and inflation. Any demand management attempt to solve one of these problems will worsen the other problem. That is, as Figure 4 indicates, an increased demand (D') designed to cure the unemployment problem (GNP_H) leads to more severe inflationary pressures (P_H'), whereas a reduced demand (D'') designed to relieve the pressure on prices (P_S) results in a deterioration of the employment picture (GNP_{LL}). However, the two-pronged problem of unemployment and inflation represents no problem for the supply-side policy. An increase in supply (S') reduces the pressure on prices (P_S) while at the same time increasing the employment levels (GNP_H).

Thus, we have the answer to our third question. If Keynesianism means demand

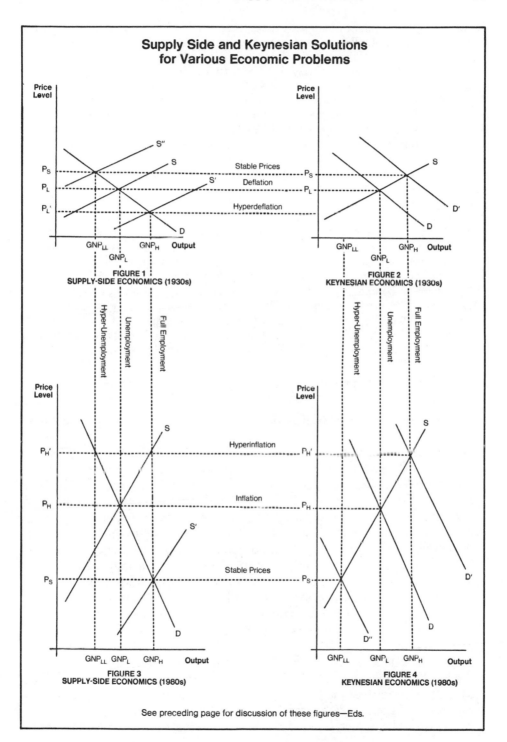

Supply Side and Keynesian Solutions
for Various Economic Problems

FIGURE 1
SUPPLY-SIDE ECONOMICS (1930s)

FIGURE 2
KEYNESIAN ECONOMICS (1930s)

FIGURE 3
SUPPLY-SIDE ECONOMICS (1980s)

FIGURE 4
KEYNESIAN ECONOMICS (1980s)

See preceding page for discussion of these figures—Eds.

management and demand management exclusively, then it cannot simultaneously solve the dual problems of inflation and unemployment. But a word of caution is necessary. Although the politics of present-day supply-side economics dictates that you accept the notion that Keynesianism is purely demand-oriented and that classical economics is purely supply-oriented, in reality both classical economists and Keynesians recognize the importance of supply and demand. As a consequence, in the 1980s you find supply-siders worrying about the aggregate demand effects caused by high interest rates and large tax cuts, while in the 1960s and 1970s Keynesians attempted to put in place manpower training programs, accelerated depreciation allowances, investment tax credits, etc., which were all designed to increase aggregate supply.

With these basic issues clearly understood, we can turn to a brief critique of the philosophical, political and economic foundations of supply-side economics. The following four essays challenge the validity of the supply-siders' view of the world. We begin with excerpts from Vassar College Economics professor, Stephen Rousseas' article, entitled "Return of the Economic Royalists." Rousseas finds little to support the assertions of supply-siders who maintain that government interference with the American economy has "sapped the vitality of capitalism." Rather Rousseas is sympathetic to Benjamin Friedman's notion that the U.S. postwar economy, which is characterized by the presence of government interference, has "entered an era of stability and prosperity." Our economy has not returned to "the years of chaos and depression" which characterized the U.S. under the old supply-siders. He argues that the present-day supply-siders would have us forget the abuses that were inflicted upon society fifty years ago. In essence he asserts that the "supply-side theory idealizes a past that never was. . . ."

A PAST THAT NEVER WAS

Stephen Rousseas, *Challenge,* January/February 1982

The Great Depression took place half a century ago. It was by far the greatest challenge American capitalism had had to face since the Civil War. On a black Thursday the stock market crash wiped out the paper wealth of the newly rich, and massive bank failures cleaned out the life savings of many of the not-so-rich. Real output fell by one-third, factories closed, and unemployment soared to 25 percent of the labor force. According to the conventional economic theory of the time, it could not and should not have happened.

True, panics and cycles were a part of our past, but they were fleeting incidents in a rapidly growing, exuberant economy engaged in the heady process of creative destruction. Cycles were seen as an unavoidable part of capitalism (attributed by some to sun spots) to be borne in stoic silence. There could therefore be no moral responsibility for the short-run suffering of the mass of people, and if the poor suffered unduly, it was because of their failure to limit their daily consumption in good times so that they could provide for the inevitable rainy days. For others, cycles were purely monetary problems which the creation of the Federal Reserve System in 1913 had solved once and for all. In the 1920s, American capitalism was seen by the economics profession as marching forward resolutely on a plateau of infinite prosperity.

Then came the collapse. One of the great axioms of our existence is: *what is, is possible.* The Great Depression was there in all its black majesty and it was not just another rainy day; it was a storm that threatened the very survival of the system. And there was no new theory to provide a quick fix; Keynes's *General Theory* came later. The political response in the United States was purely pragmatic, a groping for solutions that led to that amalgam of policies called the New Deal. Its public work projects, its relief for the poor, its civilian conservation program for unemployed youth, the National Recovery Act (NRA), and the establishment of a social security system—all these gave some measure of hope to a dispirited nation. Yet, in retrospect, the New Deal did too little rather than too much. The U.S. economy began its full recovery only with the 1939 onset of World War II in Europe, and with its own direct involvement in 1941.

As World War II was coming to an end and victory was assured, the old fears emerged. The National Planning Association was established in Washington and quickly recruited a staff of professional economists to work on a national plan for the postwar reconversion of the economy. The British White Paper of 1945, for the first time in modern history, proclaimed the government's responsibility to provide for *full* employment in the postwar world, and in the United States the Employment Act of 1946 committed the federal government to the maintenance of *maximum* employment, the concept of full employment being too controversial for the U.S. Congress. Governments were to be clearly responsible for the overall performance of their economies by adopting appropriately stabilizing fiscal measures. And it was on this basis that we entered the postwar period with some trepidation but armed with a new theory for managing aggregate demand. Government was to compensate for the occasional market failings of the capitalist system, with special emphasis on the "free" market's failure to provide for full employment.

Assessments, Pro and Con

On the occasion of its sixtieth anniversary in 1980, the National Bureau of Economic Research (NBER) held a conference on *The American Economy in Transition.* Its participants were asked to review the overall postwar performance of the American economy from the point of view of their specialties. 1980 was not a good year. The economy was once again in serious trouble. Martin Feldstein,* a leader of the current counterrevolution and host of the Conference as director of the NBER (also editor of the book emerging from the conference), attributed the poor performance of the American economy to government interference. The worm had turned. "There can be no doubt," he wrote in *The American Economy in Transition* (University of Chicago Press, 1980), "that government policies . . . deserve substantial blame for [our] adverse experience." (p. 3) Government regulations, income

*Martin Feldstein was appointed as the Chairman of the Council of Economic Advisors in the Fall of 1982—Eds.

transfer and social insurance programs, and the inhibiting tax effects on capital accumulation, had sapped the vitality of capitalism. Feldstein's views, however, were hardly reflected in the papers of his main participants. Instead of a return to "the years of chaos and depression," the postwar economy, according to Benjamin Friedman, "entered an era of stability and prosperity" with not only a higher average growth rate in the postwar years "but also a smaller variability of that growth." (pp. 11-13) The "categorical imperative" of postwar policy-makers, in the opinion of the late Arthur Okun, was the avoidance of the Great Depression, and in that they largely succeeded. The business cycle had been tamed—or at least brought within politically tolerable limits. This newfound stability, moreover, was greater than it had been at any other time. Where, from 1854 to 1937, expansions averaged 26 months and contractions 21 months, the postwar expansions had an average duration of 48 months with contractions compressed to an average of 11 months. "This quantum jump in stability," argued Okun, "must . . . be credited to public policy." *"It was made in Washington"* (italics mine) and it was "the compositional shift" to a larger public sector GNP share that constituted "the largest single stabilizing element." The American economy's sensitivity to cyclical fluctuations was markedly reduced. In this context, the growth of government transfer payments was a critical development. To Okun, the success of postwar economic policy was to be measured *"not in dollars of real GNP, but in the survival of United States capitalism."* (pp. 162-63, italics mine) . . .

The Elasticity of Capitalism

Modern post-industrial capitalism has survived as long as it has because of a unique aspect of its historical development: its flexibility and its ability to respond to changed circumstances. Unlike the regimes of the Bourbons and the Romanoffs, capitalism has been able to defuse potentially threatening situations and to adapt to changing circumstances along lines that assure its continuation. It has been this enormous elasticity of capitalism, within a relatively democratic context, that has confounded Marxian analyses of its "internal contradictions" which, according to a mechanical dialectic, guaranteed its demise in a bloody collapse. It has been capitalism's ability to place "an iron bit in nature's mouth" that has enabled it to co-opt its opponents through higher and higher levels of real income. The key has been in a virtually limitless accumulation of capital and the growth that goes along with it. And it is growth that has served, up to now, to legitimate the capitalist system and modify inequalities in the distribution of income and wealth that would otherwise have been politically destabilizing. As long as growth and capital accumulation continue, distribution is not a political problem: the system is seen and accepted as just. It is only when growth becomes problematical that the legitimacy of capitalism is cast in doubt and distribution becomes a political issue.

The Shocks of the 1970s

To a large extent, this celebration of the status quo is reflected in the sixtieth celebration of the NBER, except for one troubling development: the 1970s. The consensus politics of the 1950s and early 1960s began unraveling with the inflationary guns and butter policies of the Johnson administration. Then came a series of supply shocks that made a shambles of the fine-tuning nostrums of orthodox, neoclassical Keynesians as well as the steady-as-you-go monetary growth rule of the monetarists. Inflation was now linked with a chronic level of unemployment that made "stagflation" the faddish neologism of its time. The supply shocks started with the worldwide crop failures of 1972, quickly followed by the devastating 1973 OPEC crisis which had a shattering effect on growth and led to a rapid acceleration of the inflation rate. Lower levels of GNP were now associated with still higher price levels. These supply shocks were an addition to the inflationary bias built into the economy by the successful postwar stabilizing policies of the government. The underlying inflation rate of about 5 percent in the 1960s was, in retrospect, politically tolerable. Building on this basic inflation rate, the supply shocks pushed the economy into double-digit inflation at the same time as employment and economic growth were seriously depressed.

It is invariably during periods of great crisis, when conventional theoretical explanations no longer serve their legitimating roles, that the groundwork is laid for the rise of crackpots and assorted runaway idealogues with simple explanations for complex problems, designed explicitly for simple minds. This is the stuff of manipulated mass movements, particularly of a counterrevolutionary bent. Generally, all of society's ills are attributed to a single cause. And for single causes there are single solutions—panaceas for piping us into the good society. It was the 1970s, and the inability of existing theories to cope with dramatic, unexpected, and highly unpredictable changes in the underlying structures of society that gave rise to the ideology of supply-side economics.

Separation of Theory and Practice

The theory and praxis of supply-side economics are in different hands. The two major popularizers of the theory are Jude Wanniski and George Gilder. (I have treated the Wanniski-Gilder theory of supply-side economics more fully in a review article, "The Poverty of Wealth," for the Journal of Post Keynesian Economics, Winter 1981-82.) The main practitioners are Ronald Reagan and his now troubled Director of the Office of Management and Budget, David Stockman. Supply-side theory idealizes a past that never was or, what amounts to the same thing, it forces past history into its ideological mold. It is the world, writ large, of Andrew Mellon, Warren G. Harding, Calvin Coolidge, Ludwig Erhard and—a great hero of supply siders—John Fitzgerald Kennedy.

Supply-side economics abhors the welfare state. Indeed, it attributes all of our current ills to a misguided and overly compassionate state. It wants to go back to the *prewar* period of an unfettered and unencumbered capitalism, to a time before the onset of postwar social policy. Its program is to undo and repeal the last half-century. It is a legitimation crisis in the making.

Essentially, supply-side economics is a theory of growth, taxation, and fiscal policy—all wedded to an old and largely discredited theory of human motivation and behavior which, if realized on *its terms,* would render moot the divisive problem of redistribution. . . .   f0Cus

Thus, for Rousseas, capitalism has endured not because of some inherent rightness or some natural law; rather it has survived because it "has been able to defuse potentially threatening situations and to adapt to changing circumstances." This "enormous elasticity of capitalism" has made it possible for it to escape the "internal contradictions" that led Karl Marx to believe that capitalism would be brought to its knees. That is, modern capitalism attempts to correct for the maldistribution of income and wealth that is automatically generated by an unattended free market system. For many critics of the supply-side school, these inequalities are simply unacceptable. Consider, for example, the position put forth by journalist and editor, Michael Kinsley, who argues that it is unreasonable to expect that "voluntarism" (private good works and acts of charity) can replace "collective generosity" (public provision of social goods and services).

PRIVATE SECTOR INITIATIVES

Michael Kinsley, *Harper's,* March 1982

On January 13, Lenny Skutnik dived into the icy Potomac and saved the life of a woman who had been aboard the Air Florida plane that crashed after takeoff from Washington's National Airport. Skutnik was acting in a private capacity, not in his official government role as a $14,000-a-year gofer at the Congressional Budget Office. Speaking to some business executives in New York the next day, President Reagan praised Skutnik's courage. "Nothing had picked him out particularly to be a hero, but without hesitation there he was and he saved her life." Reagan offered Skutnik as an illustration of his theme that the proper way to solve our country's problems is through private initiative. By "private initiative," Reagan means two different things: the free-enterprise system of private capitalism, of course, but also private good works and charity. These latter activities are often grouped under the rubric "voluntarism," in implicit contrast to the compulsory nature of the government's financing arrangements.

Reagan has struck the chord of voluntarism a lot recently, as the federal social-welfare cutbacks have begun to take effect. In December, he announced the formation of a "President's Task Force on Private Sector Initiatives." Its purpose, says a task force handout, is to demonstrate the president's "concern for those people affected by the fundamental change now occurring in the servicing of social programs" by encouraging private citizens and corporations to step into the breach. In contrast to the success of voluntary good works, Reagan said on January 14, "too often those meant to benefit most from government-imposed solutions paid the highest price and bore the deepest scars when they failed." But the superiority of voluntarism is not just a matter of results; it is a matter of principle. That principle, Reagan said, is freedom: "This can be an era of losing freedom or one of reclaiming it." He went on to compare a summer job program sponsored by New York corporations (private-sector initiative) with the Soviet crackdown in Poland (Big Government). Reagan prefers the private-sector initiative.

Of all of Reagan's reasons for cutting back on government help for citizens in distress—the need for tax cuts to stimulate productivity; bureaucratic waste and fraud; the harm welfare does to its own beneficiaries; and so on—this notion of substituting private philanthropy is surely the most fatuous. Consider, for example, the problem of rescuing people who are drowning in the Potomac as the result of a plane crash. One approach—the Reagan approach, apparently—is to rely on the private-sector initiative of people like Lenny Skutnik. The other approach—the Big Government approach—is to send National Park Service helicopters to lift people out of the water. At this early stage in the Reagan revolution, the Park Service still has helicopters, and four lives were saved on January 13 through an atavistic exercise of burdensome government interference. Big Government, 4; Private Sector Initiative, 1.

But perhaps it's not that simple. Conservatives argue that the existence of massive government welfare services has numbed the charitable impulse in individuals. When the government cuts back on social welfare (cutting people's taxes in the process), the charitable instinct will flower. Perhaps, in other words, if those gawkers along the Potomac knew for sure that the government would not be sending in helicopters (and ice-cutting boats and ambulances and other paraphernalia of the welfare state), more of them might be willing to dive in themselves. Government shouldn't be discouraging such noble instincts. So cancel those helicopters. Right?

In this context the argument sounds absurd, as it's intended to. That's because nobody, not even Reagan, maybe not even libertarian philosopher Robert Nozick, treasures his freedom so much that he would rather drown than see the coercive powers of the state used to finance his rescue. Voluntarism is fine, but drowning people shouldn't have to rely on it. But this absurd example clarifies exactly what the Reagan people wish to muddle with their talk of replacing government programs with private initiative. Labeling the matter "rights" is a red flag, so let's just say it's a question of what help people ought to get. The call for "voluntarism" is a way of denying people government help while still claiming to believe that they ought to be helped. I think there are a lot of poor, sick, uneducated, jobless people who—given the resources of our society—ought to be helped. President Reagan claims to think so too, yet he would leave them to be helped by "private-sector initiative." He can't mean it. In truth, he must be willing to let them drown.

The argument for private enterprise and the argument for private philan-thropy are very different. It is one thing to say that free-market capitalism, by channeling selfishness into socially productive activity, can do more to lift people out of poverty than any number of well-meaning government programs. President Reagan says this, and he's right. It's quite another to concede that the invisible hand cannot do everything that needs to be done—that certain legitimate national goals must depend on selfless, social instincts—but to insist that the government, as society's proxy, should not do these things.

The Reagan administration has slashed federal housing subsidies. Mean-while, though, it trumpets the virtues of an organization called Habitat for Humanity, which uses private donations to build subsidized housing for the poor. This group recently opened a development in Plains, Georgia, of all places. The first tenant was a black farm worker named Johnny Murphy, who earns ten dollars a day. Now, does a just society supply subsidized housing to a person like him or not? One might well say that a healthy adult male ought to support himself. That would be principled conservatism. What the Reagan administration seems to be saying is, yes, he ought to get subsidized housing, but no, society is not going to supply it. He'll just have to wait for some Lenny Skutnik to come along.

Here is another example, from a Reagan speech to the National Alliance of Businessmen in October. José Salcido, a Los Angeles man with thirteen children, lost his wife to cancer. Shortly after, he was crushed to death in a freak accident involving his own truck. Let the president pick up the story:

> But they were not orphaned by their neighbors or even complete strangers, who immediately began collecting contributions. . . . They also discovered how kind the people of this land can be.

Very nice. But many children are orphaned in ways that do not involve freakish accidents, which get media attention. Are they any less dependent on the kindness of strangers? Why is it an act of generosity to send a small check in a well-publicized case, and an act of oppression to support a government program that will help all such people, publicized or not?

Libertarian purists like Professor Nozick would say that the difference is coercion. A government program forces all taxpayers to be generous, even those who don't feel like it. There is no answer to such purists, except to point out that their logic would have consigned four more people to an icy death on January 13. Many freedom-loving nonpurists are satisfied with the thought that in a democracy, government-imposed generosity cannot for long exceed the will of the majority. You can call government-style generosity "coercion," or you can call it "collective action." For every Lenny Skutnik, there are ten of us who aren't prepared to risk everything but are willing to make a more modest sacrifice, *if others do the same,* so that together we can maintain a certain level of generosity in our society. This process of saying, "I will if you will" is called voting.

Reagan and company may believe that by 1980 the government had exceeded the generous instincts of the majority, and they may be right. But they must have doubts about how deep the New Stinginess runs, or they wouldn't be salving people's consciences with a lot of malarkey about private initiative.

The logic of collective generosity, which Reagan rejects in the case of government, is precisely the gimmick of United Way, which he celebrates as a model of private initiative. United Way collects money from people in relatively painless amounts and aggregates it for greater effect, at the same time saving them the nuisance of weighing various worthy causes or coming into contact with the beneficiaries of their largesse, which tend to be the most traditional and uncontroversial sorts of charities, like the Boy Scouts. The more you think about United Way, in fact, the harder it is to keep in mind the difference between the coercive, bureaucratic, impersonal, stultified social welfare of the federal government, and the voluntary, personal, creative, life-enhancing nature of so-called "private" giving. United Way lacks the consummate coercive power of the government, but it does have ways of making you pledge, most of them involving solicitation by your boss. Stories like *Teller Dismissed from Job for Opposing Charity Drive* (*The New York Times,* November 29, 1981), about a bank teller fired after he refused to cough up for United Way, are never long absent from the news columns.

A recent American Enterprise Institute study compared the efficiency of government welfare and United Way in terms of how many cents of each dollar make it to the intended beneficiaries. The method of investigation was not to go and find out but, in the modern style, to take a poll. Fifteen hundred people across the country were asked, and the median answer was that fifty cents of each United Way dollar gets where it's headed, compared with only twenty-five cents of each federal dollar. A handsome chart with two circles illustrates that fifty cents is twice as much as twenty-five cents. President Reagan actually cited this poll in his January 14 speech as a reason to prefer private over public welfare services. Pardon me for challenging the consensus of 1,501 ignorant people, 1,500 of them scientifically selected, but my own little poll of two people—public information officers at United Way and the Department of Health and Human Services—concludes that the government claims an efficiency of 99.5 cents on the dollar (for Aid to Families with

Dependent Children), and United Way ninety cents on the dollar. 99.5 is larger than ninety, as the following chart demonstrates:

The main thrust of the President's Task Force on Private Sector Initiative is to increase philanthropic activity, not by individuals, but by corporations. "I plan to speak out in favor of an offensive response by business every chance that I get," is the curious way C. William Verity, Jr., chairman of Armco Corporation and head of the president's task force, put it in a recent speech. There is something a bit confused about cutting social welfare in order to give business more money to invest, then expecting business to divert money back into social welfare. And there is something very confused indeed about supposing that philanthropy by large business corporations is "voluntary" on the part of those who are really paying.

Talk about being generous with other people's money (a favorite conservative taunt about government bureaucrats)—consider Chairman Verity's suggestion of a "statewide governor's honor roll" for companies that give away more than 2 percent of their stockholders' earnings every year. "You know an annual 'Night at the Governor's Mansion' will attract a lot of attention. And for five percenters, they can stay for the weekend." We all want to encourage voluntarism, but the governor of Ohio, where Armco is located, may have second thoughts when more than 100,000 shareholders of this publicly traded corporation descend on his house for the weekend. Or perhaps what Chairman Verity has in mind is that only he—along with other top executives—should be invited to weekend with the governor, on behalf of his shareholders.

In theory, shareholders can vote out the management if they think it's being too generous, but so can taxpayers. Plunging further into theory, a miserly minority shareholder can sell his stock and get out, which a miserly citizen cannot. In practice, there is far less democratic control over philanthropy by corporations than by government. Most corporate stock today is held in trust for pensioners and insurance beneficiaries. These people have no say whatever in how much of their money is given away, or to whom. "Voluntarism is an essential part of our plan to give the government back to the people," Reagan told business executives in October. In fact, by cutting social spending and encouraging corporations to step into the breach (and by doubling the amount of philanthropy they may deduct from their taxes), Reagan is taking social decisions *away* from the people and giving them to an unelected group of corporate officers.

The growth of social welfare, according to neoconservative theology, has created a "new class" of bureaucrats, academics, political activists, consultants, and so on, who live as parasites off the productive economy and design government programs for their own benefit rather than for the poor. It is amusing to think of this "new class" while browsing through the output of the booming voluntarism industry. For example, the perennial John Gardner, founder of Common Cause, is now head of something called "Independent Sector," described as "a national forum for organizations in the voluntary sector." He is on the president's task force, along with George Romney, who once made cars but now heads the "National Center for Citizen Involvement." Another member is Michael S. Joyce, executive director of the John M. Olin Foundation, "specializing in public policy research," before that executive director of the Institute for Educational Affairs, before that executive director of the Goldseker Foundation, "a Baltimore-based foundation concerned with education, housing, medicine, and social welfare," before that assistant director of the Educational Research Council of America, and through it all a member of the Corporate Philanthropy Advisory Committee of the Council on Foundations. President Reagan told the first meeting of his task force, "A wonderful legacy of this task force could be the creation of thousands of local task forces just like yours, one for every town in America. . . ."

According to one of many reports from the Heritage Foundation, "The growth of the voluntary sector is . . . viewed by the Administration as necessary to the effective rebuilding of notions of social obligation . . . that have been eroded by the growth of government." It would be more accurate to say that Reagan's cutbacks of government aid reflect an abandonment of notions of social obligation, if the words "social" and "obligation" have any nuance at all. Reagan himself goes further, telling his task force, "What we're asking you to do is to help rediscover America—not the America bound by the Potomac River but the America beyond the Potomac River." He liked the line so much he repeated it in his January 14 speech. The next time he helicopters by, he might consider the America in the Potomac River, and think again.   focus

Kinsley underscores the fact that the differences between the "hardnosed supply-sider" and the "bleeding heart liberal" are not simply differences of opinion as to the desirability of a lot or a little of social service programs. Rather those differences are well-grounded in the philosophic foundations of the supply-sider. The individual and therefore "private initiative" is of overwhelming importance. For a supply-sider like President Reagan this means two interrelated things: "the free-enterprise system of private capital" and "private good works and charity." Government interference with one of these will affect the other.

Supply-side economics as it is practiced in the 1980s raises yet another fundamental issue which is challenged by critics. This concerns the proper role of government in the economy. Critics allege that supply-siders turn a deaf ear to social problems of our day while at the same time they are willing to allow outrageous government involvement if it benefits the business community. That is, "laissez faire" may really mean "hands on" rather than "hands off" when it refers to the business community.[2]

This issue is addressed in two essays. "Spring Fervor," the title of a "TRB from Washington" column which appeared in the *New Republic*, maintains that no matter how "you measure government intervention, our foreign competitors have more of it than we do." Thus, in spite of what the business sector says, it frequently welcomes government assistance and regulation. However, President Reagan preaches the old time religion: "reward initiative and believe in the magic of the marketplace."

2   Note, the term "laissez-faire" is a French expression which summarizes the classical economist's view of the appropriate role of government in the economy: "Leave it alone," "Hands Off," "No government involvement."—Eds.

TO REGULATE OR NOT TO REGULATE

TRB, *New Republic*, May 1982

Come with me and we will hear Ronald Reagan address the annual convention of the U.S. Chamber of Commerce. It is a dreamy day; Washington's spring is incomparable. Brigades of red tulips deploy around the equestrian statues in Lafayette Park and present arms as we pass. Over there is the White House. As we approach the great hall of the Daughters of the American Revolution, there are dogwood trees, pink and white, and azaleas. It is as though a five-year-old had taken a brush full of pink ink and splashed it along the hedges.

Now we are inside the vast DAR hall with cavernous ceilings, where the Chamber is meeting. Every seat is filled. The Marine Band bangs out spirited marches on the stage wearing uniforms as gaudy as the tulips. Old memories come back. I remember FDR's provocative grin as he addressed the annual D.A.R. convention as "Fellow immigrants!" How funny it was, and how it rankled. Washington was half segregated in those days. Marian Anderson was supposed to sing here in April 1939. She had a wonderful voice, but she was black, and they wouldn't let her. Later she sang "The Star Spangled Banner" outside. Times have changed; they have gotten better in many ways.

President Reagan arrives amid fanfares and trumpets, and he delivers his half-hour inspirational speech, the kind General Electric used to hire him to give. His voice is rich and warm and winning and the audience loves it and applauds twenty-seven times (nearly every paragraph). It only makes page A-16 of the *New York Times* the next day, and only that part where he exhorts businessmen to attempt voluntarism and reduce interest costs. I will give you some excerpts. The Chamber is the only thing that "has grown faster than the federal government" (laughter, cheers). "True wealth comes from the heart" (appreciative murmur). "Competitive enterprise is still the most revolutionary idea in the world today; it is also the most successful" (happy response). "We

cannot go back to the glory days of big, never-mind-the-cost, government"
(applause). "The best view of that kind of government is in a rear-view mirror
as we leave it behind" (more applause and laughter).

I won't go on. He warms the audience up. It is beautifully done, an earnest,
fervent, low-keyed delivery with a touch of humor. When the audience shouts
approval to three rhetorical questions he puts to them one after another, he
gives a homespun grin and says, "You get an A Plus!" Everybody laughs.

The country is in a bad recession with 9 percent unemployed, but nobody
blames business. That wasn't the way it was in 1929, after the Great Crash.
Business had been on a pedestal until then, but lost its sacred character with
the doomed Hoover, and FDR moved government from Wall Street to
Washington. The fall of business prestige marked one of America's great
social changes. Today it is different. Business isn't being chastised. General
Motors and Ford and Chrysler didn't catch the lesson of the small-car imports
from Europe and Japan until it was too late. Their response was to fire
workers. It was the reviled government that bailed out Chrysler and Lockheed.
Congress decided to assume the risks of the huge Alaska trans-Canada
natural gas pipeline. Business didn't object; it loved it. If banks begin to fail,
Washington will intervene again. That isn't what Reagan tells the Chamber.
The societies that achieve "the most spectacular progress in the shortest
period of time," he says, "are not the most tightly controlled, the biggest in size,
or the wealthiest in material resources. They are the societies that reward
initiative and believe in the magic of the marketplace."

A new book, *Minding America's Business: The Decline and Rise of the
American Economy,* has just been published by Ira C. Magaziner and Robert
C. Reich. They argue that Japan is taking away trade from the U.S. in
computers, electronics, automobiles and the like because Japanese big
business and Japanese big government are all mixed up. Other countries, too,
are going in for economic planning and for government-coordinated industrial
policies. Here is economist Lester C. Thurow's comment on the study in the
New York Review of Books: "In per capita GNP, the U.S. is now tied for 10th
place among industrial countries, after Switzerland, Denmark, Sweden,
Germany, Iceland, Norway, Belgium, Luxembourg, and the Netherlands. The
French are tied with us and the Japanese rapidly pulling up behind us.
German workers have twice as many paid holidays and vacations as American
workers." He throws in other figures. For example, America ranks 18th in
infant mortality. Life expectancy could be higher. He says that America's
problem is often attributed to too much government, but that actually "the
United States is becoming poor relative to the rest of the industrial world
because it needs more coordination and planning. The U.S. is the only
industrial country in the world that has had no growth in productivity in the
past four years. Too much government is the Reagan Administration's answer
but this argument runs into problems However you measure government
intervention, our foreign competitors have more of it than we do." No, he says,

it's not government interference—"the problem with American business is American business."

Well, maybe so, but I go back to the hypnotic rhythm of the speaker who likes simple solutions as much he dislikes big government: "I believe standing up for America also means standing up for the God who has so blessed this land," he tells us (applause). "We have strayed so far; it may be later than we think. There is a hunger in our land to see traditional values reflected in public policy again." Those who cite the First Amendment as reason "for excluding God from more and more of our institutions and everyday life," he says, "should know that the Amendment was designed to protect religious values from government tyranny and not the other way around."

The audience rises applauding and he leaves, smiling and beaming to everybody. He has done it again. He hasn't an enemy in the place. The question is, how does he do it? I walk briskly through the mellow city full of bloom and bird song.   f⊙Cʊs

Emma Rothschild, in excerpts from her review of President Reagan's *1982 Economic Report of the President*, agrees with the *New Republic* on two basic points. She rejects the notion that too much government is the cause of our current economic malaise and she finds a willingness among supply-siders to provide public assistance to the business community while they systematically eliminate public assistance for all other groups. However, she does not attribute this apparent inconsistency to the naiveté of our modern day champions of supply-side economics; rather, she finds this policy to be consistent with their understanding of a "public good." She maintains that today's supply-siders "have fallen foul of Adam Smith's own principle of . . . (the) legitimate expense of government." That is, they are more market-oriented and see a smaller role for government than Adam Smith himself. MIT professor Rothschild touches on these themes in the following selection.

ADAM SMITH AS GOVERNMENT INTERVENTIONIST

Emma Rothschild, *New York Review of Books,* April 15, 1982

. . . The first of the three main themes, concerning the government's role in general and regulation in particular, sets out from the high theoretical ground of political and economic freedom. "No nation in which the government has the dominant economic role (as measured by the proportion of gross national product originating in the government sector) has maintained broad political freedom," explain the authors of the Report. They then move to more refined distinctions. They concede that the economic role of government varies widely within the "free" nations, "without serious jeopardy to political freedom."

But even in these countries there is a "more subtle" relationship between political and economic freedom. "Expansion of the economic role of the government tends to reduce both the level of agreement on government policies and the inclination to engage in political dissent." What are we to make of this indeed subtle calculus? That throughout much of Western Europe in the 1970s people disagreed more about public policies, but complained less? That dissent flourished in Britain, where the government's share of gross domestic product (GDP) fell (under socialism) from 13.6 percent in 1976 to 12.2 percent in 1979? That dissent was buoyant in Mr. Carter's United States, where the share went from 13.3 percent to 12.4 percent? But that in Sweden, where the government share of GDP increased, under a succession of more or less neoconservative governments, from 18.5 percent in 1976 to 21.6 percent in 1979, people felt more and more subdued?[1]

In the United States, according to the Report, the growth of government has distorted the economy in many ways. The federal government has exceeded its legitimate functions, of which the most important are to correct "market failures" and to involve itself in the provision of "public goods." This judgment rests, of course, on a political choice of what constitutes a public good (or, in some cases, a "market failure"). And here the views expressed in the Report are indeed "historic"—by comparison not only with those of Carter or Barre but also with a consensus reaching back beyond Franklin Roosevelt to the reform movements of the 1870s and 1880s. Thus the authors consider that while national defense is a "true" public good, education is a good that "could be private," and indeed that the public monopoly of subsidized education should perhaps be ended in the interest of "more efficient schools." They observe that public spending leads to a regrettable reallocation of private resources: "For example, public provision of education or police services reduces the private demand for such activities."[2]

The interference with market forces involved in such forms of government activity may well lead to economic inefficiency. But they are hardly novel enough to be implicated in the sudden deterioration of the American economy since the mid-1960s. The Report's apparent enthusiasm for private bodyguard services—or other modes of the private provision of "police services"—might indeed have fallen foul of Adam Smith's own principle of 1776 that the second legitimate expense of government, after defense, was "protecting, as far as possible, every member of the society from the injustice or oppression of every other member of it"; or of Smith's strictures against the "very gross abuses" that follow when a person applies for justice "with a large present in his hand." (Smith also had a *faiblesse* for parish schools, not to mention "public works and institutions which are necessary for facilitating particlar branches of commerce.")

It is worth noting, too, that the authors have some trouble in sustaining a consistent policy against government intervention. Thus they suggest that "tax policies that distort the allocation of inputs" can lead to greater inefficiency than "neutral tax treatment." Yet eleven pages later they comment, without evident distaste, that Reagan's ("historic") Economic Recovery Tax Act of 1981 "will alter the allocation of existing capital and labor among industries," the "allocation of new business investment," and the composition of personal consumption.

The evidence they present is dramatic. Tax rates on new assets vary under the new law from a low of minus 11 percent in the motor vehicle industry to a high of plus 37 percent in services and trade. One consequence, apparently unanticipated by the administration, is that the 1981 Act will discriminate against precisely those industries that create large numbers of jobs. Thus the motor industry directly employed 770,000 people in 1980, compared to 810,000 in 1970. But the services and trade industries that are least favored by the Tax Act employed directly more than 38 million people in 1980, having supplied almost 12 million out of the 16.4 million new jobs created since 1970.[3]

Footnotes

1   Statistics for gross domestic product by kind of economic activity, including "producers of government services," taken from OECD, *National Accounts of OECD Countries 1960-1979* (Paris, 1981), vol. II, Tables 2a.
2   The authors of the Report are also concerned with the definition of market failures. Thus they write that "observed differences in safety conditions among workplaces, for example, are not sufficient evidence of a market imperfection, because employer and employee knowledge of these conditions may lead to compensating differences in wages and employment conditions."
3   US Department of Labor, *Employment and Earnings*, March 1971 and March 1981.   focus

Now that we've looked at some of the issues surrounding the historic traditions of supply-side economics and hinted at some of the implications for the 1980s, it is time to explore the modern application of these principles. Perhaps no spokesperson has been more influential than the President of the United States, Ronald Reagan. His political philosophy, his policy goals and his hope for the near-term future and the long-term future are clearly stated in the *1982 Economic Report of the President*.

THE PHILOSOPHY AND POLICY OF REAGANOMICS

Ronald Reagan, *Economic Report of the President,* 1982

In the year just ended, the first decisive steps were taken toward a fundamental reorientation of the role of the Federal Government in our economy—a reorientation that will mean more jobs, more opportunity, and more freedom for all Americans. This long overdue redirection is designed to foster the energy, creativity, and ambition of the American people so that they can create better lives for themselves, their families, and the communities in which they live. Equally important, this redirection puts the economy on the path of less inflationary but more rapid economic growth.

My economic program is based on the fundamental precept that government must respect, protect, and enhance the freedom and integrity of the individual. Economic policy must seek to create a climate that encourages the development of private institutions conducive to individual responsibility and initiative. People should be encouraged to go about their daily lives with the right and the responsibility for determining their own activities, status, and achievements. . . .

The substantially expanded role of the Federal Government has been far deeper and broader than even the growing burden of spending and taxing would suggest. Over the past decade the government has spun a vast web of regulations that intrude into almost every aspect of every American's working day. This regulatory web adversely affects the productivity of our Nation's businesses, farms, educational institutions, State and local governments, and the operations of the Federal Government itself. That lessened productivity growth, in turn, increases the costs of the goods and services we buy from each other. And those regulations raise the cost of government at all levels and the taxes we pay to support it.

Consider also the tragic record of inflation—that unlegislated tax on everyone's income—which causes high interest rates and discourages saving and investment. During the 1960s, the average yearly increase in the consumer price index was 2.3 percent. In the 1970s the rate more than doubled to 7.1 percent; and in the first year of the 1980s it soared to 13.5 percent. We simply cannot blame crop failures and oil price increases for our basic inflation problem. The continuous, underlying cause was poor government policy.

The combination of these two factors—ever higher rates of inflation and ever greater intrusion by the Federal Government into the Nation's economic life—have played a major part in a fundamental deterioration in the performance of our economy. In the 1960s productivity in the American economy grew at an annual rate of 2.9 percent; in the 1970s productivity growth slowed by nearly one-half, to 1.5 percent. Real gross national product per capita grew at an annual rate of 2.8 percent in the 1960s compared to 2.1 percent in the 1970s. This deterioration in our economic performance has been accompanied by inadequate growth in employment opportunities for our Nation's growing work force.

Reversing the trends of the past is not an easy task. I never thought or stated it would be. The damage that has been inflicted on our economy was done by imprudent and inappropriate policies over a period of many years; we cannot realistically expect to undo it all in a few short months. But during the past year we have made a substantial beginning.

Policies for the 1980s

Upon coming into office, my Administration set out to design and carry out a long-run economic program that would decisively reverse the trends of the past, and make growth and prosperity the norm, rather than the exception for the American economy. To that end, my first and foremost objective has been to improve the performance of the economy by reducing the role of the Federal Government in all its many dimensions. This involves a commitment to reduce Federal spending and taxing as a share of gross national product. It means a commitment to reduce progressively the size of the Federal deficit. It involves a substantial reform of Federal regulation, eliminating it where possible and simplifying it where appropriate. It means eschewing the stop-and-go economic policies of the past which, with their short-term focus, only added to our long-run economic ills. . . .

Last February I promised to bring a halt to the rapid growth of Federal spending. To that end, I made budget control the cutting edge of my program for economic recovery. Thanks to the cooperation of the Congress and the American people, we have taken a major step forward in accomplishing this objective, although much more remains to be done.

The Congress approved rescissions in the fiscal 1981 budget of $12.1 billion, by far the largest amount ever cut from the budget through this procedure. Spending for fiscal 1982 was subsequently reduced by another $35 billion. The Omnibus Budget Reconciliation Act of 1981 also cut $95 billion from the next 2 fiscal years, measured against previous spending trends. Many of these cuts in so-called "uncontrollable" programs were carried out by substantive changes in authorizing legislation, demonstrating that we can bring government spending under control—if only we have the will. These spending cuts have been made without damaging the programs that many of our truly needy Americans depend upon. Indeed, my program will continue to increase the funds, before and after allowing for inflation, that such programs receive in the future.

In this undertaking to bring spending under control, I have made a conscious effort to ensure that the Federal Government fully discharges its duty to provide all Americans with the needed services and protections that only a national government can provide. Chief among these is a strong national defense, a vital function which had been allowed to deteriorate dangerously in previous years.

As a result of my program, Federal Government spending growth has been cut drastically—from nearly 14 percent annually in the 3 fiscal years ending last September to an estimated 7 percent over the next 3 years—at the same time that we are rebuilding our national defense capabilities.

We must redouble our efforts to control the growth in spending. We face high, continuing, and troublesome deficits. Although these deficits are undesirably high, they will not jeopardize the economic recovery. We must understand the reasons behind the deficits now facing us: recession, lower inflation, and higher interest rates than anticipated. Although my original timetable for a balanced budget is no longer achievable, the factors which have postponed it do not mean we are abandoning the goal of living within our means. The appropriate ways to reducing [sic] the deficit will be working in our favor in 1982 and beyond: economic growth, lower interest rates, and spending control. **foCus**

President Reagan could not be more explicit in underscoring his philosophic foundations: "My economic program is based on the fundamental precept that *government must respect, protect, and enhance* the freedom and integrity of the individual" (emphasis added). Nor could he be more explicit in signaling to the American public how he intended to implement this philosophy in public policy: ". . . my first and foremost objective has been to improve the performance of the economy by reducing the role of the Federal Government in all its many dimensions."

Thus we have come full circle. We have looked over our shoulder at the beginnings of supply-side economics. We have listened to its critics. And we have glimpsed the future the modern day advocates would shape for us. What are these policies in detail? How will they affect us? This is the story that will unfold in the next five chapters.

CHAPTER 3

The Perils of Government Intervention

Introduction

One feature which clearly identifies supply-side economists and distances them from their more "liberal" colleagues is their concern for—indeed in some cases, a devotion to—a freely operating marketplace. Not only does this concern set them apart from Keynesians and others further to the left, but, in a most fundamental way, it also differentiates supply-siders from other conservative classical economists.

As we have noted, economists on the right find the virtues of the marketplace to be self-evident. They believe the market which operates freely, without interference from government and/or unions, generates the most amount of output with the least amount of expenditures in terms of time and money. This highly efficient system also guarantees an equally important by-product: It preserves and restores individualism and self-determination. Although most economists of a conservative persuasion share this view, *only the supply-siders are so confident in the market that they are willing to endure the presence of temporary "budget deficits" in order to unleash the power of the marketplace.*

This point may require emphasis. In all too many instances supply-side programs are looked upon as warmed-over traditional classical economics. There is good justification for this confusion. Those on the right have long contended that government tax and regulation policies are becoming increasingly intrusive. All camps on the right share this belief. Their basic concern is that these policies interfere with the free choice of individuals and business and that this interference, by definition, must result in a loss of economic efficiency.

As economic efficiency falters, total output must decline. Thus, for the free market advocates, no evidence of the costs of government taxes and regulations is more compelling than the poor performance of the American economy in recent years. For these economists, the presence of high taxes which discourage production initiatives and misguided government regulations which impose unreasonable costs on the business community are the true villains. These intrusions into the marketplace have resulted in a sluggish economy. They have caused the excess capacity in our plants and the long lines at the unemployment office. They are why we no longer have the highest per capita income in the world, and, more ironically, why more and more Americans have been pushed to the edge of poverty.

Thus, the supply-side theorists and policy makers have focused their attention on these market distortions. They maintain that if these impediments to a freely operating market were removed, a massive amount of new economic activity would be stimulated. More labor, capital, raw materials and creative business leadership would be brought to the marketplace. As these factors of production were put to work, output would gush forward at an unprecedented rate.

No one has articulated this view more persuasively than Arthur Laffer of the University of Southern California. He rightly deserves to be remembered as the "father of supply-

side economics." His simple and extremely understandable construct, the 'Laffer Curve,"
has stopped Keynesianism and the old liberals in their tracks, led to the election of the
New Right, and set in motion a massive restructuring of social programs in the U.S. Here,
former Wall Street Journal editor, Jude Wanniski, explores this curve.

THE LAFFER CURVE

Jude Wanniski, *Public Interest,* Winter 1980

As Arthur Laffer has noted, "There are always two tax rates that yield the
same revenues." When an aide to President Gerald Ford asked him once to
elaborate, Laffer . . . drew a simple curve, shown on the next page, to
illustrate his point. The point, too, is simple enough—though, like so many
simple points, it is also powerful in its implications.

When the tax rate is 100 percent, all production ceases in the money
economy (as distinct from the barter economy, which exists largely to escape
taxation). People will not work in the money economy if all the fruits of their
labors are confiscated by the government. And because production ceases,
there is nothing for the 100-percent rate to confiscate, so government
revenues are zero.

On the other hand, if the tax rate is zero, people can keep 100 percent of
what they produce in the money economy. There is no governmental "wedge"
between earnings and after-tax income, and thus no governmental barrier to
production. Production is therefore maximized, and the output of the money
economy is limited only by the desire of workers for leisure. But because the
tax rate is zero, government revenues are again zero, and there can be no
government. So at a 0-percent tax rate the economy is in a state of anarchy,
and at a 100-percent tax rate the economy is functioning entirely through
barter.

In between lies the curve. If the government reduces its rate to something
less than 100 percent, say to point A, some segment of the barter economy will
be able to gain so many efficiencies by being in the money economy that, even
with near-confiscatory tax rates, after-tax production would still exceed that of
the barter economy. Production will start up, and revenues will flow into the
government treasury. By lowering the tax rate, we find an increase in
revenues.

On the bottom end of the curve, the same thing is happening. If people feel
that they need a minimal government and thus institute a low tax rate, some
segment of the economy, finding that the marginal loss of income exceeds the
efficiencies gained in the money economy, is shifted into either barter or
leisure. But with that tax rate, revenues do flow into the government treasury.
This is the situation at point B. Point A represents a very high tax rate and very
low production. Point B represents a very low tax rate and very high
production. Yet they both yield the same revenue to the government.

THE LAFFER CURVE *

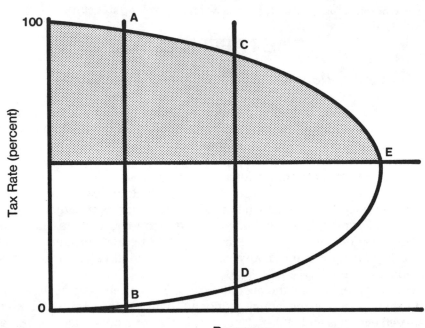

*Professor Arthur Laffer's projection of the effects of different tax rates on revenue—Eds.

The same is true of points C and D. The government finds that by a further lowering of the tax rate, say from point A to point C, revenues increase with the further expansion of output. And by raising the tax rate, say from point B to point D, revenues also increase, by the same amount.

Revenues and production are maximized at point E. If, at point E, the government lowers the tax rate again, output will increase, but revenues will fall. And if, at point E, the tax rate is raised, both output and revenue will decline. The shaded area is *the prohibitive range for government,* where rates are unnecessarily high and can be reduced with gains in *both* output and revenue.

Tax Rates and Tax Revenues

The next important thing to observe is that, except for the 0-percent and 100-percent rates, there are no numbers along the "Laffer Curve." Point E is not 50 percent, although it may be, but rather a variable number: *It is the point at which the electorate desires to be taxed.* At points B and D, the electorate desires more government goods and services and is willing—without reducing its productivity—to pay the higher rates consistent with the revenues at point E. And at points A and C, the electorate desires more private goods and services in the money economy, and wishes to pay the lower rates consistent with the revenues at point E. It is the task of the statesman to determine the location of point E, and follow its variations as closely as possible.

This is true whether the political leader heads a nation or a family. The father who disciplines his son at point A, imposing harsh penalties for violating both major and minor rules, only invites sullen rebellion, stealth, and lying (tax evasion, on the national level). The permissive father who disciplines casually at point B invites open, reckless rebellion: His son's independence and relatively unfettered growth come at the expense of the rest of the family. The wise parent seeks point E, which will probably vary from one child to another, from son to daughter.

For the political leader on the national level, point E can represent a very low or a very high number. When the nation is at war, point E can approach 100 percent. At the siege of Leningrad in World War II, for example, the people of the city produced for 900 days at tax rates approaching 100 percent. Russian soldiers and civilians worked to their physical limits, receiving as "pay" only the barest of rations. Had the citizens of Leningrad not wished to be taxed at that high rate, which was required to hold off the Nazi army, the city would have fallen.

The number represented by point E will change abruptly if the nation is at war one day and at peace the next. The electorate's demand for military goods and services from the government will fall sharply; the electorate will therefore desire to be taxed at a lower rate. If rates are not lowered consistent with this new lower level of demand, output will fall to some level consistent with a point along the prohibitive side of the "Laffer Curve." Following World War I, for example, the wartime tax rates were left in place and greatly contributed to the recession of 1919-20. Warren G. Harding ran for president in 1920 on a slogan promising a "return to normalcy" regarding tax rates; he was elected in a landslide. The subsequent rolling back of the rates ushered in the economic expansion of the "Roaring Twenties." After World War II, wartime tax rates were quickly reduced, and the American economy enjoyed a smooth transition to peacetime. In Japan and West Germany, however, there was no adjustment of the rates; as a result, postwar economic recovery was delayed. Germany's recovery began in 1948, when personal income-tax rates were reduced under Finance Minister Ludwig Erhard, and much of the government regulation of commerce came to an end. Japan's recovery did not begin until 1950, when wartime tax rates were finally rolled back. In each case, reduced *rates* produced increased *revenues* for the government. The political leader must fully appreciate the distinction between tax rates and tax revenues to discern the desires of the electorate.

The easiest way for a political leader to determine whether an increase in rates will produce more rather than less revenues is to put the proposition to the electorate. It is not enough for the politician to propose an increase from, say, point B to point D on the curve. He must also specify how the anticipated revenues will be spent. When voters approve a bond issue for schools, highways, or bridges, they are explicitly telling the politician that they are willing to pay the high tax rates required to finance the bonds. In rejecting a bond issue, however, the electorate is not necessarily telling the politician that taxes are already high enough, or that point E (or beyond) has been reached. The only message is that the proposed tax rates are too high a price to pay for the specific goods and services offered by the government.

Only a tiny fraction of all government expenditures are determined in this fashion, to be sure. Most judgments regarding tax rates and expenditures are made by individual politicians. Andrew Mellon became a national hero for engineering the rate reductions of the 1920's, and was called "the greatest Treasury Secretary since Alexander Hamilton." The financial policies of Ludwig Erhard were responsible for what was hailed as "an economic miracle"—the postwar recovery of Germany. Throughout history, however, it has been the exception rather than the rule that politicians, by accident or design, have sought to increase revenues by lowering rates. . . .

The Politics of the "Laffer Curve"

The "Laffer Curve" is a simple but exceedingly powerful analytical tool. In one way or another, all transactions, even the simplest, take place along it. The homely adage, "You can catch more flies with molasses than with vinegar," expresses the essence of the curve. But empires are built on the bottom of this simple curve and crushed against the top of it. The Caesars understood this, and so did Napoleon (up to a point) and the greatest of the Chinese emperors. The Founding Fathers of the United States knew it well; the arguments for union (in The Federalist Papers) made by Hamilton, Madison, and Jay reveal an understanding of the notion. Until World War I—when progressive taxation was sharply increased to help finance it—the United States successfully remained out of the "prohibitive range."

In the 20th century, especially since World War I, there has been a constant struggle by all the nations of the world to get down the curve. The United States managed to do so in the 1920's, because Andrew Mellon understood the lessons of the "Laffer Curve" for the domestic economy. Mellon argued that there are always two prices in the private market that will produce the same revenues. Henry Ford, for example, could get the same revenue by selling a few cars for $100,000 each, or a great number for $1,000 each. (Of course, Ford was forced by the threat of competition to sell at the low price.) The tax rate, said Mellon, is the "price of government." But the nature of government is monopolistic; government itself must find the lowest rate that yields the desired revenue.

Because Mellon was successful in persuading Republican Presidents —first Warren G. Harding and then Calvin Coolidge—of the truth of his ideas the high wartime tax rates were steadily cut back. The excess-profits tax on industry was repealed, and the 77-percent rate on the highest bracket of personal income was rolled back in stages, so that by 1925 it stood at 25 percent. As a result, the period 1921-29 was one of phenomenal economic expansion: G.N.P. grew from $69.6 billion to $103.1 billion. And because prices fell during this period, G.N.P. grew even faster in real terms, by 54 percent. At the lower rates, revenues grew sufficiently to enable Mellon to reduce the national debt from $24.3 billion to $16.9 billion.

The stock market crash of 1929 and the subsequent global depression occurred because Herbert Hoover unwittingly contracted the world economy with his high-tariff policies, which pushed the West, as an economic unit, up the "Laffer Curve." Hoover compounded the problem in 1932 by raising personal tax rates almost up to the levels of 1920.

The most important economic event following World War II was also the work of a finance minister who implicitly understood the importance of the "Laffer Curve." Germany had been pinned to the uppermost ranges of the curve since World War I. It took a financial panic in the spring of 1948 to shake Germany loose. At that point, German citizens were still paying a 50-percent marginal tax rate on incomes of $600 and a 95-percent rate on incomes above $15,000. On June 22, 1948, Finance Minister Ludwig Erhard announced cuts that raised the 50-percent bracket to $2,200 and the 95-percent bracket to $63,000. The financial panic ended, and economic expansion began. It was Erhard, not the Marshall Plan, who saved Europe from Communist encroachment. In the decade that followed, Erhard again and again slashed the tax rates, bringing the German economy farther down the curve and into a higher level of prosperity. In 1951 the 50-percent bracket was pushed up to $5,000 and in 1953 to $9,000, while at the same time the rate for the top bracket was reduced to 82-percent. In 1954, the rate for the top bracket was reduced again, to 80 percent, and in 1955 it was pulled down sharply, to 63 percent on incomes above $250,000; the 50-percent bracket was pushed up to $42,000. Yet another tax reform took place in 1958: The government exempted the first $400 dollars of income and brought the rate for the top bracket down to 53 percent. It was this systematic lowering of unnecessarily high tax rates that produced the German "economic miracle." As national income rose in Germany throughout the 1950's, so did revenues, enabling the government to construct its "welfare state" as well as its powerful national defense system.

The British empire was built on the lower end of the "Laffer Curve" and dismantled on the upper end. The high wartime rates imposed to finance the Napoleonic wars were cut back sharply in 1816, despite warnings from "fiscal experts" that the high rates were needed to reduce the enormous public debt of £900 million. For the following 60 years, the British economy grew at an unprecedented pace, as a series of finance ministers used ever-expanding revenues to lower steadily the tax rates and tariffs.

In Britain, though, unlike the United States, there was no Mellon to risk lowering the extremely high tax rates imposed to finance World War I. As a result, the British economy struggled through the 1920's and 1930's. After World War II, the British government again made the mistake of not sufficiently lowering tax rates to spur individual initiative. Instead, the postwar Labour government concentrated on using tax policy for Keynesian objectives—i.e., increasing consumer demand to expand output. On October 23, 1945, tax rates were cut on lower-income brackets and surtaxes were added to the already high rates on the upper-income brackets. Taxes on higher incomes were increased, according to Chancellor of the Exchequer Hugh Dalton, in order to "continue that steady advance toward economic and social equality which we have made during the war and which the Government firmly intends to continue in peace."

From that day in 1945, there has been no concerted political voice in Britain arguing for a reduction of the high tax rates. Conservatives have supported and won tax reductions for business, especially investment-tax income credits. But while arguing for a reduction of the 83-percent rate on incomes above £20,000 (roughly $35,000 at current exchange rates) of earned income and the 98-percent rate on "unearned income" from investments, they have insisted that government *first* lower its spending, in order to permit the rate reductions. Somehow, the spending levels never can be cut. Only in the last several months of 1977 has Margaret Thatcher, the leader of the opposition Conservative Party, spoken of reducing the high tax rates as a way of expanding revenues.

In the United States, in September 1977, the Republican National Committee unanimously endorsed the plan of Representative Jack Kemp of New York for cutting tax rates as a way of expanding revenues through increased business activity. This was the first time since 1953 that the GOP had embraced the concept of tax cuts! In contrast, the Democrats under President Kennedy sharply cut tax rates in 1962-64 (though making their case in Keynesian terms). The reductions successfully moved the United States economy down the "Laffer Curve," expanding the economy and revenues.

It is crucial to Western economic expansion, peace, and prosperity that "conservative" parties move in this direction. They are, after all, traditionally in favor of income growth, with "liberals" providing the necessary political push for income redistribution. A welfare state is perfectly consistent with the "Laffer Curve," and can function successfully along its lower range. But there must be income before there can be redistribution. Most of the economic failures of this century can rightly be charged to the failure of conservatives to press for tax rates along the lower range of the "Laffer Curve." Presidents

Eisenhower, Nixon and Ford were timid in this crucial area of public policy. The Goldwater Republicans of 1963-64, in fact, emphatically opposed the Kennedy tax rate cuts!

If, during the remainder of this decade, the United States and Great Britain demonstrate the power of the "Laffer Curve" as an analytical tool, its use will spread, in the developing countries as well as the developed world. Politicians who understand the curve will find that they can defeat politicians who do not, other things being equal. Electorates all over the world always know when they are unnecessarily perched along the upper edge of the "Laffer Curve," and will support political leaders who can bring them back down. **focus**

It is important to keep in mind Laffer's understanding of tax cuts. Although the consequences of a supply-side tax cut appear to be identical to the consequences of a Keynesian demand side tax cut, *they are not*. A Keynesian tax is designed to increase demand in the marketplace. It is hoped that producers would respond to this increased demand by increasing supply. But note, the consequences of a Keynesian tax cut is to first increase demand. In an economy that is already experiencing inflation, this can only intensify that problem.

Compare this to the Laffer response. A tax cut is not intended to work on the demand curve. Rather, a tax cut is expected to stimulate supply. This, of course, is a very desirable consequence in a price-inflated economy. But how does this happen? Supply-siders tell us it happens by increasing the rewards paid for economic effort: work, investment and innovation. That is, in addition to the investment that is directly stimulated by cutting the taxes of those who provide investment funds—relatively high income people[1]—a large tax cut changes the cost/benefit ratio of economic activity. Thus, an income tax cut reduces the cost of work effort and increases the benefit. Supply-siders hypothesize that if the rewards to economic effort are improved, not only will more economic effort be expended, but this additional economic effort will lead to an upward spiral in economic activity. GNP will increase. The greater incomes associated with this larger GNP will lead to an increased consumer demand. Business firms will have to increase their capacity to produce and hire more workers to meet this increased demand. This will, in turn, generate yet another increase in income which will continue to spin the economy to higher and higher levels. Thus, a tax reduction unleashes the power of the market system. The net result of this reduction is not a loss of tax receipts. Quite the contrary, a tax reduction will result in an increase in tax receipts.

1 This raises the important question of whose taxes are to be cut. If we ignore for the moment equity considerations and only examine the supposed economic consequences, then we might hypothesize how identifiable groups will react to a tax cut. Conventional wisdom suggests that, since families with low to moderate incomes spend most of their income (that is they save little), a tax cut focused on this group—a Keynesian tax cut—would result in an increase in demand. In a like manner, conventional wisdom suggests that since higher income groups save a significant portion of their income (that is they can satisfy their basic wants and have money left over) a tax cut focused on this group—a supply-side tax cut—would result in more funds being available for investment, which in time would lead to an increased "supply."—Eds.

So sayeth Arthur Laffer. He and his economics are right in the middle of the classical economics camp, yet separate from it. Belief in his curve sets him apart. For Laffer and those who follow his path, the "magic of the marketplace" lets you work political magic. You can cut taxes and not make a corresponding cut in expenditures. *You can have a temporary budget deficit,* because tax cuts don't lead to reductions in tax receipts: They result in increases in tax collections.

Although most non-supply-siders on the right are more comfortable with Laffer and his followers than they are with the heretical notions of the Keynesians, they plead with the supply-siders to return to "economic orthodoxy": classical economics. They implore Laffer and his camp of economists to forsake their policy recommendations which call for budget deficits. They remind their wayward brothers that government spending is a corrupting influence and should be avoided and/or minimized whenever possible.

Once again we underscore the fact that *the right is not necessarily united behind supply-side economics.* As hard-line as it may appear to Keynesian factions in U.S. society, the group of economists and journalists we know as the supply-siders are viewed as liberals by those further to the right.

North Carolina State University professor, E.C. Pasour Jr., identifies five lessons of the "economic orthodoxy" that have been forgotten or ignored by the supply-siders. These lessons all focus upon government spending: (i) public expenditures should be held to a "necessary minimum"; (ii) deficits "weaken the responsibility of legislators"; (iii) serious inflation can't be cured without a "steep recession"; (iv) it is a matter of "inference and judgment" as to whether a tax rate cut will increase or decrease tax revenues; and (v) since public policy can't be "fine tuned," constraints on government spending must take the form of "constitutional constraints."

If Pasour is correct in asserting—or at least in implying—that high profile conservative economists such as Fredrick Hayek, Ludwig von Mises, Milton Friedman, and others oppose some very fundamental aspects of supply-side economics, they have kept their public criticisms to a minimum. Perhaps this is because the alternatives of Keynesianism are so odious to them. Perhaps it is because these economists do not wish to cause a deeper split in the conservative camp now that one group of conservatives has captured control of public policy. Perhaps it's because the supply-siders' public champion, President Reagan, is too effective to be challenged. Whatever the reason, the reality is that until recently, criticism of supply-side economics has come largely from the left rather than the right.

What exactly is the thrust of the criticism? It is directed toward the economic programs of President Ronald Reagan.

Supply-Side Tax Cuts

The following material outlines the Reagan administration's economic program directed toward stimulating economic activity. The first selection examines the Reagan tax cut proposals, while the selections in the next section explore his plea for a substantial cut in government regulations. Taken together, these statements represent the foundation of the supply-side experiment in the U.S. Once these policies have been initiated, it is assumed that the economy will leap forward and spin to higher and higher levels of economic achievement. The income and wealth that will be generated by this economic growth will lay the foundation for the remaining policy initiatives of the supply-siders in the Reagan administration.

TAX CUTS REWARD WORK, SAVINGS AND INVESTMENT

Ronald Reagan, *Program for Economic Recovery,* 1981, and *Economic Report of the President,* 1982

Any increase in nominal income moves taxpayers into higher tax brackets, whether the increase is real or merely an adjustment for higher costs of living. As a consequence, taxes rise faster than inflation, raising average tax rates and tax burdens. In fact, every 10 percent increase in income—real or nominal— produces about a 15 percent increase in Federal personal income tax receipts. An average family requiring a $1,500 cost-of-living increase to maintain its standard of living must have $1,900 in wage increases to keep even after taxes.

Individual tax liabilities rose from 9.2 percent of personal income in 1965 to 11.6 percent last year. The average tax burden would have risen far more had not much of the inflation-related tax increases been offset by periodic tax cuts. Marginal tax rates, however, have been allowed to rise sharply for most taxpayers. In 1965, 6 percent of all taxpayers faced marginal rates of 25 percent or more. Today nearly one of every three taxpayers is in at least the 25 percent bracket.

As taxpayers move into higher brackets, incentives to work, save, and invest are reduced since each addition to income yields less after taxes than before. In the late 1960s and the early 1970s, Americans saved between 7 to 9 percent of personal disposable income. In 1979 and 1980, the saving rate was between 5 to 6 percent. The combination of inflation and higher marginal tax rates is undoubtedly a major factor in the lower personal saving rate.

To correct these problems and to improve the after-tax return from work and from saving, the President is asking the Congress to reduce the marginal tax rates for individuals across the board by 10 percent per year for the next 3 years starting July 1, 1981. This would reduce rates in stages from a range of 14 to 70 percent to a range of 10 to 50 percent effective January 1, 1984. These rate reductions will contribute materially above those which would be attained under present laws. At these higher income levels the reductions in Federal tax revenues, compared with those which would be obtained under present law, are $6.4 billion in fiscal 1981, $44.2 billion in fiscal 1982, and rise to $162.4 billion in fiscal 1986.

The effect of these tax cuts on a 4-person family whose 1980 income is $25,000 would be a $153 tax reduction this year, and a $809 tax reduction for 1984, assuming no increase in income. If the family's nominal earnings rise to $30,300 in 1984, their reduction would be $1,112 in that year.

The Administration's proposals will bring down average individual tax receipts to 10.8 percent of personal income in 1984, still 1.6 percentage points above where it was in 1965. Without these marginal tax rate cuts, however, individual tax would rise to 14.7 percent of personal income by 1984. Failure to enact these proposals is thus tantamount to imposing a tax increase on the average American taxpayer.

Tax Incentives for Investment

Since the late 1960s the rate of net capital formation (excluding spending mandated to meet environmental standards) has fallen substantially. For the 5 years ending in 1979, increases in real net business fixed capital averaged just over 2 percent of the Nation's real net national product, or one-half the rate for the latter part of the 1960s.

One of the major tasks facing the U.S. economy in the 1980s is to reverse these trends and to promote more capital investment. To combat the decline in productivity growth, to hasten the replacement of energy-inefficient machines and equipment, to comply with government mandates that do not enhance production, we must increase the share of our Nation's resources going to investment. Both improvements in productivity and increases in productive jobs will come from expanded investment.

Inflation and an outdated capital equipment depreciation system have combined to lower the after-tax real rate of return on capital investments by business. High inflation causes a large discrepancy between the historic and the current replacement costs of physical assets of business. Thus, corporate financial records, utilizing historic costs and current dollar sales figures, significantly overstate nominal profits and understate true economic costs.

In 1980 alone, the replacement cost of inventories exceeded by over $43 billion the cost of the inventories claimed for tax purposes. Depreciation charges based on historical cost fell short of the replacement cost of capital assets consumed by another $17 billion. These arose from a failure to record inventory and capital assets at their true replacement cost.

On an inflation adjusted basis, many firms are now paying out more than their real income in the form of taxes and dividends. The result is that real investment in equipment, maintenance, modernization, and new technology is falling further behind the needs of our economy. Clearly, present incentives for business capital formation are inadequate.

As a consequence, the President is asking the Congress to provide for an accelerated cost recovery system for machinery and equipment and certain structures according to the following classes:

- Ten years on an accelerated write-off schedule for long-lived public utility property (with a 10 percent investment credit) and factories, stores, and warehouses used by their owners (no investment credit, consistent with present law).
- Five years on an accelerated write-off schedule (plus 10 percent investment credit) for all other machinery and equipment except long-lived utility property.
- Three years on an accelerated write-off schedule (plus 6 percent investment credit) for autos and light trucks and capital costs for research and development.

In addition, audit-proof recovery periods would be established for other depreciable real estate:

- Fifteen years straight line (and no investment credit) for other nonresidential buildings and low-income housing.
- Eighteen years straight line (and no investment credit) for other rental residential structures.

A 5-year phase-in of the accelerated recovery rates for the 5-year and 10-year classes is proposed, but the effective date would be January 1, 1981, so that no pending investment plans are deferred in anticipation of the new system. These tax changes will make important contributions to raising economic activity above the levels of which would be attained under present laws. At this higher income, Federal tax revenues would be less than those which would be obtained under present law, by $2.5 billion in fiscal 1981, $9.7 billion in fiscal 1982, and $59.3 billion in fiscal 1986.

DIRECT REVENUE EFFECTS OF PROPOSED TAX REDUCTIONS*
(In billions of dollars)

| | (Fiscal Years) | | | | | |
	1981	1982	1983	1984	1985	1986
Individual 30 Percent Phased Rate Reduction	−6.4	−44.2	−81.4	−118.1	−141.5	−162.4
Business Accelerated Cost Recovery System After Interaction with Individual Tax	−2.5	−9.7	−18.6	−30.0	−44.2	−59.3
TOTAL	−8.8	−53.9	−100.0	−148.1	−185.7	−221.7

*Administration projections—Eds.

Economic Report of the President

. . . We often hear it said that we work the first few months of the year for the government and then we start to work for ourselves. But that is backwards. In fact, the first part of the year we work for ourselves. We begin working for the government only when our income reaches taxable levels. After that, the more we earn, the more we work for the government, until rising tax rates on each dollar of extra income discourage many people from further work effort or from further saving and investment.

As a result of passage of the historic Economic Recovery Tax Act of 1981, we have set in place a fundamental reorientation of our tax laws. Rather than using the tax system to redistribute existing income, we have significantly restructured it to encourage people to work, save, and invest more. Across-the-board cuts in individual income tax rates phased-in over 3 years and the indexing of tax brackets in subsequent years will help put an end to making inflation profitable for the Federal Government. The reduction in marginal rates for all taxpayers, making Individual Retirement Accounts available to all workers, cutting the top tax bracket from 70 percent to 50 percent, and reduction of the "marriage penalty" will have a powerful impact on the incentives for all Americans to work, save, and invest.

These changes are moving us away from a tax system which has encouraged individuals to borrow and spend to one in which saving and investment will be more fully rewarded.

To spur further business investment and productivity growth, the new tax law provides faster write-offs for capital investment and a restructured investment tax credit. Research and development expenditures are encouraged with a new tax credit. Small business tax rates have been reduced.   **focus**

The Economic Recovery Act of 1981, which was passed by the 97th Congress, incorporated the major tax relief proposals of the Reagan administration. This legislation provided for an across-the-board tax cut for individuals (approximately 25 percent over a three-year period[2]), rapid write-offs for capital investments, a newly fashioned investment tax credit, a reduction of the top bracket rate from 70 percent to 50 percent and a number of other reforms. One year after the enactment of this law President Reagan noted: "As a result of the historic . . . Tax Act of 1981, we have set in place a fundamental reorientation of our tax laws. Rather than using the tax system to redistribute existing

2   Much confusion surrounds this legislation. The tax bill passed in 1981 will not reduce the total tax liability of an individual by 25 percent by the year 1983. Rather, it is scheduled to reduce the marginal tax rate by 25 percent. Thus, if the money income of an individual taxpayer remains constant over this three year period and if his or her marginal tax rate was 20 percent in 1981, that marginal tax rate—not the tax bill—will fall by 25 percent. At the end of that period this individual's marginal tax rate will be 15 percent (20% minus 25% of 20%). This reduction in rates will reduce the taxes this individual pays, but this reduction will be far less than the amount which is popularly believed to be the case.

income, we have significantly restructured it to encourage people to work, save, and invest more."

But not everyone was willing to give up using the tax system to "redistribute existing income." Not everyone was willing to "significantly restructure" the tax system.

Indeed, some critics see this change in tax/government expenditure policy as nothing more than "an attack on the living standard of the poor." This is so because taxes, at least in absolute terms, are paid mostly by the more affluent, while the services which these taxes support are used primarily by the poor.

Harvard professor, J.K. Galbraith, takes up this argument when he implies that the conservative/supply-side economic policies currently being implemented are "a generalized assault on all the civilian services of modern government." Galbraith agrees with the supply-siders that taxes limit individual economic freedom. However, he sheds a different light on this argument when he looks at the amount of liberty *lost* by the taxpayer as compared with the amount of liberty *gained* by the recipients of tax-funded government services. Specifically, Galbraith argues, "the difference for liberty between considerable income and a little less income (due to payments of taxes) can be slight; in contrast, the effect on liberty of the difference between no income and some income (from tax-supported government programs) is always very, very great."

THE SOCIAL CONSENSUS AND THE CONSERVATIVE ONSLAUGHT

John Kenneth Galbraith, *Millenium Journal of International Studies,* Spring 1982

The Economic and Social Consensus

In economic and social affairs we value controversy and take it for granted; it is both the essence of politics and its principal attraction as a modern spectator sport. This emphasis on controversy regularly keeps us from seeing how substantial, on occasion, can be the agreement on the broad framework of ideas and policies within which the political debate proceeds.

This has been the case with economic and social policy in the industrial countries since the Second World War. There has been a broad consensus which has extended to most Republicans and most Democrats in the United States, to both Christian Democrats and Social Democrats in Germany and Austria, to the Labour and Tory Parties in Britain, and to Liberals and Progressive Conservatives in Canada. In France, Italy, Switzerland and Scandinavia also, policies have generally been based on a consensus. Although the rhetoric in all countries has been diverse, the practical action has been broadly similar.

All governments in all of the industrial countries, although differing in individual emphasis, have agreed on three essential points. First, there must be macroeconomic management of the economy to minimise unemployment and inflation. This, particularly in the English-speaking countries, was the legacy of Keynes. Second, there must be action by governments to provide those services which, by their nature, are not available from the private sector, or on which, like moderate-cost housing, health care and urban transportation, the private economy defaults. Finally, there must be measures—unemployment insurance, old age pensions, medical insurance, environmental protection, job-safety and product-safety regulation, and special welfare payments—to protect the individual from circumstances with which he or she, as an individual, cannot contend, and which may be seen as a smoothing and softening of the harsh edges of capitalism.

There is no accepted term for the consensus which these policies comprise. 'Keynesian' policy refers too narrowly to macroeconomic action; 'liberal' or 'social democratic' policy has too strong a political connotation for what has been embraced in practice by Dwight D. Eisenhower, Gerald Ford, Charles de Gaulle, Konrad Adenauer, Winston Churchill and Edward Heath. I will not try to devise a new term; instead I will refer to the broad macroeconomic, public-service and social-welfare commitment as the economic and social consensus, or just 'the consensus.' It is the present attack on this consensus—notably by Mrs. Thatcher's government in Britain and by Ronald Reagan's government in the United States—that I wish to examine.

The Conservative Challenge to the Consensus

The ideas supporting the economic and social consensus have never been without challenge. Keynesian macroeconomic management of the economy, the first pillar of the consensus, was powerfully conservative in intent. It sought only to correct the most self-destructive feature of capitalism (the one Marx thought decisive), namely its tendency to produce recurrent and progressively more severe crisis or depression, while leaving the rôle of the market, the current distribution of income and all property rights unchallenged. Despite this, numerous conservatives, especially in the United States, for a long time equated Keynesian economics with subversion. There was discomfort among conservatives when, thirty years after Keynes's *General Theory*[1] was published and the policy it prescribed was tending visibly towards obsolescence, Richard Nixon, in an aberrant moment, was led to say that all Americans, including Republicans, were Keynesians now. A reference to the welfare policies of the consensus—'the welfare state'—has always encountered a slightly disapproving mood; something expensive or debilitating, it was felt, was being done for George Bernard Shaw's undeserving poor. The need to compensate for the failures of capitalism through the provision of lower-cost housing, lower-income health care and mass transportation has been accepted in all countries; but, in the United States at least, not many have wanted to admit that this is an unavoidable form of socialism. In contrast, in all countries at all times there has been much mention of the cost of government, the level of taxes, the constraints of business regulation and the effect of these on economic incentives.

There has always been a likelihood, moreover, that an attack on the economic and social consensus would be taken to reflect the views of a larger section of the population than was actually the case, because a large share of all public comment comes from people of relatively high income, while the consensus is of greatest importance to those of lowest income. High social, business and academic position gives access to television, radio and the press, and those who are professionally engaged in the media are, themselves, relatively well off. It follows that the voice of economic advantage, being louder, regularly gets mistaken for the voice of the masses. Furthermore, since it is so interpreted by politicians, it has much the same effect on legislatures and legislation as a genuine shift of opinion.

In the last thirty-five years we have had many such shifts of opinion—all drastically to the right. Professor Friedrich Hayek with his *Road to Serfdom*;[2] Senator Goldwater in 1964; the unpoor, non-black, distinctly unradical Dayton, Ohio housewife, the supposed archetype discovered by two American scholars; Vice-President Spiro Agnew; George Wallace; and Enoch Powell in Britain—they were all, in their turn, seen to represent a growing new conservative mood, before being, each in his turn, rejected.

However, even if proper allowance is made for the dismal success, in the past, of conservative revival, it seems certain that there is now not only in the United States but in other industrial countries as well, an attack on the economic and social consensus that has a deeper substance. Mrs. Thatcher and Mr. Reagan have both won elections. Of course, much, if not most, of Mr. Reagan's success in 1980 must be attributed to President Carter's economists—to the macroeconomic management that combined a severe recession with severe inflation with a drastic slump in the housing industry with particular economic distress in the traditional Democratic industrial states, and all these in the year of the election. (Economists do some things with precision.) But *Effective* macroeconomic management was one part of the consensus and, obviously, there is something wrong with the way it now functions.

The Conservative Onslaught

There is, indeed, substance to the conservative attack on the economic and social consensus, especially in Britain and the United States. It strikes at genuine points of vulnerability. This, however, is not true of all of the attack; some of it is merely a rejection of reality—or of compassion. The conservative onslaught we now witness needs careful dissection and differentiation. . . .

The Simplistic Attack

The *simplistic* attack, which is currently powerful in the United States, consists in a generalised assault on all the civilian services of modern government. Education, urban services and other conventional functions of government; government help to the unemployed, unemployable or otherwise economically incapable; public housing and health care; and the regulatory functions of government are all in the line of fire. People, in a now famous phrase, must be left free to choose.

In its elementary form this attack on the consensus holds that the services of government are the peculiar malignity of those who perform them; they are a burden foisted on the unwilling taxpayer by bureaucrats. One eloquent American spokesman for this view, Mr. William Simon, the former Secretary of the Treasury, has said that,

> Bureaucrats should be assumed to be noxious, authoritarian parasites on society, with a tendency to augment their own size and power and to cultivate a parasitical clientele in all classes of society.[3]

There must, he has urged, 'be a conscious, philosophical prejudice against any intervention by the state into our lives.'[4] If public services are a foisted malignancy—if they are unrelated to need or function—it follows that they can be reduced more or less without limit and without significant social cost or suffering. This is implicit, even explicit, in the simplistic attack.

Other participants in this line of attack are, superficially at least, more sophisticated. Professor Arthur Laffer of the University of Southern California has supported the case with his now famous curve, which shows that when no taxes are levied, no revenue is raised, and that when taxes absorb all income, their yield, not surprisingly, is also zero. Taxes that are too high, as shown by a curve connecting these two points, have at some point a reduced aggregate yield. The Laffer Curve—which in its operative ranges is of purely free-hand origin—has become, in turn, a general case against all taxes. Let there be large horizontal reductions, it is argued, and the resulting expansion of private output and income—for those who will believe anything—can be great enough to sustain public revenues at more or less the previous level. For the less gullible, the Laffer Curve still argues for a large reduction in the cost and rôle of government.[5]

Another, stronger attack on the public services comes from Professor Milton Friedman and his disciples. It holds that these services are relentlessly in conflict with liberty: the market accords to the individual the sovereignty of choice; the state, as it enlarges its services, curtails or impairs that choice—a cumulative and apocalyptic process. By its acceptance of a large service and protective rôle for the state, democracy commits itself to an irreversible descent into totalitarianism and to Communism. Professor Friedman is firm as to the prospect. He argues that,

If we continue our present trend, and our free society is replaced by a collectivist society, the intellectuals who have done so much to drive us down this path will not be the ones who run the society; the prison, insane asylum, or the graveyard would be their fate.[6]

Against this trend he asks

shall we have the wisdom and the courage to change our course, to learn from experience, and to benefit from a 'rebirth of freedom'?[7]

I have called this attack on the social consensus simplistic: it could also be called rhetorical and, by the untactful, vacuous, because it depends almost wholly on passionate assertion and emotional response. No one, after reflection, can conclude that publicly rendered services are less urgently a part of the living standard than privately purchased ones—that clean water from the public sector is less needed than clean houses from the private sector, that good schools for the young are less important than good television sets. In most countries public services are not rendered with high efficiency, a point worthy of real concern. But no way has ever been found for seriously reducing outlays for either efficiently or inefficiently rendered services without affecting performance. Public bureaucracy has a dynamic of its own, but so does private bureaucracy. As road builders promote public highways and public educators promote public education, so private weapons firms promote weapons and other corporate bureaucracies promote tobacco, alcohol, toothpaste and cosmetics. This is the common tendency of organisation, as we have known since Max Weber. Good education, health care and law enforcement do not impair liberty or foretell authoritarianism. On the contrary, the entire experience of civilised societies is that these services are consistent with liberty and enlarge it. Professor Friedman's belief that liberty is measured, as currently in New York City, by the depth of the uncollected garbage is, as I have previously observed, deeply questionable.

Taxes on the affluent do reduce the freedom of those so taxed to spend their own money. 'An essential part of economic freedom is freedom to choose how to use our income.'[8] But, unemployment compensation, old-age pensions and other welfare payments serve even more specifically to increase the liberty of their recipients. That is because the difference for liberty between considerable income and a little less income can be slight; in contrast, the effect on liberty of the difference between *no* income and *some* income is always very, very great. It is the unfortunate habit of those who speak of the effect of government on freedom that they confine their concern to the loss of freedom for the affluent. All but invariably they omit to consider the way income creates freedom for the indigent.

The differential effect of taxes and public services on people of different income is something we must not disguise. Taxes in industrial countries are intended to be moderately progressive; in any case, they are paid in greatest absolute amount by people of middle income and above. Public services, in contrast, are most used by the poor. The affluent have access to private schools, while the poor must rely on public education. The rich have private golf courses and swimming pools; the poor depend on public parks and public recreation. Public transportation is most important for the least affluent, as are public hospitals, public libraries and public housing, the services of the police and other municipal services. Unemployment and welfare benefits are important for those who have no other income, while they have no similar urgency for those who are otherwise provided.

We sometimes hesitate in these careful days to suggest an apposition of interest between the rich and the poor. One should not, it is felt, stir the embers of the class struggle. To encourage envy is uncouth, possibly even un-American or un-British. However, any general assault on the public services must be understood for what it is; it is an attack on the living standard of the poor. . . .

Footnotes

1 John Maynard Keynes, *The General Theory of Employment Interest and Money* (London: Macmillan, 1936).
2 Fredrich von Hayek, *Road to Serfdom* (London: Routledge and Kegan Paul, 1944).
3 William Simon, *A Time for Truth* (New York: McGraw Hill, 1978), p. 219.
4 *Ibid.*, p. 218.
5 Professor Laffer's inspired use of purely fortuitous hypotheses, it is only fair to note, has been a source of some discomfort to some of his more scrupulous academic colleagues.
6 Professor Friedman's foreword in William Simon, *op. cit.*, p. xiii.
7 Milton and Rose Friedman, *Free to Choose* (New York: Harcourt Brace Jovanovich, 1979). p. 7.
8 *Ibid.*, p. 65.   focus

Galbraith's argument is that if you want to couch the argument about taxes in terms of freedom and disincentives, you cannot forget to count the gains in freedom acquired by those people who rely on government to soften some of what Galbraith calls the harsh edges of capitalism. For a fair and honest appraisal of any tax program, you must include all of the gains as well as all of the costs.

Although the criticism hurled at supply-side economics often is focused upon the equity considerations, opponents aren't simple-minded, bleeding heart liberals who ignore the hard realities of the marketplace. The right has been quite successful in cultivating that image, but it is an image that many critics of supply-side economics find as lacking in substance as the policies of the supply-siders.

Consider the criticisms of supply-side economics that are articulated by Emma Rothschild in the following selection containing further excerpts from the article presented in Chapter 2. They can hardly be characterized as the utterings of a "bleeding heart liberal." She challenges the supply-siders on their own terms: efficiency considerations.

Rothschild provides us with a lengthy and detailed review of the supply-side policy proposals which were articulated in the *1982 Economic Report of the President.* Her review of President Reagan's blueprint for success in the 1980s appeared in the *New York Review of Books*. Her review suggests that the assertions made by the Reagan administration about the causes and cures of our current economic malaise are just not supported by the economic data supplied in the *Economic Report*.

DO THE FACTS SUPPORT THE SUPPLY-SIDE CASE?

Emma Rothschild, *New York Review of Books*, April 1982

. . . [One] of the [President's] Report's indictment is taxation. Taxes are bad for the economy not only because of what the government does with its tax revenues but also because of the ways in which taxes affect the economic behavior of the people and corporations who pay taxes. The main charge is that high and increasing levels of taxes in the 1960s and 1970s led people to work too little and to save too little. "Income tax progressivity," in particular, "encourages current consumption and leisure and discourages saving for the future."

The argument about taxes is developed at considerable length in the Report, and is linked to the view that low savings and an excessively high "rate of household consumption" are among the most important causes of the American economic "deterioration." The administration's view of taxes is embodied, moreover, in the 1981 tax legislation. As the Report explains, the "dominant thrust" of the Tax Act is to "provide increased incentives to household and business saving." It has "changed the basic character of the tax system by shifting the burden of taxation away from capital income, thereby providing substantially greater incentives for capital investments and personal saving."

One can see why the Reagan program is such an inspiration to conservatives around the world. As the Gotha Program did for the socialists of 1875, it summarizes the economic and political theories of the conservative International, of the tax "revolution" which has stirred the right in Britain, Sweden, and elsewhere. And it is actually being carried out: the Wilhelm Liebknecht of neoconservatism is in the White House, having signed the Economic Recovery Tax Act and the Omnibus Budget Reconciliation Act of 1981.[1]

The Reagan economists' philosophy of taxation purports, nonetheless, to reflect real economic conditions. Its value thus depends on the answers to two questions. To what extent do changes in taxation lead to changes in the supply of labor and savings? And to what extent have any such changes contributed to economic deterioration in the 1960s and 1970s?

The answer to the first question can only come from empirical investigations, which the present Report hardly cites, sticking fairly resolutely to the high ground of generalization: "In making the decisions that determine national output and capital formation, households consider their options." It is worth noting, however, that the "households" with which the Report is concerned are distinctly prosperous ones. "Most people," the authors write, "earn income from both capital and labor over their lifetimes. But some people may have few or no valuable things to sell, and these people will have low incomes." The tax-related decisions the Report envisages are lofty: on the basis of anticipated tax rates, whether to "invest in durable capital, to invest in land or other tax-sheltered capital, or to consume."

The implicit view of all Americans as inherently capitalist is not new. Tocqueville saw the "business-like qualities" of Americans everywhere, and for Engels America was the "last Bourgeois Paradise on earth," where "everyone could become, if not a capitalist, at all events an independent man, producing or trading with his own means, for his own account." But this may not be a useful simplification for understanding the economic behavior of most Americans in the 1980s. It is indeed the case that more than half of all American households receive some income from dividends, interest, or rent. But these sources account for only 3 percent of the total money income of what the US government calls "nonaged" families—less than the 4 percent of total money income which they receive from public programs. For poor (nonaged) families, only 1 percent of income comes from dividends, interest, and rent, compared to 48 percent from public programs.[2]

No one would question that taxes affect the economic choices of taxpayers in general and rich taxpayers in particular. What seems possible, however, is that responses to taxes are swamped by other effects. With lower taxes, the authors of the Report write, people will have more "incentive to work more hours, or accept a more demanding job." But can they even find such a job, with the unemployment rate at 8.8 percent for all workers, 12.7 percent for blue-collar workers, 21.5 percent for teenagers? The authors concede that tax changes will have their strongest "labor supply effects" on married women, who presumably will be encouraged by lower tax rates to find jobs. But in this case the comparable discouraging effects of high taxes were convincingly swamped by other forces during the postwar period, since the female labor force participation rate increased 1.0 percent a year in the 1950s, 1.4 percent a year in the 1960s, and 1.9 percent a year in the 1970s.[3]

What of the second question? Even if taxes do affect economic behavior, does this matter? The Report suggests that tax disincentives have contributed to economic deterioration by reducing labor supply and savings. Yet such effects on the supply of labor have hardly been decisive, since the civilian labor force grew about twice as fast in the 1970s as in the preceding three decades, adding more than 20 million new workers, compared to less than 30 million during the 1940s, 1950s, and 1960s. It is of great social importance that people be free to join or to remain in the labor force; and an expanding American economy may well need millions of workers in the late 1980s. But the slow growth of labor supply cannot plausibly be blamed for the economic problems of the 1970s. A simple extrapolation suggests that if participation in the labor force had been no higher in 1980 than in 1970, there would have been, with the same civilian population and employment, 5.6 million fewer people unemployed in 1980. If unemployment remained at its actual 1980 level, with 1970 labor force participation, productivity (real GNP per employed person) would have grown at 1.4 percent a year during the 1970s, instead of its actual rate of below 0.8 percent per year.

The argument about taxes and savings is far more important, since it is at the heart of the entire Reagan program. Yet here again, the real economy is peskily intrusive. A low savings rate can lead to economic problems—notably slow economic growth—if it results in a low rate of investment. (It seems unilluminating to speculate whether the Reagan economists believe that savings determine investment, or investment savings. . . .) The US has virtually the lowest investment rate of any OECD country, lower even than Britain's. But this rate was in fact no lower in the 1970s than it had been in the earlier postwar period. Gross private domestic investment—according to statistics taken from the appendix to this Report—amounted to 15.9 percent of GNP in the 1950s; 15.5 percent in the 1960s; and 15.9 percent in the 1970s.

Personal savings also contribute only part of the funds available for domestic investment: less than a third in the 1970s, with the balance coming from business "saving." The authors of the Report indeed contemplate an ingenious way of finding funds for investment from sources other than personal (or corporate) savings. The solution, not likely to endear the administration to America's allies, already restive at high US interest rates, is to seduce savings from countries that save more: "Some saving could also come from abroad." As the authors continue, discussing the effects of US government borrowing on private investment, "If international credit flows respond sufficiently to only slightly higher interest rates, significant crowding out of US private investment may be prevented."[4]

The most conclusive objection to the Reagan view of savings is, finally, that personal savings have declined only slightly in the 1970s. Personal savings accounted for 6.8 percent of disposable (after tax) personal income in the 1950s (still according to the Report's statistical appendix); for 6.9 percent in the 1960s; and for 6.6 percent in the 1970s.

Footnotes

1 The German Social Democratic Workers' Party, led by Liebknecht and August Bebel—later founders of the Second International—merged with the General Association of German Workers at the Gotha Unity Congress of May 19, 1875. The "Gotha Program"—which called, among other things, for universal suffrage, public elementary education, and a uniform progressive income tax—was the major document of the economic and political philosophy of social democracy. It was bitterly criticized by Marx and Engels for its implicit economic theory and for including such "bourgeois liberal" demands as "freedom for science" and "freedom of conscience."

2   US Department of Health and Human Services, *Social Security Bulletin*, Annual Statistical Supplement, 1980, page 62. Shares of money income for nonaged households, families with head under age 65, 1978. According to this Supplement, 21.3 million "nonaged" Americans were poor in 1978 (p. 61).

3   Here and in what follows, all statistics are taken from the statistical appendix to the present Report. We also follow the practice adopted in the text of defining the decade of the 1970s as lasting from 1971-1980, the 1960s from 1961-1970, and so on.

4   This flow of foreigners' "savings" would presumably be offset—as the Report does not point out—by an increase in US imports of goods and services. Gross investment is of course only one measure of national investment. Economists concerned with paucity of US investment also cite the decline in "net private domestic investment" (gross investment less capital consumption allowances) as a share of GNP: from 6.6 percent in the 1950s, to 7 percent in the 1960s, to 6 percent in the 1970s. Some decline is however to be expected in a decade which included two recession years when the ratio of net to gross investment fell sharply.   **focus**

Rothschild maintains that the supply-side tax policies of the Reagan administration are based upon the notion that our sluggish economic performance in the late 1970s and early 1980s can be traced to low productivity, which in turn is a result of deteriorating incentives to work, save, and invest. The Economic Recovery Act of 1981 was designed to change this. It was explicitly designed to encourage work effort, savings and investment. But Rothschild questions the basic assertions of the supply-siders. She asks them: "To what extent do changes in taxation lead to changes in the supply of labor and savings? And to what extent have any changes contributed to economic deterioration in the 1960s and 1970s?"

Rothschild finds little factual support for the supply-siders' assertions. Indeed, she systematically finds that work effort, savings and investment were, at worst, about the same in the 1970s as they were in the 1950s and 1960s and, at best, more encouraging in the 1970s than they were in the previous two decades. Thus, for Rothschild, the factual foundation upon which the supply-side tax policy is built is non-extant. It is rhetoric, not reality. It is illusionary.

Director of the Center for Economic and Anthropogenic Research at Rutgers University, Alfred Eichner, examines the other major component of the 1981 Recovery Act. He challenges the legitimacy of reducing business taxes. Although supply-siders maintain that business taxes are too high and that these high taxes have a detrimental influence on the decisions of businesses to invest, Eichner argues that: "the fact is that corporate investment, which accounts for at least 80 percent of all business fixed investments, is almost surely self-financed.... Thus, the so-called 'capital-shortage,' given as the rationale for cutting the taxes of upper income groups, is an illusion...." Eichner and Rothschild agree that the factual foundations for the supply-side tax policy are non-extant, rhetorical, and illusionary.

TAX RELIEF FOR THE WEALTHY

Alfred S. Eichner, *Challenge*, May/June 1981

. . . The Reagan administration itself has emphasized the reduction in tax rates as the hallmark of its sharp break with the past. And indeed tax reduction as a remedy for inflation is a novel idea, one that goes against the grain of the orthodox "Keynesian" (actually neoclassical) synthesis that previously dominated economic policy-making in the United States. The administration has defended its advocacy of tax reduction as an anti-inflation measure on the grounds that it reflects a new "supply-side" approach, one that seeks to stimulate production rather than being forced to curtail demand as a means of holding down prices. In particular, it is argued that tax reduction will spur savings and capital formation, thereby producing high growth rates and increased productivity in the future. This is why the tax reduction must, according to the Reagan advisors, favor businesses, rentiers, and the wealthy generally.

There is every reason to believe that the tax relief now being advocated by the administration will have little or no effect on capital formation in the United States—other than the general stimulus to investment that is provided by any measure which raises the level of aggregate demand. In fact, the advocacy of tax relief for the wealthy to spur savings and capital formation is based on at least two fallacies. One is that capital formation has previously been hindered by a lack of personal savings. A second fallacy is that tax reduction or—what amounts to the same thing—liberalized depreciation allowances will induce business firms to invest more and thereby increase the rate of capital formation.

The first notion reflects an anachronistic view of how business investment is actually financed. It is not that individuals, particularly wealthy ones, first decide how much *not* to spend on consumption and that this amount of personal savings then sets a limit on the amount of investment that can be funded. That is the pre-Keynesian view and, as Paul Davidson pointed out in a paper recently published by the Joint Economic Committee of Congress, it confuses personal savings with business finance. The two are not the same, since business firms are able to finance investment expenditures out of the working capital provided by commercial banks independently of what the level of personal savings may be. (Business firms have the recourse of borrowing additional working capital, should their own cash flow be insufficient to cover the current rate of capital spending.) If business firms lack finance, it is not because personal savings are too low but rather because the banks, straitjacketed by the Federal Reserve, are unable to provide it.

The fact is that corporate investment, which accounts for at least 80 percent of all business fixed investment, is almost entirely self-financed. This means it is funded out of the cash flow generated by profit margins. Only on rare occasions are the nation's largest corporations forced to turn to outside financing—public utilities, because they are regulated, being an exception. Indeed, as Eli Schwartz and Duane Graddy have pointed out in a joint study, the corporate sector normally returns to individuals more in dividends than individuals supply to corporations in the way of funds for investment, making the household sector a net recipient of funds. Personal savings would appear to be important as a source of finance only for residential construction, and not for capital formation by private enterprises. Thus the so-called "capital shortage," given as the rationale for cutting the taxes of upper-income groups, is an illusion created by equating personal savings with total savings, and thereby ignoring the funds, or savings, generated by business firms themselves out of profits and depreciation allowances.

The second notion which needs to be challenged is that tax relief, as proposed for businesses by this administration, will induce firms to invest more. Here there is confusion over what the principal determinant of business investment is. As a large number of studies have shown (Robert Eisner's is the most systematic body of work), it is the level of industry sales which exerts the decisive influence on investment. When the economy is booming and industry sales are growing apace, capital outlays by business can be expected to follow suit. When the economy slows down or stagnates, leading to a fall in sales, investment will fall. Our own estimates, based on the econometric model being constructed at the Center for Economic and Anthropogenic Research, is that for every one percent the economy expands above (or below) the average growth rate, corporate plant and equipment expenditures will rise (or fall) 1.9 percent above (or below) the growth trend of investment. And if the higher (or lower) growth rate is maintained for four consecutive quarters it will, with a further lag of one quarter, boost (or lower) corporate plant and equipment expenditures another 1.9 percent. These findings point to the major reason why capital formation has not been as high as some might like: the relatively low growth rates during the 1970s have acted, via what is termed the accelerator effect, to depress business investment. The solution does not lie in reducing the taxes on business. Indeed, the same empirical studies suggest that liberalized depreciation allowances and similar tax relief measures are likely to have little or no effect on investment. Only consistently higher growth rates for the economy as a whole will make a significant difference.

If the tax relief advocated by the Reagan administration is likely to produce few, if any, of the "supply-side" effects being claimed for it, then how is this feature of the overall economic game plan to be understood? The answer is that it is simply an old-style Keynesian cut in taxes which, together with the vastly increased outlays for national defense and the resulting federal deficit, can be expected to stimulate the economy further—much as similar measures did under the Kennedy-Johnson administrations in the 1960s. Paradoxically, the combined set of policies will achieve the stated goal of stimulating investment—though from the demand side rather than from the supply side. . . .   focus

Deregulation of the Marketplace

Supply-side advocates are quick to point out that the economic stimuli put in place by the Reagan administration are not limited to tax incentives. Indeed, an extremely successful campaign has been waged against ever-present government regulation. Supply-siders maintain that government regulation of the private marketplace has resulted in massive inefficiencies and increased costs; costs which far exceed any benefits which might be associated with such government interference. Thus, they are confident that as these regulations are relaxed, the business community will respond with an increase in supply.

The importance of deregulation for the supply-side policy makers is demonstrated by its prominence in the following excerpts from the *1982 Economic Report of the President.* In President Reagan's words: "The redirection of work and effort away from trying to cope with or anticipate Federal regulation toward more productive pursuits is how regulatory reform will make its greatest impact in raising productivity and reducing costs."

REGULATORY REFORM WILL INCREASE PRODUCTIVITY

Ronald Reagan, *Economic Report of the President,* 1982

My commitment to regulatory reform was made clear in one of my very first acts in office, when I accelerated the decontrol of crude oil prices and eliminated the cumbersome crude oil entitlements system. Only skeptics of the free market system are surprised by the results. For the first time in 10 years, crude oil production in the continental United States has begun to rise. Prices and availability are now determined by the forces of the market, not dictated by Washington. And, helped by world supply and demand developments, oil and gasoline prices have been falling, rather than rising.

I have established, by Executive order, a process whereby all executive agency regulatory activity is subject to close and sensitive monitoring by the Executive Office of the President. During the first year of my Administration, 2,893 regulations have been subjected to Executive Office review. The number of pages in the *Federal Register,* the daily publication that contains a record of the Federal Government's official regulatory actions, has fallen by over one-quarter after increasing steadily for a decade.

But the full impact of this program cannot be found in easy-to-measure actions by the Federal Government. It is taking place outside of Washington, in large and small businesses, in State and local governments, and in our schools and hospitals where the full benefits of regulatory reform are being felt. The redirection of work and effort away from trying to cope with or anticipate Federal regulation toward more productive pursuits is how regulatory reform will make its greatest impact in raising productivity and reducing costs.   foCus

President Reagan's interest and concern for deregulation can be traced to his respect for the views of Murray L. Weidenbaum who is perhaps the most visible and successful champion of deregulation. Dr. Weidenbaum, in his capacity as the Chairman of President Reagan's Council of Economic Advisors and as the academic spokesman for the business community, has traveled across the country on speaking tours and published numerous professional and popular articles. In the process, he has been extremely successful in alerting U.S. voters to the evils of government regulation. His message is simple: Government regulation costs money. His recommendations are equally clear: Don't impose a regulation unless the dollar benefits of that regulation are equal to or greater than the dollar costs of that regulation.

At times, Weidenbaum and his associates have been unrelenting in their assault upon regulatory authority. They have often asserted that it costs U.S. consumers extraordinary amounts of money. Indeed, one study by Weidenbaum's Center for the Study of American Business, which was quoted by President Reagan in his first State of the Union Message, alleged that government regulations cost the American consumer $102.7 billion in 1979. Although this study and others like it have been criticized for the liberties that were taken in estimating costs, these studies served their purpose. They galvanized public opinion.

Building upon the success of his campaign against government regulation, Weidenbaum and the current policy makers in Washington have been far more moderate in their rhetoric. They no longer need to shout that "all regulation is bad." They can now argue, as Weidenbaum argues in our next reading, that "To an economist, 'over regulation' is not an emotional term, it is merely short hand for the regulatory activities in which the costs to the public are greater than benefits." Because of the widespread exposure the supply-siders have given to the costs of regulation, Weidenbaum's plea for a "market test" of government regulation has fallen upon very receptive ears. His approach is detached and free of emotion, objective and measureable; it is, in short, a "scientific test."

LET'S PUT GOVERNMENT REGULATIONS TO THE MARKET TEST

Murray L. Weidenbaum, *Across the Board,* February 1982

Discussions of government regulation of product hazards, such as toxic substances, frequently conclude that decision-makers would be aided by the results of benefit-cost studies and related economic analyses. This article tries to explain the role of such quantitative analyses in the regulatory process.

The motive for incorporating benefit-cost analysis into public decision-making is to lead to a more efficient allocation of government resources by subjecting the public sector to the same type of quantitative constraints as those in the private sector. In making an investment decision, for example, business executives compare the costs to be incurred with the expected revenues. If the costs exceed the revenues, the investment usually is not considered worthwhile. If revenues exceed costs, further consideration usually is given the proposal, although capital constraints require another determination of the most financially attractive investments.

The government agency decision-maker does not face the same type of economic constraints. If the costs and other disadvantages to society of an agency action exceed the benefits and other advantages, that situation may not have an immediate adverse impact on the agency. However, such an action would have an immediate impact on a private business if one of its executives made an error. Such analytical information rarely exists in the public sector, so that, more often than not, the governmental decision-maker is not aware that he or she is approving a regulation that is economically inefficient. The aim of requiring agencies to perform benefit-cost analysis is to make the government's decision-making process more effective, and to eliminate regulatory actions that, on balance, generate more costs than benefits. This result is not assured by benefit-cost analysis, since political and other important, but subjective, considerations may dominate. This may result in actions that are not economically efficient, but are desired on grounds of equity or income distribution. Yet benefit-cost analysis may provide valuable information for government decision-makers.

It may be useful to consider the economic rationale for making benefit-cost analyses of government actions. Economists have long been interested in identifying policies that promote economic welfare, specifically by improving the efficiency with which a society uses its resources.

Benefits are measured in terms of the increased production of goods and services. Costs are computed in terms of the foregone benefits that would have been obtained by using those resources in some other activity. The underlying aim of benefit-cost analysis is to maximize the value of the social income, usually measured by the gross national product (GNP). For many years, certain Federal agencies (such as the Corps of Engineers and the Bureau of Reclamation) have used benefit-cost analysis to evaluate prospective projects.

[Typically,] initial regulatory effort—such as cleaning up the worst effects of pollution in a river—may well generate benefits greater than costs. But the resources required to achieve additional cleanup become disproportionately high, and at some point the added benefits may be substantially less than the added costs. For example, a study of the impact of environmental controls on the fruit and vegetable processing industry revealed that it costs less to eliminate the first 85 percent of the pollution than the next 10 percent. In beet sugar plants, it costs more than $1 a pound to reduce biological oxygen demand (BOD)—a measure of the oxygen required to decompose organic wastes—up to a level where 30 percent of pollution is eliminated. But it costs an additional $20 for a one-pound reduction at the 65 percent control level and an additional $60 for a one-pound reduction when over 95 percent control is achieved.

Another comparison is equally telling. The pulp and paper industry spent $3 billion between 1970 and 1978 complying with Federal clean-water standards, and achieved a 95 percent reduction in pollution. But to reach the new reduction goal proposed by the Environmental Protection Agency (EPA)—98 percent by 1984—would cost $4.8 billion more, a 160 percent increase in costs to achieve a 3 percent improvement in water quality. Thus, it is important to look beyond the relationship of the costs and the benefits of a proposed governmental undertaking to the additional (marginal) benefits and costs resulting from each extension of or addition to the governmental activities.

If regulatory activity goes unchecked, the result could be an excess of costs over benefits. Thus, benefit-cost analyses should be viewed as a tool for identifying the optimum amount of regulation, rather than as a means of debating the pros and cons of regulation in general. To an economist, "overregulation" is not an emotional term; it is merely shorthand for the regulatory activities in which the costs to the public are greater than the benefits. . . .

If a business decision in the private sector places an external burden on its neighbors, such as pollution, the firm does not include such a cost in its accounting, since it does not bear the burden. Public sector decision-makers, however, must, or at least ought to, consider all the effects of such a decision. Because their vantage point is the entire nation, government regulators—unlike their private sector counterparts—should attempt to include all costs and benefits, including those external to the government.

The agencies should do so because most regulatory actions have indirect effects on the economy. For example, requiring safety belts in automobiles has a direct impact on the cost of automobiles and on sales in the safety belt industry. It also influences the severity of auto accidents and has a ripple effect on the suppliers of the safety belt industry and their suppliers, and so on. If a regulatory decision is to be good, these indirect effects, as well as the direct impacts, must be taken into account.

The benefits and costs attributable to regulation are measured by the difference between the benefits and costs that occur in the presence of regulation and those that would prevail in its absence. Although the idea may seem straightforward, its application can be complex. Determining what would occur in the absence of regulation—which establishes a reference point for the calculations—may involve a considerable amount of judgment.

<table>
<tr><th colspan="2">Table 1
Calculation of Incremental Cost of Regulation</th></tr>
<tr><th>Steps</th><th>Example</th></tr>
<tr><td>Company identifies an action taken to comply with a specific regulation.</td><td>Installation of wastewater pretreatment system to remove 99 percent of pollutants in compliance with Title 40 of the *Code of Federal Regulations,* Chapter 1, Part 128.</td></tr>
<tr><td>Would action have been taken otherwise?</td><td>Pretreatment system without Title 40 would have been designed to remove 95 percent of pollutants.</td></tr>
<tr><td>What was the cost of the action?</td><td>$1,200,000 (from fixed-asset ledger data).</td></tr>
<tr><td>How much would the action that would have been taken in the absence of regulation have cost?</td><td>$800,000 (the cost of installing a 95-percent system).</td></tr>
<tr><td>What was the incremental cost?</td><td>$1,200,000 − $800,000 = $400,000.</td></tr>
</table>

Table 1 shows how the incremental costs (the expenses that would not have been made in the absence of regulation) were computed in one study of water pollution control. Apparently the bulk of the costs would have been undertaken voluntarily.

Sometimes the indirect effects of regulation may be as important as the direct. Consider, for example, the question of mandatory standards to ensure the production of less hazardous consumer products. From time to time, suggestions have been made to require more protection in helmets and other recreational equipment used in playing football. Those using the safer helmets would be expected to receive the benefit of fewer or less severe injuries. However, such a safety standard could impose substantial costs on lower-income youngsters. Perhaps of greater concern, the standards might even contribute to more injuries since the price increases might result in more people playing football without any protective equipment at all. That example illustrates another basic thrust of benefit-cost analysis—to examine the proposed government action not only from the viewpoint of the impact on the business firm but also from the vantage point of the effects on the consumer.

A type of regulatory cost that is large, but difficult to measure, is a grouping that economists refer to as deadweight losses. Regulation often limits the range of permissible prices, practices, or processes. Those legal restrictions may inhibit the most productive use of resources. The loss of the higher output that would result in the absence of the regulatory activity—those deadweight losses—arises from an inefficient combination of factors. For example, the total efficiency of the economy is reduced when regulated surface transportation rates make it necessary for freight to be moved by rail rather than hauled at a lower cost by truck. That is so because more resources are used to achieve the same objective.

When political judgment suggests that it is not feasible to put a dollar sign on the benefits, a benefit-cost analysis still can be helpful by ranking the cost-effectiveness of alternatives. By using this method, which was originally developed for military programs, estimates are made of the costs of different ways to accomplish an objective. Cost-effectiveness analyses permit policy-makers to identify least-cost solutions. In this more limited approach, the analyst assumes that the objective is worth accomplishing. In the regulatory field, this approach may be particularly useful in dealing with programs to reduce personal hazards. Instead of dealing with such an imponderable question as the cost of a human life, the emphasis shifts to identifying regulatory approaches that would maximize the number of lives saved after use of certain resources (such as people or capital), or minimize pain. Rather than a cold, systems approach, such attempts at objective analysis show true compassion for our fellow human beings by making the most effective use of the limited resources available to society.

A regulatory action has an impact not only in the present but also in the future. It is necessary, therefore, to place a lower value on future costs and benefits than on present costs and benefits. The basic notion here is that a given benefit is worth more today than tomorrow, and a given cost is less burdensome if borne tomorrow than today. (This is a restatement of the economic principle that a dollar received today is worth more than a dollar received tomorrow, because today's dollar could be invested and earn a return.) For this reason, future benefits and costs have less weight than today's benefits and costs.

This practice is important in evaluating regulatory actions. If the costs and benefits of two actions appear equal, and most of the benefits of one action occur after five years, while the benefits of the other action occur immediately, then the latter is the preferred alternative. Discounting of the future thus implies that the timing of any proposed action's costs and benefits is an important consideration in its evaluation.

Reliable measures of costs and benefits are not easily achieved or always possible. Should the loss of a forest be measured by the value of the timber eliminated? What of the beauty destroyed? What of the area's value as a wildlife habitat? In view of such questions, it is unlikely that agency decision-makers will be faced with simple choices.

However, the difficulties in estimating the benefits or costs of regulatory actions need not serve as a deterrent to pursuing the analysis. Merely identifying some of the important and often overlooked impacts may be useful in the decision-making process. Examples on the cost side include the beneficial drugs that are not available because of regulatory obstacles, the freight not carried because empty trucks are not permitted to carry back-hauls, and the television stations that are not broadcasting because they were not licensed. On the benefit side, examples include a more productive work force that results from a lower rate of accidents on the job, savings in medical care because of safer products, and a healthier environment that results from compliance with governmental regulations.

At times the imperfections of benefit-cost analysis may seem substantial. Nevertheless, this analysis can add some objectivity to the government's decision-making process. While benefit-cost analysis is capable only of showing the effectiveness of an action, the subsequent decisions of elected officials and their appointees might be envisioned as representing society's evaluations of the equity effects of that action. Economists can provide benefit-cost analyses and studies of the distribution of those benefits and costs, leaving the final decision to society's representatives. Presumably, those individuals are better able to make political decisions on the impacts of the actions they contemplate. Despite its shortcomings, benefit-cost analysis is a neutral concept, giving equal weight to a dollar of benefits and to a dollar of costs.

Not all the criticism of benefit-cost analysis may be valid. The idea of attempting to quantify the effects of regulation outrages some persons. They forget the objectives that economists have in developing such measurements. The goal is not to eliminate all regulation. As economists of all political persuasions have testified before a variety of Congressional committees, it is not a question of being for or against government regulation of business. A substantial degree of intervention in private activities is to be expected in a complex, modern society.

Critics who are offended by the notion of subjecting regulation to a benefit-cost test may unwittingly be exposing the weakness of their position: they must be convinced that some of their pet rules would flunk the test. After all, showing that a regulatory activity generates an excess of benefits is a strong justification for continuing it.

Despite talk of cold, systems approaches, economists are deeply concerned about people as well as dollar signs. The painful knowledge that resources available to safeguard human lives are limited causes economists to become concerned when they see wasteful use of those resources because of regulation.

General Motors, for example, calculates that society spends $700 million a year to reduce carbon monoxide auto emissions to 15 grams per mile, thus prolonging 30,000 lives an average of one year, at a cost of $23,000 for each life. To meet the 1981 standard of 3.4 grams per mile, the company estimates that it will cost $100 million in addition, and prolong 20 lives by one year at an estimated cost of $25 million for each life. Human lives are precious, which is why it is so sad to note another use of that money. It has been estimated that the installation of special cardiac-care units in ambulances could prevent 24,000 premature deaths each year, at an average cost of approximately $200 for each year of life. Thus spending the $100 million for the special ambulances conceivably could save 500,000 lives a year.

Part of the problem in setting regulatory policy is that at times the benefits are more visible than the costs—not necessarily greater, but more evident. If the required scrubber for electric utilities results in cleaner air, we see the benefits. The costs are merely part of the higher electric bills we pay. Thus, the cost of regulation takes on the characteristics of a hidden sales tax that is paid by the consumer.

In the final analysis, the political factors in regulatory decision-making cannot be ignored. Many social regulations involve a transfer of economic resources from a large number of people to a small group of beneficiaries. The Occupational Safety and Health Act's coke-oven standard, for example, protects fewer than 30,000 workers, but is paid for by everyone who buys a product containing steel. So long as regulators avoid concentrating the costs on a small group that could organize political counterpressures, costly regulations can be promulgated easily.

Despite the limitations, there is a useful role for formal economic analyses of regulatory impacts in providing, at least, an ancillary guide to policymakers. As a Federal court stated in striking down [a proposed OSHA regulation]: "Although the agency does not have to conduct an elaborate cost-benefit analysis, . . . it does have to determine whether the benefits expected from the standards bear a reasonable relationship to the costs imposed by the standard." That court's commonsense approach might be the direction to which the public policy debates on regulation could profitably shift.   focus

Thus, Weidenbaum moves the debate over government regulations to a new plane. For the supply-side community, this is not a debate over fairness, equity or consumer rights. It is an attempt to "eliminate inefficiencies in the marketplace," to subject "the public sector to the same type of quantitative constraints as those in the private sector," and to identify an "optimum amount of regulation." That is, government regulations impose costs upon the private sector, and these costs are translated into a *reduced supply*. If supply-side policy is to be successful, these costs must be minimized.

But is Weidenbaum's benefit-cost rule as scientific, objective and detached as he would have us believe? Some say it is not.

Consider the textile worker who asked us how we are going to "decide on a dollar value for a long healthy life, or retirement with dignity." He is concerned that too low a value will be placed on his life and too high a value will be placed on the costs industry will bear. His anxiety is not totally unrealistic.

THE COTTON INDUSTRY PASSES THE BOLL

Dollars and Sense, May/June 1982

In 1970 the Department of Labor estimated that about 35,000 cotton workers were permanently disabled and over 100,000 (18% of the industry's workforce) were afflicted by byssinosis, commonly called "brown lung." Only a year earlier, a leading textile trade journal had scoffed, "We are particularly intrigued by the term 'byssinosis,' a thing thought up by venal doctors who attended last year's (International Labor Organization) meeting in Africa where inferior races are bound to be affected by new diseases more superior people defeated years ago."

Those superior people must be the bosses, because byssinosis has been diagnosed in workers of every color since it was first mentioned in medical literature in 1705. Almost three centuries later the manufacturers have finally had to face reality, coping with cotton dust exposure limits mandated by the federal Occupational Health and Safety Administration (OSHA) during the 1970s.

Unfortunately for textile workers, the manufacturers have found a new ally in current OSHA head Thorne Auchter, who is weaving a tangle of complex economic tales to justify severely weakening those cotton dust standards. Blatant racism is no longer used to discredit efforts to fight brown lung, but it has been replaced by a more subtle attempt to do the same thing through technical comparisons of "cost effectiveness."

Cutting Down Dust

Byssinosis, a crippling respiratory disease affecting cotton mill workers, has been recognized in England since 1942 as an occupational illness for which workers deserve compensation. It causes shortness of breath, chest tightness, and coughing upon the employee's return to work on Mondays. Later these symptoms extend to other workdays, and the disease may eventually result in permanent disability or contribute to death.

The exact cause of brown lung is not known, although it is accepted that high cotton dust levels accompany high incidence of the disease. Particularly troubling, it appears, is the dust that comes from "trash" (twigs and the bract that grows at the base of the cotton boll) mixed with the cotton.

Mechanical harvesters, now in common use, yield cotton with a much higher trash content than the old hand-picking method. The cotton is ginned on site, at the fields, to remove seeds, and is then sold to the mills in huge bales. Unbaling, carding (combing into small strands), weaving, and other processing stages take place at the mills.

One way to reduce the risk of brown lung at all stages would be to improve the ginning process to remove more trash more safely. Ginning, however, is controlled by a different set of owners than milling. It is a seasonal, highly competitive, fluctuating, and low-profit business run by thousands of small operators. Ginners insist that the capital outlays needed for improved equipment would put them out of business.

OSHA proposed weak regulations on ginning in 1977, but the ginners' lobby prevented their adoption. Mill operators claim the high trash content of the cotton they must process is not *their* problem. In short, the ginners and mill owners pass the boll—but neither pays for the damaged health of the workers.

At the mills, however, cotton dust exposure regulations have been in effect since OSHA was created in 1970. The original standard was weak and often unenforced. Political pressure, lawsuits, and direct action by groups like the Brown Lung Association (a group of disabled workers and their supporters) and the Amalgamated Clothing and Textile Workers Union (ACTWU) resulted in stricter standards in 1976 and again in 1978.

These new standards specified that engineering controls (changes in the workplace, including ventilation and new machinery) had to be the primary long-range solution to the dust problem. Cheaper and less effective measures— such as wearing of respirators and removing workers who show signs of byssinosis—were recommended only as interim methods.

Instant Policy—Just Add Numbers!

The American Textile Manufacturers Institute challenged the 1978 standard on the grounds that OSHA had not justified it on a "cost-benefit" basis, nor proved its economic feasibility. This reasoning had frightening implications for potential regulation of thousands of other hazardous substances and suspected carcinogens. In effect, the companies proposed that a certain number of human lives had to be lost before OSHA could regulate a substance.

Cost-benefit analysis has a certain simple logic: Add up total costs to industry of a regulation and total benefits to workers from the regulation, and then compare. Instant social policy! All you have to do is look out there in the marketplace and see exactly what the regulation will cost, and what the improved health of the workers will be worth.

In fact, there is nothing simple or objective about the method. Any calculation about the size of costs or benefits involves political judgments that will be made differently by different observers. It is precisely because the economic system does not place a high enough value on workers' health (you can't sell it, after all) that regulations are needed in the first place.

On the practical side, how do you decide on a dollar value for a long healthy life, or retirement with dignity? How can you add up the benefits of regulation when the full health impact of brown lung—or asbestos or chemical poisoning—is not yet known? And where to do you get reliable figures on the costs to industry?

One way to figure "benefits" to workers is to calculate how much more money a worker who dies or is forced to retire would have made if he or she had worked a normal lifetime. Depending on the prevailing wage, which for cotton mill workers is only 60% of the national average, that could be pretty low. For the 48% of the cotton workforce that is female, and the 20% that is black, expected earnings are particularly low. Does this mean that their lives are worth less?

It doesn't take an economic whiz to realize that "benefits," as industry figures them, don't place much value on workers' lives. As a lawyer from the U.S. Chamber of Commerce put it, "Is a human life worth $10? Of course it is. But when you start going up the ladder, you have to start making some judgments, no matter how cold and callous it sounds."

As for costs to industry, the history of vinyl chloride regulation provides a clue to the abuse of cost-benefit techniques. When vinyl chloride standards were debated within OSHA in 1975, plastic manufacturers complained of compliance costs of $90 billion. Not only did that estimate turn out to be 300 times too high, but some manufacturers ended up making money from their efforts at compliance, because the new, safer equipment also saved labor and materials.

The same may be true for cotton dust compliance. During the 1977 OSHA hearings, the manufacturers insisted that compliance with new standards would cost upwards of $2.3 billion. The figures supporting this estimate were left to the imagination. The companies refused to release information they had about cost of new equipment that could meet OSHA's standards.

The Textile Workers Union was able to get some of that information from Czechoslovakia, where the more advanced technology is already in use. They also produced copies of requests cotton firms had made to the Treasury Department for rapid depreciation allowances on the old machinery that would have to be replaced. These requests included the industry's estimate of what the new machinery would cost: $450 million over a three-year period, not $2.3 billion.

The union claimed the true cost would be even lower, because one factor overlooked by the cotton millers (and generally overlooked by manufacturers in any such cost-benefit analysis) was the improved productivity and durability of the new machines.

Back to the Dictionary

The manufacturers' challenge to the '78 regulations went all the way to the Supreme Court, which finally didn't buy it. In June 1981, the Court ruled that "Congress has already defined the basic relationship of costs to benefits when it passed the Occupational Safety and Health Act of 1970." That relationship "places the benefit of worker health above all other considerations except the feasibility of achieving that benefit."

That decision sent industry racing back to the dictionary, but by this time they had a new ally—Reagan-appointed OSHA director Thorne Auchter. Less than a year after the Supreme Court decision, the cotton dust standard is again up for grabs, though this time the challenge has come in more subtle garb. Ostensibly because of "new health data," OSHA is now studying the "cost effectiveness of compliance (which) may result in reconsideration of the present standard."

In the new "cost-effectiveness" approach, unlike the cost-benefit analysis, benefits are not weighed against costs. Rather, different methods of complying with a given regulation are compared according to their costs. This makes sense only if the different methods can all reach the same standard, and if they don't compromise the goal of a health workplace. That is hardly what's going on, as OSHA's new management attempts to talk itself around the Supreme Court victory the agency's own lawyers won in 1981.

In the cotton dust case, the varying methods under consideration are engineering controls, respirators, and medical surveillance of workers. Only engineering controls—that is actual changes in the machinery used—decrease the dust levels associated with the disease.

Respirators are difficult to work with, and a study by the National Institute of Occupational Safety and Health has found that they are unreliable under real working conditions. Medical surveillance, therefore, has been a favorite of the industry. This involves monitoring of workers' health by the employer, and removal of any worker for whom byssinosis symptoms appear. It can help identify brown lung victims before the disease becomes chronic, but it is not foolproof and often comes too late.

In challenging the 1978 regulations at the time they were proposed, the textile firms argued that medical surveillance would be as effective as engineering controls. In the study that was supposed to back up this claim, however, anyone with a 60% or better breathing capacity was considered "normal" and unaffected by any work-related disease.

What's more, all the data in this study came from company doctors, to whom workers fear admitting brown lung symptoms because the result will be firing or rotation to lower-paying jobs. To top it off, the "study" had no control groups or standard statistical evidence, no clear methodology, no review by other scientists, and no authors willing to answer questions about it!

Yet strangely enough, when these same folks now submit a similar study,

Auchter says "new health data" justify reviewing the standard. This time, the manufacturers' association claims that brown lung affects only 0.5% of cotton workers, not 18% as previously thought.

OSHA has not only bought this argument, but is going ahead with the companies' dirty work by commissioning its own "Regulatory Impact Analysis" study, once again relying on the medical and scientific data supplied by the industry. The union charges that four of the five guidelines for this analysis explicitly violate the 1981 Supreme Court decision.

The only way to conduct a meaningful cost-effectiveness study would be to have independent scientists do rigorous long-term studies of the two methods of preventing brown lung—engineering controls and medical surveillance—on two distinct test populations. Instead, it's likely that OSHA will "find" in the existing company health data enough justification to forget about engineering controls altogether, thereby saving millions for the employers.

A victory for the companies on this issue would set a precedent for "reevaluating" other current standards in other industries as well. The potential benefit to industry from avoiding government regulation and investment in a clean workplace is enormous—but the potential cost to workers' health is also.   fOCus

Although benefit-cost analysis appears to be scientific, judgments must be made as to how we will measure these costs and benefits. As our last essay points out, benefits are usually measured by how much more money a worker would have earned if the worklife of the individual had not been shortened by the brown lung. That is, if the cause of byssinosis is removed from the working environment and worker A is not forced to retire at age 50, but can work to age 70, the benefit is determined by multiplying the extra 20 years of work by the average wage this worker would earn. It is precisely at this point where the scientific character of the benefit-cost rule begins to break down. What happens if by chance worker A's average wage is one-half, one-third, or one-fourth of worker B's wage? Is worker B's life worth twice as much, three times as much, or four times as much as worker A's? Just because wages are low in the textile industry, do we as a society want to say that the lives of the workers in that industry are worth less than the lives of workers in the steel industry, the auto industry, or the oil industry? It is unlikely that a daughter, son, mother, or father of a textile worker would think that.

In short, benefit-cost analysis is plagued by an inherent social bias. It places a lower value on poor people than it places on wealthy people. It says that just because you are less successful in the marketplace, you will receive less benefit from a clean environment than that received by a more successful market participant. Therefore, plumbers are worth more than high school teachers; fathers are worth more than mothers; and college graduates are worth more than high school graduates.

The critics of supply-side economics do not stop here. They also argue that the insistence upon benefit-cost analysis is a purely diversionary tactic on the part of supply-siders, and that insisting on applying benefit-cost rules simply provides the supply-siders time to dismantle existing regulatory agencies. No case is more to the point than the EPA. A recent article in the *New Republic* asserts that: "The lowest priority at the Environmental Protection Agency these days is environmental protection." The authors go on to note that "the EPA has become the Reagan Administration's most faithful outrider in the long march to a deregulated—or, more accurately, degoverned—America."

POISON AT THE EPA?

New Republic, March 24, 1982

The lowest priority at the Environmental Protection Agency these days is environmental protection. The EPA has become the Reagan Administration's most faithful outrider in the long march to a deregulated—or, more accurately, de-governed—America. The agency's latest outrage is its scrapping of rules that ban the wanton dumping of liquid "hazardous wastes" in landfills and open pits, a practice with a proven tendency to poison water supplies, causing such nasty side effects as cancer and birth defects. When industry complained about these "onerous" rules, the heart of Anne Gorsuch, the Administrator of the EPA, melted. She overrode her staff's recommendations and announced that in ninety days the agency will issue much weaker standards, allowing up to 25 percent of the capacity of dump sites to be filled with barrels of poisonous liquid. For the interim, Ms. Gorsuch suspended the rules entirely. The result is a three-month binge that has already begun, as the chemical industry and others clear out their overstocked barrels and dump whatever they want, wherever they want, whenever they want.

The regulations on hazardous waste disposal, ordered by Congress in 1976 and promulgated by the Carter EPA in 1980, were the first attempts to do something about the 94 billion pounds of toxic garbage that the U.S. produces each year. It was hoped that, with these rules in place, another costly Love Canal nightmare could be averted. Given the many preferable alternatives to landfill dumping—such as incineration and recycling—that hope was not unreasonable. But at today's EPA, such wise, long-term environmental planning has been obscured by an obsession with short-term money costs. Ms. Gorsuch proposes to cut such costs by eliminating the quarterly checks on groundwater that flows under hazardous waste facilities, as well as the requirement that those facilities have plans for coping with toxic disasters. The agency even turned aside a proposal made by the chemical industry that dump sites be lined with impermeable material to catch the leaks. These actions fly in the face of Congressional intent; worse, they reveal the EPA's short-sightedness. In addition to the obvious health hazards posed by the policy, the expense of cleaning up tomorrow's Love Canals will far outweigh any savings that industry and government gain today.

Ironically, some of the loudest criticism of the EPA's proposed revisions have come from segments of industry. The few businesses that had the prescience to set up alternative forms of toxic liquid disposal now find themselves at a competitive disadvantage with the many more that didn't. The EPA's actions have rewarded the polluters and penalized the long-term planners and the environmentally conscious. Two firms that have invested heavily in alternative technology—ENSCO and SCA Services Inc.—have joined the Environmental Defense Fund in a suit to reimpose the ban. Faced with a barrage of complaints, the EPA has announced that it will begin hearings on March 11 to reconsider its decision.

The EPA's suspension of the dumping ban is only one of the most visible expressions of the agency's reverse approach to environmental protection. Throughout the agency, programs continue to be cut with the same ruthless abandon that has characterized the entire budget exercise. The average American's exposure to toxic chemicals is expected to double in the 1980s. In the wake of Love Canal, Congress required the agency to tackle the massive job of researching and controlling environmental toxics, a task which would have doubled the EPA's workload. Having invested over $130 million in the program, the EPA was ready to start regulating some 120 priority poisons this year. But the Reagan-Gorsuch budget calls for an overall 42 percent reduction in the agency, which has entailed the virtual elimination of its toxic control program. Specifically, Ms. Gorsuch's plans would result in a cut in staff from 11,400 to 6,000, and in the agency's purchasing power from $1.4 billion to about $525 million (after inflation) over the next two years. If Congress permits this to go through, not only will the EPA be unable to tackle its new job of regulating environmental poisons, it will no longer have the means to do its old job of keeping the air and water clean. As former assistant administrator William Drayton points out, "To think that half an agency can do twice as much is sheer illusion."

The EPA's sharp move away from enforcement and prosecution is equally alarming. As soon as she took office, Ms. Gorsuch abolished the agency's enforcement division and scattered its staff among the various other programs. Yet for the past eleven years that division has been the key to the EPA's effectiveness. If the Clean Air Act and the Clean Water Act have had impressive results, it is primarily because polluting industries were brought to court and sued. The EPA's new approach to enforcement can be easily gauged by the number of cases it has filed involving hazardous waste sites. In the last eighteen months of the Carter Administration, when the regulations took effect, fifty-five cases were filed. In the fourteen months since Mr. Reagan came into office, six cases have been filed, and only two of them since Ms. Gorsuch took over in May.

Furthermore, Ms. Gorsuch plans to stop spending money on those sites already determined to be dangerous health hazards. In one of its last gasps, the 96th Congress imposed a tax on chemical companies to create a

"Superfund" to pay for cleaning up other existing Love Canals. Next year $283 million from the fund will be made available to the EPA. Even though Ms. Gorsuch herself has listed 114 toxic dumping sites that pose an immediate danger to the public, she has asked for only $190 million, and intends to spend far less than that. Indeed, only a minute fraction of the money she received in 1981 has been spent.

Given the enthusiasm with which Ms. Gorsuch has used the Reagan budget cuts to undermine her own agency, how does she plan to control pollution and protect the environment? One answer, apparently, is voluntarism, which she expects will fill the gap when the EPA's regulations are stripped away. Since the agency will no longer enforce the laws on the books, it must assume that American business will suddenly cease pursuing short-term profits in favor of the long-term health considerations of us all.

The other answer, of course, is the new federalism. Gorsuch has repeatedly proclaimed her belief that more responsibility for pollution control should be handed over to the states. But even if the idea of having fifty different sets of regulations didn't make the concept impractical, the Reagan budget would make it unfeasible. Grant money allocated to the states has been drastically slashed: state water grants by 51 percent, state air program grants by 20 percent, state drinking water grants by 23 percent, state hazardous waste grants by 9 to 16 percent. Moreover, state governments have shown no great enthusiasm for the idea. The state legislatures of Idaho, Iowa, and Wyoming have already responded to Gorsuch's attempts to increase their role in pollution control by voting to hand that responsibility right back to Washington.

The fact is that pollution cannot be handled state by state because pollution does not respect state lines. It plumes into the air, seeps into water that flows across state borders, and washes up on beaches and banks lapped by interstate oceans, rivers, and lakes. Nor can pollution be tamed by the intangible laws of voluntarism. Even libertarians agree that this is one problem the market isn't equipped to solve. All the market can do is make matters worse, by punishing those companies that spend money on what the Constitution calls the general welfare, and by allowing industry to play the states off each other. The Reagan-Gorsuch approach to environmental protection is suitable only for a world in which pollution grows on trees.

The EPA is fast becoming a mere facade, like a mock building on a Hollywood set. Half the agency's top positions are still vacant and the existing staff is melting away by attrition at an annual rate of 12 percent. To avoid carrying out its mandate, the Reagan EPA has followed a consistent pattern of delaying tactics, nonenforcement of standards, and, as Representative Toby Moffett, Democrat of Connecticut, recently wrote, "deciding which programs to kill or cripple, then cynically using the budget as a justification of those political decisions." It is time for bipartisan action in Congress to put an end to this appalling pattern, before the EPA itself is added to the list of endangered species.   f⊙Cⅰs

Conclusion

So, the debate rages on. Supply-side advocates maintain that taxes and regulation interfere with the operation of an efficient marketplace. Their opponents retort that the market won't be measurably more efficient if taxes and regulations are kept to a minimum while equity will certainly be sacrificed. Only time will tell who is right and who is wrong.

We do know that the supply-side community has staked its future on the impact of these cutbacks in taxes and regulations. It is these programs that will stimulate the economy and provide the support upon which a streamlined, more functional government sector will be built, say supply-siders. These programs are only one step, however, in the overall Reagan economic program. Another important element involves cuts in expenditures, and this is the topic of the next chapter.

CHAPTER 4

Slowing the Growth in Federal Government Spending

Introduction

A second major component of the Reagan supply-side economic program was a reduction in the growth of Federal government expenditures. The Reagan administration estimated that these outlays had been growing at an annual rate of 14 percent over the three fiscal years ending in September, 1981. This growth pattern had resulted in an increase in the absolute size of the Federal government, as well as an increase in the relative importance of Federal spending in the national economy. Indeed, Federal government spending as a percent of Gross National Product has increased steadily over the past 30 years. In 1951-60, the average was 18.7 percent, increasing in 1961-70 to an average of 19.5 percent. This rose in 1971-80 to an average of 21.5 percent, and then to an estimated *24 percent for calendar year 1982*. Thus, the goal of the administration was to reduce the growth rate of Federal government spending to a level below that of the Gross National Product. If this could be accomplished, it would mean the Federal government would lose some of its economic power, and the private sector would gain that power.

The substance of the Reagan administration's expenditure initiatives was contained in the Omnibus Budget Reconciliation Act, signed into law on August 13, 1981. This legislation was designed to reduce the growth rate of Federal government expenditures from the aforementioned 14 percent to an annual growth rate of 7 percent for the three fiscal years beginning in October, 1981. Since this growth rate was below that estimated for the Gross National Product, Federal government spending was expected to fall below 20 percent of Gross National Product by 1985. Thus, the legislation was seen as a major victory in the struggle to decrease the relative importance of the Federal government in economic affairs.

This attempt to reduce the growth rate of Federal government expenditures legislatively was not simply a case of Republican-conservative goals prevailing over those of the Democratic-liberal camp. A large number of Democrats voted with Republicans to reduce Federal government spending. For example, in his last *Economic Report,* President Carter stated: "It is my view that we must strike the balance so as to restrict for some time the overall growth of Federal spending to less than the growth of our economy, . . ."

This is not to say that there was no disagreement. However, the disagreements were over specifics. How much should the growth rate in government spending be reduced, and which programs should be affected? The supply-side Reagan administration demanded cuts in the growth rate of government spending that were far deeper than many Democrats would allow. The supply-siders also demanded a sharp *increase* in defense spending and a sharp *decrease* in social welfare spending. The traditional liberal

Democratic camp resisted the cuts in the social welfare programs while admitting there was a need for an increase in the growth rate of defense spending. In regard to this last point, it is interesting to consider President Carter's position on this issue. Carter was also quoted as indicating that there was a need for . . . faster increase of the military component of the budget."

We must not over-emphasize the apparent agreement on the need to decrease the growth of Federal government spending and the need to increase the growth of military spending. There was an extensive and acrimonious debate over these expenditure issues. Supply-side proponents defended both the size of the budget reductions and the cuts in specific programs by stressing the gains that would be achieved by reducing the rate of inflation, strengthening incentives, and increasing the economic freedom of the private sector. Their critics, on the other hand, charged that the proposed changes unfairly burdened the poor and the disadvantaged, and that this broke the social contract which had been a foundation of American society since the 1930s.

Chapter four surveys this debate. The first section provides an overview of the debate over expenditures. The second and third sections then focus on the programmatic changes. Social welfare program cuts are examined in the second section, and the issues surrounding the build-up in defense expenditures are considered in the third.

A Supply-Side Budget: An Overview

Our first two selections are taken from *America's New Beginning: A Program for Economic Recovery* and the *1982 Economic Report of the President.* These statements indicate that the supply-side community sees three roles for the Federal government: (i) to provide for the improved economic performance of the private marketplace, (ii) to provide for national defense, and (iii) to provide some measure of economic protection for those unable to provide for themselves. Underlying the first supply-side proposal is the notion that changes in the Federal budget will enhance economic performance, because a reduction in government spending will free up resources for use by the private sector. This will increase the overall level of efficiency, which, in turn, will reduce the rate of inflation because of the increase in "supply." The second proposal, which calls for an increase in the growth rate of defense spending, will strengthen U.S. defense capabilities and make the nation better able to deal with international political problems. The last proposal, which assumes that the growth of other Federal spending programs will be cut substantially, asserts that these cuts will not jeopardize those who are "truly needy."

IT'S TIME TO CONTROL THE SIZE
OF THE FEDERAL BUDGET

Ronald Reagan, *A Program for Economic Recovery* and
Economic Report of the President, 1982

The uncontrolled growth of government spending has been a primary cause of the sustained high rate of inflation experienced by the American economy. Perhaps of greater importance, the continued and apparently inexorable expansion of government has contributed to the widespread expectation of persisting—and possibly higher—rates of inflation in the future.

Thus, a central goal of the economic program is to reduce the rate at which government spending increases. In view of the seriousness of the inflationary pressures facing us, the proposed reductions in the Federal budget for the coming fiscal year are the largest ever proposed.

Despite the tendency to refer to "cutting" the budget, it is clear that an expanding population, a growing economy, and a difficult international environment all lead to the need for year-to-year rises in the level of government spending. Thus, the badly needed effort to "cut" the budget really refers to reductions in the amount of increase in spending requested from one year to the next.

The magnitude of the fiscal problem facing the United States can be seen when we realize that, despite the $49.1 billion of savings including $5.7 billion in off-budget outlays that is being recommended for fiscal 1982, the total amount of Federal outlays for the year is likely to be $41 billion higher than the current year. (A separate document is being issued by the Office of Management and Budget that outlines the major spending reductions in considerable detail.)

It is essential to stress the fundamental principles that guided the development of that program.

First, and most importantly, all members of our society except the truly needy will be asked to contribute to the program for spending control.

Second, we will strengthen our national defense.

Finally, these fundamental principles led to nine specific guidelines that were applied in reducing the budget:

- Preserve "the social safety net."
- Revise entitlements to eliminate unintended benefits.
- Reduce subsidies to middle- and upper-income groups.
- Impose fiscal restraint on other national interest programs.
- Recover costs that can be clearly allocated to users.
- Stretch-out and retarget public sector capital investment programs.
- Reduce overhead and personnel costs of the Federal Government.
- Apply sound economic criteria to subsidy programs.
- Consolidate categorical grant programs into block grants.

The application of these guidelines has required great care, judgment, and sensitivity. However, we are putting forward over 80 proposals that will carry out these guidelines and affect virtually every segment of our economy except the truly needy. The Administration's insistence on this fundamental principle has meant that programs benefiting millions of truly needy beneficiaries have not been affected by the spending control effort. These programs include social insurance benefits for the elderly, basic unemployment benefits, cash benefits for the chronically poor, and society's obligations to veterans.

The selection of specific reductions has been a difficult task involving the entire Administration as well as much consultation with representatives of business, labor, agriculture, minority groups, and State and local governments.

The spending reduction plan will shift Federal budget priorities so that Federal resources are spent for purposes that are truly the responsibility of the national government. As the table below indicates, our budget plans reflect the increased importance attached to national defense, maintain the Federal Government's support for the truly needy, and fulfill our responsibilities for interest payments on the national debt. The spending reductions will restrain Federal involvement in areas that are properly left to State and local governments or to the private sector.

	SHIFT IN BUDGET PRIORITIES		
Dollar Amounts (in billions)	**1962**	**1981**	**1984**
DOD - Military	46.8	157.9	249.8
Safety net programs	26.2	239.3	313.0
Net interest	6.9	64.3	66.8
All other	26.9	193.2	142.0
Total	106.8	654.7	771.6
Outlay Shares (percent)			
DOD - Military	43.8	24.1	32.4
Safety net programs	24.5	36.6	40.6
Net interest	6.4	9.8	8.6
All other	25.2	29.5	18.4
Total	100.0	100.0	100.0

Carrying out this program of budget restraint will also halt and begin to reverse the tendency of government to take an ever-larger share of our economic resources. From a high of 23 percent of the gross national product (GNP) in fiscal 1981, Federal outlays are now scheduled to decline to 21.8 percent in fiscal 1982 and to reach approximately 19 percent beginning in 1984.

In conjunction with the tax program that is being proposed, the present excessively high deficit in the budget will be reduced and, in a few years, eliminated. Because of the legacy of fiscal commitments that were inherited by this Administration, balancing the budget will require tough action over several years.

THE FEDERAL BUDGET AND GNP

Fiscal Year	Outlays as Percent of GNP
1981	23.0
1982	21.8
1983	20.4
1984	19.3
1985	19.2
1986	19.0

From a deficit of $59.6 billion in 1980—and of a similar deficit this year if past policies had continued—Federal expenditures are now estimated to exceed revenues by $45.0 billion in 1982, and $23.0 billion in 1983. By fiscal 1984—under the policy recommendations presented in this document—the Federal budget should be in balance. And that will not be a one-time occurrence. As shown in the table below, the Federal budget will actually generate a surplus in 1985 and 1986, for the first time since 1969.

FEDERAL REVENUES AND OUTLAYS

Fiscal Year	Revenues	Outlays	Deficit (−) or Surplus (+)
	(in billions of dollars)		
1981	600.2	654.7	−54.5
1982	650.5	695.5	−45.0
1983	710.1	733.1	−23.0
1984	772.1	771.6	+ 0.5
1985	851.0	844.0	+ 7.0
1986	942.1	912.1	+30.0

The Federal Budget and the Economy

The rewards that the economy will reap with enactment of the spending control plan are many and substantial. In the past, excessive deficit spending has been a major contributor to the initiation and persistence of inflation. Not only have Federal budget deficits at times of expanding private sector activity fueled inflationary pressures, but government's tendency to stop fighting inflation with the first signs of a slackening economy has persuaded firms and workers that they need not fear pricing themselves out of business with inflationary wage and price increases. With the plans for controlling government spending, the Federal budget will become a weapon against inflation, rather than one of its major causes.

During the decade of the 1970s, the Federal budget was in deficit every year. In 1970 the deficit was a relatively modest $2.8 billion; in 1980 it was nearly $60 billion. Outlays soared by almost 200 percent. When this Administration began, the prospect was for a continuation of these alarming trends.

Fiscal Year	Receipts	Outlays	Deficit (−)
	(in billions of dollars)		
1970	193.7	196.6	−2.8
1971	188.4	211.4	−23.0
1972	208.6	232.0	−23.4
1973	232.2	247.1	−14.8
1974	264.9	269.6	−4.7
1975	281.0	326.2	−45.2
1976	300.0	366.4	−66.4
1977	357.8	402.7	−44.9
1978	402.0	450.8	−48.8
1979	465.9	493.6	−27.7
1980	520.0	579.6	−59.6

Many of the program reductions that are being proposed will contribute to a more efficient use of resources in the economy and thereby higher levels of production and income. No longer will the average American taxpayer be asked to contribute to programs that further narrow private interests rather than the general public interest. In many cases, such services are more appropriately paid for with user charges. By consolidating a variety of categorical grant programs into a few block grant programs, the resources spent will provide greater benefits because the levels of government closer to the people can better recognize their needs than can Washington. And by reducing Federal deficits and off-budget Federal financing we will ensure that Federal borrowing requirements do not crowd more productive private activities out of the market.

The budget that is being proposed will restore the Federal Government to its proper role in American society. It will contribute to the health of the economy, the strength of our military, and the protection of the less fortunate members of society who need the compassion of the government for their support. Many special interests who had found it easier to look to the Federal Government for support than to the competitive market will be disappointed by this budget, but the average worker and businessman, the backbone of our Nation, will find that their interests are better served.

Economic Report of the President

The federal budget presents economic policymakers with three fundamental questions. First, how much should the Federal Government spend? Second, how should that spending be allocated? Third, how should the spending be financed—by current taxes only, by borrowing to cover a deficit in tax revenues, or by adding to the monetary base. Without spending there would be no need to impose taxes or to borrow to cover deficits. The composition of a given level of spending has implications for how it should be financed. And the choice of the level of spending is influenced by the recognition that government spending cannot indefinitely grow faster than the economy and that the financing mechanisms available to the government impose costs on the economy. . . .

The Administration's spending policies rest on both philosophical beliefs and economic judgments. As discussed in Chapter 2, the view that the size and scope of the Federal Government are too large reflects the belief that most individuals know best what they want and how best to attain it. In the aggregate their actions will generally result in the most appropriate distribution of our economic resources. This belief is accompanied by the judgment that resources left in the private sector generally are more effective in generating growth and productive employment than resources moved to the public sector.

Because of these philosophical beliefs and economic judgments, the Administration has initiated a major transformation of the role of the Federal Government in the U.S. economy. The Administration's economic recovery program will change both the size and the nature of government involvement, reversing the trend of recent decades when the Federal budget usually grew faster than the rest of the economy as the Federal Government took upon itself responsibilities that had previously been left to the private sector or to State and local governments. . . .

The shift in the role of the Federal Government is more than a reduction in size. It also encompasses a restructuring of priorities at the Federal level and a reallocation of responsibilities and resources between the Federal and the State and local levels of government. Within the Federal budget, spending will shift toward those activities that, in this Administration's view, reflect truly national needs, such as strengthening the Nation's defenses and maintaining the integrity of the social insurance programs.

Economic criteria will be applied to various spending programs to help ensure that the resulting benefits offset the costs to the taxpayers who ultimately must bear them. These criteria should apply not only to direct Federal spending, but also to on- and off-budget credit activities. Such Federal credit programs reallocate national resources by financing activities that might not be attractive to investors in the private market.

The first step in the realignment of responsibilities among Federal, State, and local jurisdictions was the consolidation of a number of categorical grant programs into block grants in fiscal 1982. The second step, proposed in the budget for fiscal 1983, is to shift responsibility for some programs now jointly operated by the States and the Federal Government either to the States or to the national government, and to turn some other programs that are now wholly federally funded back to the States. The proposed restructuring of functions should be accompanied by a phased withdrawal of the Federal Government from the excise tax base. These proposals are intended to strengthen the Federal system by improving the operation of government at all levels, making it more responsive to the people. . . .   **focus**

The first selection outlines the philosophical goals behind Reagan's expenditure proposals, while the second underscores the practical policy proposals of the Reagan administration. These essays express the fundamental conservative belief that it is desirable—indeed, mandatory—to reduce the role of the Federal government contending "most individuals know best what they want and how best to attain it. In the aggregate their actions will generally result in the most appropriate distribution of our economic resources." But these statements are more than a plea for a reduction in the relative importance of the Federal government. These budget changes must also be seen as a "restructuring of priorities" for the Federal government, with defense becoming more important, and as a "reallocation of responsibilities and resources between the Federal and the State and local levels of government."

These selections should help to place the Reagan supply-side expenditure initiatives into their proper perspective. The Reagan administration hoped to achieve a reduction in the growth of government spending which would decrease the relative importance of the Federal government and increase the relative importance of the private sector. The anticipated consequence of this policy would be to increase economic growth and economic freedom, and to reduce the rate of inflation. But spending rates were not to be cut for all programs; in the case of defense, the rate was to be increased not decreased. Still, for the remaining programs, the Reagan administration stated that it would preserve "the social safety net."

Critics of supply-side economics found many aspects of these proposals disturbing. Even those who agreed with the general supply-side prescriptions of decreased overall growth of government spending, increased defense spending and a balanced budget, disagreed with many specific issues. There were those who wanted broader definitions of the terms "truly needy" and "the social safety net," and those who wanted more narrow definitions. There were those who feared the changes benefitted the rich at the expense of the poor, and those who feared that the policy makers had not gone far enough in reducing expenditures. There were those who argued that we must rearm, and those who argued that it was too expensive. It is to these issues that we now turn.

Changes in Social Welfare—Income Security Expenditures

There will be at least two difficulties when discussing the changes in social welfare expenditures. First, some programmatic changes were proposed for fiscal year 1982 and became law with the Omnibus Budget Reconciliation Act; these must be differentiated from a second set of changes which were proposed for fiscal year 1983. Second, it is not always clear whether the lawmakers are talking simply in terms of increasing or decreasing the absolute dollar level of expenditures, or whether they are referring to increases or decreases in the "current service levels." This latter distinction is important and complex enough to merit further discussion.

A "current service outlay" represents an estimate of how much a program would cost if the service level were to remain unchanged while economic parameters were allowed to change. For example, current service outlay of unemployment compensation would assume no changes in eligibility requirements, level of benefits, or length of benefits. However, economic conditions will change, and this change will affect the cost of the program. In this case, the key element is an estimation of what the unemployment rate will be. If the unemployment rate falls and the service level is constant, the programmatic costs will fall. If, on the other hand, the unemployment rate is expected to rise, a constant service level will necessitate a larger budget commitment. For other programs, the rate of inflation may be a key determinant of outlays and, thus, must be anticipated when estimating current services outlay. Costs of new policy initiatives can now be isolated. The costs are simply the difference between the estimates of current services outlay for a particular fiscal year and the administration's proposed budget for that fiscal year, for the latter budget includes the impact of the new policy initiatives.

With this in mind, consider that one forecast estimates there is a $34 billion difference between the fiscal 1982 current services budget for social programs, which would have been in effect under the Carter administration, and the budget proposed by the Reagan administration. That is, the Reagan administration would be spending $34 billion less. This estimated difference increases for fiscal 1983, when the supply-siders propose to cut an additional $41 billion from the current service level budget. However, it is important to recognize that even though the proposed outlay figure is below the current services outlay figure for a fiscal year, the proposed figure may still be higher than the amount actually spent in the preceding year. That is, the supply-siders recommended and were successful in enacting a reduction in the rate of growth in spending, not a reduction in the absolute level of spending.

The specific actions taken by the Reagan administration during 1981 and reflected in the Omnibus Budget Reconciliation Act were summarized by the *Congressional Digest* as follows:

. . . abolition of the public service employment program and the Young Adult Conservation Corps, substantial reductions in the CETA [Comprehensive Employment Training Act] program, trade adjustment assistance, extended unemployment benefits, medicaid payments to the States, AFDC [Aid to Families With Dependent Children], Economic Development Administration, Appalachian Regional Commission, child nutrition, food stamps, subsidized housing, mass transit aid, synthetic fuel development, pay raises for Federal Workers, cost of living increases for Federal retirees among others. Additionally, cuts were made in veterans programs, the Legal Services Corporation, endowments for the arts and humanities, community action programs, foster care and child adoption, postal subsidies, and public broadcasting.

These major programmatic cutbacks were enthusiastically justified by many in the supply-side community. In our next essay, John Cogan, Assistant Secretary of Labor for Policy, Evaluation and Research, argues that the nature of today's unemployment is quite different from the unemployment that was experienced in the 1930s. It is important to differentiate between the unemployment we are experiencing in the 1980s from the unemployment of the 1930s for two reasons. First, the supply-siders had to demonstrate that the budget cuts in social services would not really hurt the unemployed. To this end, they argued that: (i) today's unemployed person is young, with about one-quarter of all the unemployed being teenagers; (ii) the average person is usually unemployed for a "very short time"; and (iii) the typical unemployed person is from a family whose income is quite close to the average income for all families. In short, they contend unemployment is not necessarily an indication of severe financial hardship; to be unemployed is not as bad as it used to be. Second, given this understanding of unemployment, the supply-siders could underscore the need for their policy prescriptions. They could call for programs to spur economic growth and to curtail programs which made unemployment attractive. In this way, workers would have a real economic incentive to take the jobs that would be created by the economic expansion the supply-siders forecasted.

UNEMPLOYMENT ISN'T AS BAD AS IT LOOKS

John F. Cogan, *Vital Speeches,* April 1982

Last Friday the Labor Department reported that unemployment had reached 8.9 percent of the labor force. At only one other time since the second World War has it been this high.

That certainly should give cause for concern. Unemployment puts a strain on people, both economic and emotional. Many unemployed people are being priced out of the housing market and are starting to wonder if they'll ever be able to afford what has long been part of the American dream. Some are living in poverty, and even for those who are not in economic straits, unemployment often takes an emotional toll as they start to question whether they are of use to anyone.

But our concern for the unemployed should not lead us to propose solutions that are based on misconceptions. We have probably all had our views affected significantly by direct or indirect experience with the Great

Depression. Back then, the labor force was largely comprised of male heads of household. Most of the unemployed had been involuntarily separated from their jobs. If a male head of household lost his job, there was generally no secondary income to fall back on since few married women worked, families had very little savings to draw upon, there was no unemployment insurance program, and there were no welfare programs to speak of. In short, unemployment created severe economic hardship and nothing mitigated its harshness.

But unemployment today is very different. Half of the unemployed are younger than age 25 and half of these are teenagers. Only one-seventh of the unemployed are husbands with children at home. And over half of *these* husbands are in households that have one or more family members employed.

Today's average person remains unemployed for a very short time. In 1978, the last time the Labor Department conducted a survey of length of unemployment spells, they found that the average length of unemployment was 6 weeks, sixty percent of all spells of unemployment lasted 4 weeks or less, and only 3.4 percent of the unemployed were out of work for more than six months.

Now it's true that 1978 was a boom year so that unemployment durations may be a little longer today. Nevertheless, it is still true that unemployment is usually temporary and transitional.

Family incomes of people who are unemployed are not far below the incomes of all families. In 1980, the average family income for an unemployed person was $19,400. And in case you think that a large portion of that is unemployment insurance, you're wrong. A full 86 percent of the family income of the unemployed was *earned* either by the unemployed person or by other working family members. Even for individuals who were unemployed for more than six months, the average family income was $16,000, and three quarters of this was earnings. Moreover, only 18 percent of all of the unemployed had family incomes which placed them below the official poverty level.

To summarize, in today's economy the typical person who experiences unemployment lives with other family members who work, is unemployed for a relatively short period of time, and has a family income that's not much below the average income of all families. Losing one's job is a traumatic experience but is far less a financial trauma than it used to be.

Is this to say that we should not be concerned about unemployment? Not at all. For some groups in society, unemployment is a particularly severe problem. And government policies are often the cause of their problems. Black teenagers are a prime example. Their unemployment rate is currently above 40 percent. A substantial fraction of this unemployment is caused by the minimum wage law.

Now you might wonder how a law that says that teenagers must be paid a certain minimum hourly rate could end up hurting teenagers. After all, farmers seem to benefit from laws that set minimum prices on their products. Why the difference? The reason is that when the government sets minimum prices on agricultural products, it buys up the surplus, whereas when it sets a minimum wage it does not. The imposition of a minimum wage induces employers to cut back on the amount of labor they demand. Although that benefits some workers, it prices others out of the labor market altogether. The minimum wage prevents them from acquiring skills and permanently scars a large number of black youths. A special program in the form of a youth sub-minimum would do much to solve their unemployment problem and get them on the first rung of the economic ladder.

For the vast majority of the unemployed, the appropriate policy is one that leads to a healthy economy. The President's economic program, in my view, will lead to a lower unemployment rate in 1982. This is because most of the recent employment reductions have been in durable goods manufacturing. History has shown that if anything spurs production and employment in these industries, it is increased defense expenditures. History has also shown that durable goods industries are particularly sensitive to changes in tax policy. As we are all aware, increased defense expenditures and tax cuts are important components of the President's program.

Now in the coming months you will probably hear about proposals to provide retraining and relocation assistance for "displaced workers." Several bills to that effect are about to be introduced to Congress. The issue is also currently being considered in the Labor Department and at the White House. Now you're probably all wondering, "What is a displaced worker?" From looking at the bills, it's not at all clear. But the basic idea is that a displaced worker is one who has permanently lost his job because of technological change or changes in the composition of demand. The usual examples given are workers in industries like autos, rubber and steel.

The Administration has not yet taken a position on this issue primarily because we are not yet sure about the extent and causes of the problem. It is true that unemployment in these industries is of longer duration than in other industries. However, should we assume that workers can't transfer skills to jobs in other industries? Or is it perhaps a problem with incentives?

While I won't try to answer these questions now, I will offer the following statistics. The average family income of an unemployed worker in these industries in 1980 was over $21,000. Compare this to the average family income for all workers which was $23,200. Even for those who were unemployed for more than six months, family income in 1980 was over $17,000.

Now some of these workers will have to find jobs in other industries and could benefit from adjustment assistance. But can we identify those workers? Our experience with the Trade Adjustment Assistance Program provides an answer. That program was supposed to provide adjustment assistance to workers who had lost jobs due to competition from imports. We found that 70 percent of the people who received benefits returned to work, not just in the same industry, but with the same employer. The fact is that we don't know who is "displaced" and who is not.

Even if we did know, it's still not clear that we would want a displaced worker program. We would first have to know what caused the problem. Take the auto industry. One reason for the employment problem is the changes in the level and composition of demand. These took management by surprise. They also surprised the UAW, which had bargained for and received wage increases which were inconsistent with a contracting industry. The inevitable result of the decline in demand coupled with a high, inflexible wage was a reduction in employment.

We should be sympathetic to the plight of the unemployed auto worker, but policies that cushion labor and management from the consequences of their actions would lead to similar problems in the future. And sympathy for the auto worker should not lead us to ignore the taxpayers who would have to pay for the policies.

Now you know my view. Two months down the road, when you read that the Administration has proposed a program for displaced workers, you'll know how much weight I carry around here.

An unemployment rate of close to 9 percent is cause for great concern. However, rational policies require that we put the unemployment figures in perspective. I hope that my remarks have done so.   **focus**

An examination of the desirability and need for expenditure cuts in social programs, which were initiated by the Reagan administration, is continued in our next selection. Here Professor Yale Brozen of the University of Chicago suggests that a number of social expenditure programs have proven to be counterproductive. He argues that disability pensions have caused the number of disabled workers to increase more rapidly than the size of the total work force, while income maintenance programs have increased both the number of unemployed people and the number of people living in poverty. Thus, these supply-side economists reach the same conclusion as Assistant Secretary of Labor Cogan. They believe that, by making unemployment and poverty less attractive and spurring economic growth, the Reagan administration initiatives will lead to "a greater affluence for everyone, with a reinvigoration of American industry and re-establishment of American leadership in innovation and productivity."

GOVERNMENT REDISTRIBUTION PROGRAMS INCREASE THE NUMBER OF PEOPLE LIVING IN POVERTY

Yale Brozen, *National Review,* July 1982

We have a wide range of interests at the University of Chicago—from pure science and outer space to income distribution and the inner city. In all these activities, we are basically concerned with the discovery of laws that will enable us to understand various phenomena. We, of course, don't have a monopoly on the discovery field, although the association of fifty Nobel Prize winners with the University indicates that we have some eminence in contributions made to knowledge.

Discoveries also occur elsewhere. Professor C. Northcote Parkinson, for example, the former Raffles Professor at the University of Malaya, through many years of painstaking research discovered the law that "Expenses rise to meet income." If he had spent a little time observing the Federal Government, he might have amended his law to read, "Expenditures always exceed income, no matter how great income is."

Lee Loevinger, formerly of the Federal Communications Commission, discovered a very useful law which helps us to understand many things. His law might be called the Law of Irresistible Use. Loevinger's law says, "If a boy has a hammer, it proves something needs pounding." The political-science analogue is, "If there is a government agency, this proves something needs regulating."

I am going to propound a law. Brozen's law is this: *Whenever the government attempts to redistribute income from the rich to the poor, it creates more poor people, impoverishes the nation, and decreases the portion of the tax burden borne by the rich.*

First, what are the means used by government to redistribute income? They are many and varied in design. They range from minimum-wage laws to welfare programs to a steeply progressive income-tax structure that taxes high incomes disproportionately more than it taxes low incomes. A more complete list would have to include rent and other price controls (such as those imposed on natural gas and the lifeline rates for telephone service); unemployment insurance; laws granting power to unions and exempting them from antitrust laws and laws against the use of violence; the bend in the formula relating Social Security benefits to the amount of Social Security tax paid; provision of educational services at no charge or at a nominal charge; medicaid, housing, and urban-renewal programs; toll-free waterways constructed or maintained by the Federal Government; overpayment of low-echelon civil servants and postal workers; agricultural and maritime subsidies; taxation on corporate earnings and property; subsidies provided to the Tennessee Valley Authority;

Rural Electrification Administration loans at 2 and 5 per cent; etc. Some of these programs actually redistribute income from the poor to the rich, while others redistribute in the opposite direction. The net effect of all these programs, however, is to impoverish the rich without producing marked benefits for the poor. Some of the poor are helped, but most of them are worse off than they would be without the programs that are supposed to help them. . . .

Let us turn now to the effect of government largesse on the recipients. The largesse is passed out through many channels—Social Security disability pensions, aid to families with dependent children, general welfare assistance, supplementary security income, food stamps, school lunch programs, basic educational opportunity grants, price supports for farmers, maritime subsidies, mass transit subsidies, heating-cost allowances for low-income families, and many more. Let us take Social Security disability pensions for analysis.

You would think that the supply of disabled people would be completely inelastic. To get a disability pension, you must have been unable to work for at least five months and there must be no prospect that your disability will be cured in the next 12 months. That would seem to fix the population eligible for disability pensions with no possibility for expansion due to an incentive factor.

Disability pensions were first provided under the Social Security system in mid-1957 for workers aged fifty to 64. They were expanded to cover all workers late in 1960. In addition, the monthly payment has grown from $97 in 1961 to over $400. The monthly payment has gone up relative to the wage rate. As it has done so, the number of disabled workers has grown much faster than the total work force. From two million in 1961, the number has expanded to five million currently.

Professor Donald Parsons investigated this phenomenon as part of a project in which he was trying to find out why so many men of prime working age—35 to 64—had dropped out of the work force. The proportion of men 35 to 44 years of age who do not work has more than doubled since 1953, rising from 1.8 to 4.3 per cent. In the 45 to 54 age group, the proportion has increased from 3.5 to 8.7 per cent. And in the 55 to 64 age group the proportion has increased from 12 to 27 per cent.

Professor Parsons measured the effect of a number of factors. He found that the primary factor causing an increase in the proportion of men withdrawing from the labor force was a rise in the pay for not working. He found that a 10 per cent increase in disability pensions increased the rate of nonparticipation in the work force by 6 per cent, other things being equal. A 10 per cent increase in monthly general welfare payments increased the non-participation rate by 3 per cent.

Parsons's findings are illustrative of a general principle. If we tax people for working and subsidize them for not working, we will create more poverty to be subsidized by income-redistribution schemes. We see this same effect in many areas. We can look, for example, at the consequences of different levels of unemployment compensation. The higher the level of benefits relative to previous take-home pay, the longer workers remain unemployed and the more frequent their spells of unemployment. In the states which provide early unemployment benefits—i.e., those in which no waiting period or only a short waiting period is required before unemployed workers can start drawing benefits—and also in states which provide benefits to workers who quit voluntarily and early benefits for people who are on strike, unemployment rates are higher than in states which are less open-handed.

The whole potpourri of "income maintenance" programs, which has only been touched on in this discussion, has had the effect of inducing people to give up employment. Formerly, the majority of the lowest quintile of families (ranked by income) obtained income from employment. Now, only a minority do so, since income without work has become available on increasingly generous terms. In 1953, 58 per cent of the heads of low-income families were employed. In 1978, a prosperous year, only 41 per cent of the heads of low-income families chose to work. Income maintenance programs have been sufficiently generous that many households whose head does not choose to work are in the second quintile of families ranked by income despite that choice. The proportion of households in the second quintile whose head does not choose to work has doubled in the past twenty years, rising from 12 per cent in 1960 to 24 per cent in 1978. The proportion of families in this quintile where the head of household does work has dropped from 81 to 69 per cent.

Nonetheless, the withdrawal of a male head of household from the work force appears (albeit from very sketchy evidence) to reduce family income by about one-third despite the replacement of lost income from other sources. In other words, our income-maintenance programs have provided an incentive to become poverty-stricken. Many prefer leisure to the income obtainable by working even when it means some sacrifice of income, provided the sacrifice does not exceed one-half of the earnings obtainable from a job. As Edgar K. Browning reports in *Redistribution and the Welfare System,* "The low-income population appears to have become less self-supporting and more dependent on government transfers over the past two decades."

Another consequence of this withdrawal from participation in the work force is that our capital stock is focused on a smaller work force. Because of this, the productivity of our tools and other equipment is reduced. With a less productive capital stock, the incentive to save and invest is dampened, in turn, and the growth rate of our national income is slowed.

The course down which public policy has been proceeding is one which has been increasing poverty, destroying capital, and decreasing the rate of capital formation. Many plants are being shut down and the capital invested in them disposed of even though they would still be economically useful if resources were appropriately priced. Some steel mills owned by U.S. Steel are being junked, for example, because the over-pricing of labor makes them uneconomic to operate. Because we pay the unemployed and those living in poverty so well, we are getting a rise in unemployment and a rise in the number living in poverty. The amount of unemployment responds to the demand for unemployment and poverty. The Reagan Administration understands this, fortunately, and has been taking action to help those in poverty *without increasing the demand for poverty*—for example, by persuading Congress to repeal the 8-cent-a-gallon increase in milk prices that was scheduled to go into effect on April 1 of last year, saving the government and us taxpayers $147 million and saving consumers $1.4 billion. It is proposing to further decrease poverty by actually decreasing the demand for poverty.

President Reagan is being criticized for reducing the generosity of the programs which subsidize unemployment and withdrawal from the work force. But if we do not decrease the rewards for not working, there will continue to be a decreasing participation rate, falling productivity, and declining real wages. Poverty will increase because people do what they are rewarded for doing. As long as poverty pays well, the number in poverty but for the various "income security" programs will continue to grow and our affluence will continue to decline. It is that slide into the abyss that Reagan has worked hard to reverse by developing proposals for changes in government programs that, if instituted, will turn the country around.

President Reagan has proposed the course of action that will begin to do that job. In doing so, he has stepped on the toes of almost every group feeding at the federal trough. His proposals, *if enacted,* will cause some pain for awhile as we adjust our expectations and rid ourselves of the "cargo cult" mentality that has grown up in the last two decades. But the reward will be greater affluence for *everyone,* with a reinvigoration of American industry and a re-establishment of American leadership in innovation and productivity. **focus**

For Brozen, Cogan and other supply-siders, the issue is undeniably clear: "If we tax people for working and subsidize them for not working, we will create more poverty to be subsidized by income redistribution schemes." Put a bit more starkly: "Because we pay the unemployed and those living in poverty so well, we are getting a rise in unemployment and a rise in the number living in poverty." In the view of the supply-side community, we have simply gone too far. We have taken programs that were intended to help people in a truly "difficult period of our history" (the Depression) and made these programs available when times are more normal. The supply-siders contend the consequences of this policy drift is also undeniably clear: ". . . it creates more poor people, impoverishes the nation, and decreases the portion of the tax burden borne by the ride."

According to these supply-siders, we must reverse this drift in policy. We must realize, as the Reagan administration realizes, that these programs are designed to relieve conditions which prevailed at a different time. Because times have changed, it is time to change our social programs to make them more consistent with a free enterprise, market economy which provides strong incentives for work. If we do, maintain supply-siders, we will *increase supply, reduce prices, and make everyone, including those who live in poverty, better off.*

The first issue raised by the critics of supply-side economics is whether or not social welfare programs perform the functions for which they were designed. More specifically, the issue is whether or not programs such as food stamps and Aid to Families with Dependent Children create "a welfare class" or whether those programs, as designed, give support to families and individuals who find themselves in temporary economic trouble. The answer provided by the liberal community is that the programs are functioning as they were designed to function. In the words of Richard Coe, "Even for the most disadvantaged of groups, the welfare system does not appear to promote long term dependency." He believes there is little evidence to support the widely-held belief that these programs erode "incentives to work, save or support families" or that these programs are responsible for "a tragic wreckage of demoralization, rage, unemployment and crime." Simply, Notre Dame economics professor Coe contends these programs have not created a permanent and growing welfare class.

DOES A LARGE PART OF OUR POPULATION GET CAUGHT IN THE "SAFETY NET"?

Richard D. Coe, *Challenge,* September/October, 1982

The decade of the eighties has been ushered in by a rising conservative attack on the liberal social welfare policies of the 1970s and late 1960s. The attack has been focused most sharply on those public welfare programs which grew rapidly in the last decade, most notably Aid to Families With Dependent Children (AFDC) and the Food Stamp Program. The most damaging criticism is the argument that these programs actually hurt the poor rather than help them. The central tenet of this argument is that the growth in public welfare programs has resulted in the concomitant growth of a "welfare class"—a group of people who go through life subsisting on government welfare checks, trapped in a system which perpetuates their poverty and dependence. In his widely noted book *Welfare,* Martin Anderson succinctly summarizes this view: "In effect we have created a new caste of Americans—perhaps as much as one-tenth of this nation—a caste of people free from basic wants but almost totally dependent on the State, with little hope or prospects of breaking free. Perhaps we should call them the Dependent Americans."

On the op-ed page of *The Wall Street Journal* last spring, two articles expanded on this theme. In one Charles Murray presented aggregate time-series statistical evidence which indicated that when the effects of increases in GNP are held constant, increases in social welfare expenditures resulted in an *increase* in the percentage of the population living in poverty. In an accompanying piece George Gilder provided the theoretical explanation for this counter-intuitive result. "These redistributional schemes, by eroding the incentive to work, save, or support families, have created in our inner cities a tragic wreckage of demoralization, rage, unemployment, and crime . . . In this heartbreaking harvest of liberal 'compassion,' all the necessary disciplines of upward mobility and small business activity have given way to the vandalism and chaos of gangs and drugs, illegitimacy, and prostitution. Thus poverty has been intensified and perpetuated by income redistribution." Backed by anecdotal stories of the "three-generation" welfare family, the impression conveyed is that welfare is akin to heroin, locking its victims into long-term dependency detrimental to their well-being.

Does the evidence support such a contention? Until now the data have not been available for a thorough examination of the long-term dynamics of welfare use and dependency. With the advent of large-scale panel studies, we are now in a position to determine the pattern of welfare use over an extended period of time. Utilizing data from the Panel Study of Income Dynamics (PSID) initiated at the University of Michigan, this paper examines the welfare experience of a representative sample of the U.S. population over the 10-year period 1969-1978, inclusive. The PSID originated in 1968. Since that time it has followed approximately 5,000 families, interviewing them (and any offshoots from the original sample families) each year. Detailed questions are asked concerning the sources of income of the household, including public welfare income. Based on these data, we answer the following set of questions:

1. What percent of the population received welfare at some time over the ten-year period? What were the characteristics of the welfare recipients?

2. What percent of these recipients were long-term users of welfare? What percent short-term? What characteristics distinguished these groups?

3. Of the welfare recipients, how many were *dependent* on welfare income as their primary source of support? What were the characteristics of this dependent group?

4. What percent of welfare recipients were long-term dependents on the system? What percent short-term? What are the characteristics of the long-term welfare dependent population?

The answers to these questions will shed light on the issue of whether the welfare system promotes and perpetuates dependency among welfare recipients. . . .

What Do the Figures Tell Us?

Over the ten-year period 1969-1978 the proportion of the population in 1969 which was in a household that received welfare in any one year was relatively constant, as shown in Table 1. (Note that the 1972 figure is unusually low due to the lack of data on food stamp use for that year.) From 1970 on, the proportion varied from a low of 9.3 percent in the boom year of 1973 to a high of 11.6 percent in the recession year of 1975. One interpretation often drawn from such results is that there is a relatively stable group of individuals who receive welfare virtually every year, this group being temporarily augmented in times of severe economic downturn and somewhat lowered in times of exceptional growth in the economy. On first inspection, in fact, the results in Table 1 would seem to lend support to Martin Anderson's contention that one-tenth of the population has become trapped in the welfare system in the decade of the seventies.

Table 1
**Percent of the 1969 Population Which Received
Welfare In a Given Year, 1969-1978
(N = 12,563)**

Year	Percent of 1969 Population Receiving Welfare
1969	7.1
1970	10.6
1971	10.7
1972	6.3
1973	9.3
1974	10.5
1975	11.6
1976	10.5
1977	9.6
1978	9.6

Food Stamps are not included in 1972.

A closer examination of individual household experience, however, casts considerable doubt on this conclusion, for it appears evident that these relatively stable cross-sectional figures mark considerable movement on and off the welfare rolls between years. Although only about 10 percent of these individuals were in a household which received some welfare income in any one year, fully *one-quarter* (25.2 percent) were in a household receiving welfare at some time in the ten-year period. The conclusion to be drawn from this simple fact is that the welfare experience is not limited to a stable, relatively small percent of the population. On the contrary, a surprisingly large segment of the population (one out of every four) received some support from the welfare system at some time over the ten year period. . . .

Table 2
Composition of the Population of Welfare Recipients

Characteristic	(1) Percent of entire population	(2) Percent of annual welfare recipients (1977)	(3) Percent of all welfare recipients	(4) Percent of short-term welfare recipients	(5) Percent of long-term welfare recipients
All individuals	100.0	9.6	25.2	12.3	4.4
Head or Wife in 1970					
1. Elderly	12.4	12.8	9.5	7.8	11.7
2. Nonelderly male					
White	16.3	5.3	9.3	13.4	2.5
Black	1.3	1.6	1.8	1.9	1.1
3. Nonelderly female					
White	20.2	12.2	14.4	16.9	10.4
Black	2.4	8.6	5.8	3.4	11.2
Child less than age 10 in 1970					
White	17.0	16.6	17.5	18.4	13.8
Black	2.9	14.0	8.3	2.7	20.9
Other	27.5	18.7	33.4	35.5	28.4
Total					
White	88.3	59.4	71.2	84.5	44.7
Black	11.7	40.4	28.8	15.5	55.3

Time Span

The fact that there is considerable turnover in the welfare population from year to year suggests that welfare recipients spend varying lengths of time on welfare. It is illustrative to divide the population of welfare recipients into three categories: short-term, intermediate-term, and long-term. Short-term recipients are defined as those who received welfare in only one or two of the ten years covered; intermediate-term received welfare in three to seven of the ten years; and long-term recipients received it in at least eight of the ten years. Table 3 shows the distribution of welfare recipients by the number of years of welfare receipt.

Table 3
**Distribution of Welfare Recipients by Length
of Time of Welfare Receipt, 1969-1978**

Length of time of welfare receipt	Percent of all welfare recipients	Percent of entire population
Short-term recipient	48.8%	12.3%
Intermediate-term recipient	33.7%	8.5%
Long-term recipient	17.5%	4.4%
Total	100.0%	25.2%

The most notable result is that one-half (48.8 percent) of all welfare recipients fall into the short-term category; that is, they received welfare in at most two of the ten years examined. On the other hand, less than one-fifth of the welfare recipients (17.5 percent) were long-term, accounting for less than 5 percent of the population as a whole. The results are straightforward—when viewed over a ten-year period, long-term utilization of the welfare system is the exception rather than the rule among the population of welfare recipients.

Are there differences in the characteristics of short-term and long-term welfare recipients? The last two columns of Table 2 provide the answer to this question. The composition of the short-term welfare population closely parallels the composition of the population as a whole (columns 4 and 1). Whites composed 84.5 percent of the short-term welfare recipients, virtually equal to their 88.3 percent share of the population. Nonelderly white male heads of households, who comprise 16.3 percent of the sample, accounted for 13.4 percent of the short-term welfare population. The implication of these results is that no one—in terms of broad demographic groups—is immune from an occasional bad year which temporarily forces him or her to turn to welfare in order to make ends meet.

A look at the composition of the long-term welfare population reveals a different story. This group is disproportionately composed of blacks, who account for 55 percent of the total. The situation is particularly acute for nonelderly black females, who constitute 11.2 percent of the long-term welfare population as compared to 2.4 percent of the population as a whole. As one might expect, long-term welfare use is strongly associated with having young children, particularly for blacks. While young black children comprise only 2.9 percent of the entire population, they accounted for 20.9 percent of the individuals who were in households which were long-term recipients of welfare income.

It should be noted, however, that although blacks, especially black females with children, comprise a disproportionately large share of the long-term welfare population, the fact remains that even for the majority of this group, contact with the welfare system does not appear to result in long-term use. Of all black females who were either heads of households or wives in 1970, 58.9 percent received welfare at some time over the ten-year period 1969-1978. Of this group, only 30 percent were long-term recipients, as defined above. Approximately 60 percent (57.6 percent) of those who received welfare did so for five or fewer years. Thus, even for this group, which was especially prone to spend extended periods of time on welfare, long-term receipt was nevertheless the exception in the decade of the seventies.

Welfare Dependency

The above results cast serious doubt on the idea that the welfare system traps those it touches into a continual state of dependency. But even those figures overstate the extent of *dependency*, for they refer to the receipt of *any* welfare income, no matter how small. The word "dependency" connotes an idea that recipients rely on welfare income as their primary means of support (as Martin Anderson's words imply in the quotation at the beginning of this article.) In the view of its critics, the welfare system instills into recipients an attitude that they are not obligated to provide the basic necessities of life for themselves. The government will supply those necessities if the recipient doesn't make too much money on his own. The end result is a group of people who are dependent on the system to provide them with the necessities of life, but who have little incentive to leave the system and find alternative means of support.

Table 4

Percent of 1969 Population which was Dependent on Welfare Income in a Given Year, 1969-1978

Year	Percent of population dependent on welfare income	Percent of welfare recipients in that year who were dependent
1969	2.9	40.8
1970	2.3	21.7
1971	3.3	30.8
1972	2.5	39.7
1973	2.6	28.0
1974	3.1	29.5
1975	3.2	27.6
1976	2.8	26.7
1977	3.0	31.3
1978	2.7	28.1

Food stamps are not included in 1972.

Dependency is difficult to define, but a reasonable beginning would be to define a household (and the individuals in it) as dependent if more than one-half of the total annual income of the head and wife of the household comes from welfare sources. Under this definition (in which the cash value of food stamps is added to household income), in any given year only about 30 percent of the persons who received welfare were dependent on welfare income in that year as their primary means of support (see Table 4). (This does not mean that the remaining 70 percent of welfare recipients were not dependent on welfare income at some time within the year, for example, in one month.) This dependent group accounted for approximately 3 percent of the entire 1969 population in any given year. But as was the case with welfare, this year-to-year stability in the percent of the population dependent on welfare income disguises considerable turnover in that group, as shown in Table 5. Over the entire ten-year period about three times as many individuals were dependent on welfare income in some year, as would be inferred from the one-year figures. The ever-dependent group (that is the group who were dependent on welfare at any time), accounted for 8.7 percent of the entire population and 34.4 percent of the individuals who ever received welfare income over the ten-year period.

Table 5
**Percent of Population Dependent on Welfare Income,
1969-1978, by Length of Time Dependent**

Length of time dependent on welfare income	Percent of population ever dependent	Percent of all welfare recipients	Percent of entire population
Ever dependent	100.0%	34.4%	8.7%
Short-term dependent	38.1%	13.1%	3.3%
Long-term dependent	22.3%	7.7%	1.9%

How long do people who become dependent on the welfare system remain dependent? Does the system *perpetuate* as well as promote dependency? Defining short-term and long-term dependency analogously to short-term and long-term welfare receipt, the results in Table 5 indicate that approximately 40 percent of those individuals who were ever dependent on welfare income were so for a short term—that is, they were dependent in only one or two of the ten years covered. A little more than one-fifth (22.3 percent) of the ever-dependent population was long-term dependent—dependent on welfare income in at least eight of the ten years. The long-term dependent population accounted for 1.9 percent of the entire population, and only 7.7 percent of the individuals who received welfare income at some time. To summarize, in the ten-year period between 1969 and 1978 only one-third of all individuals who came into contact with the welfare system were ever in a household which was dependent on welfare income in some year. And of those who ever were dependent, only one-fifth were dependent in eight or more of the ten years.

Who were the long-term welfare dependents of the 1970s? Female heads (and wives) and young children accounted for the predominant share (62.9 percent) of this group. Nonelderly male heads were very unlikely to be long-term dependent. One-half of the long-term dependents were white, half black. Because blacks comprise only one-tenth of the population, this means that blacks are heavily overrepresented among the long-term dependent group.

The major contributing factor to this overrepresentation of blacks is the status of black children. Young black children, who comprise only 2.9 percent of the total population, account for 22.8 percent of the long-term dependent population. Their mothers (nonelderly black female heads or wives) likewise account for a disproportionately large share of the long-term dependent (11.8 percent compared to 2.4 percent of the entire population). Perhaps this is not surprising. Black women in general have low expected wages in the labor market, a result of a combination of low human capital and double discrimination (being black and female). With child care responsibilities piled on top of bleak labor market prospects, welfare may be the only source of livelihood for this group. But as was the case with welfare receipt, for the majority of black females who at some time received welfare, or indeed were ever dependent on welfare, long-term dependency was the exception rather than the rule. Of all nonelderly black female heads or wives in 1969 who were ever in a household which received welfare at some time in the 1969-1978 period, only slightly more than one-half (53 percent) were ever dependent on welfare income. Only 15 percent were long-term dependent. Even for the most disadvantaged of groups, the welfare system does not appear to promote long-term dependency.

Conclusions

Over a ten-year period a surprisingly large percentage of the population had some experience with the welfare system. In the aggregate, a relatively stable percent of the population (approximately 10 percent) received welfare income each year. However, over the decade fully one-quarter of the population was in a household which received welfare income at some time.

While the receipt of welfare income was surprisingly widespread, it was also usually of relatively short duration. Of the 25 percent of the population which received welfare in the decade, one-half received it in only one or two of the ten years between 1969 and 1978 (inclusive). Less than one in five (17.5 percent) received welfare in eight or more of the ten years.

Receiving welfare income was clearly not synonymous with being *dependent* on welfare income as the primary source of a person's means of support. Of all persons who were *ever* in a household which received welfare, only one-third were *ever* in a household which was dependent on welfare income.

Long-term welfare dependency was the exception rather than the rule in the decade of the seventies, both for welfare recipients and, perhaps more important, also for that subset of welfare recipients who were at some time dependent on welfare income. Of all welfare recipients, less than one-tenth (7.7 percent) were dependent on welfare income in eight or more of the ten years between 1969 and 1978. Of all welfare recipients who were ever dependent on welfare income, only one in five (22.3 percent) were long-term dependent.

It is difficult on the basis of these results to conclude that there is something inherently pernicious about the welfare system—that it poisons those who touch it with a debilitating dose of dependency. Quite the contrary. The welfare system would seem to be more accurately portrayed as a temporary fallback position for those individuals who suffer unexpected shocks to their more normal style of life. For nonelderly men, these shocks would most likely be an involuntary job loss; for married women, a divorce or separation; for an unmarried woman, the birth of a child. For the vast majority of these people, the welfare system serves as a stepping-stone back to a more normal standard of living. In essence, the welfare system, despite its numerous flaws, by and large fulfills the role that most people probably believe it should fulfill—that of an insurance system against unforeseen (and largely uncontrollable) adverse circumstances. If this characterization of the welfare system is correct, as the findings of this paper strongly indicate, then the idea that the welfare system promotes and perpetuates long-term dependency must be rejected as a myth with little grounding in reality. Unfortunately, like all good myths, there is a germ of truth underlying it. A small subset of all welfare recipients—a subset consisting mainly of individuals (and their dependents) who face extremely unfavorable labor market prospects—are indeed dependent on the welfare system for an extended period of time. The question which the reader, and our society, must answer is whether the existence of such a group justifies the wholesale condemnation of the liberal welfare state.   **fOCus**

The last selection in this section challenges the supply-siders in the Reagan administration head-on. Priven and Cloward, in their book *The New Class War*, readily accept the notion that reductions in income maintenance programs will enlarge the number of people looking for work. But, they argue that there is something fundamentally wrong with how the supply-siders view this phenomenon. Priven and Cloward assert that since supply-siders believe the rich and the poor are fundamentally different, they have established a system where the rich are expected to respond to rewards (tax cuts) while the poor are only expected to respond to punishment (reductions in social welfare programs). According to political scientist Priven and Columbia professor Cloward, the conclusion which emerges from this two-class view of the world is that the Reagan administration's supply-side economic program is a "concerted attack by the privileged and the powerful with Ronald Reagan serving as chairman of the board."

KEEPING LABOR LEAN AND HUNGRY

Frances Fox Priven and Richard A. Cloward,
Nation, November 1981

Almost immediately upon taking office, President Ronald Reagan asked Congress to slash billions of dollars from Federal allocations for social programs. Aid for the unemployed and the poor was the primary target, while spending for defense remained sacrosanct. But the all-out assault on social programs, many of which date back to the New Deal, was launched for reasons that had little to do with defense, tight money or even the New Federalism.

The White House, of course, cited the need to reduce budgetary deficits as the primary reason for the cuts in spending for social programs. Its spokesmen also interpreted the 1980 election as a "mandate" for shrinking the size of the Federal government, especially the part of it that is concerned with social welfare.

But neither of these rationalizations will wash. Even if we accept the need for budget cuts, and even if we buy the unsubstantiated claim that "the electorate" wants less government, we are left with a case for overall reductions in Federal spending—not a license to sock it to the poor.

Actually, the progressive philosophy behind the programs—the idea that government should help the poor and the unemployed—was the real target of the Reagan budget ax. Programs that do not require the applicant to demonstrate need or submit to a means test, like Social Security, Medicare and a variety of veterans' benefits, were left relatively unscathed, while most of the cuts were made in funding for public-service jobs, unemployment insurance, Medicaid, welfare, low-income housing, workers' compensation and food stamps. A reason other than fiscal prudence was the motivating force; conservatives believe that, in an industrial society, aid to the needy reduces business profits by enhancing the bargaining power of the labor force.

The nexus between social programs and the labor market is to be found in the relationship between unemployment and wage levels. A large number of unemployed workers exercises a downward pressure on wages because people who need work will generally accept wages below the going rate. A large pool of unemployed people also acts as a check on the pay and benefit demands of those who have jobs, because the latter, aware of the long line of applicants at the factory gate, are reluctant to jeopardize their own positions. When the unemployed are absorbed by an expanding job market, however, worker demands increase and cut into profits. This, some analysts say, is what happened in the late 1960s, when the long post-World War II boom reached its crest.

Manipulating the relationship between unemployment and wages has been an objective of economic policy in the United States since the Great Depression. Government planners used fiscal and monetary policies that raised or lowered aggregate demand to smooth out the business cycle. Instead of being allowed to swing from trough to peak to trough again, it was regulated. Moderate recessions were induced every few years, however, to increase unemployment without driving it to dangerous levels. The large number of people looking for work lowered wage demands. The promotion of limited unemployment became a major tool for stabilizing the economy and controlling inflation. In 1958, the publication of the Phillips curve, which shows the inverse correlation between unemployment and wage inflation, lent this strategy the cachet of social science.

In the two decades following World War II, the strategy worked. Cyclical increases in the unemployment rate produced the expected fall-off in the rate of wage increases. By the 1960s, however, the relationship was beginning to weaken, and by the early 1970s it no longer existed. According to Barry Bosworth, head of President Jimmy Carter's Council on Wage and Price Stability from 1977 through 1979, an unemployment rate of 6 percent failed to curb inflation following the recession of 1969-71:

> Economists, at first, viewed the problem as one of lags in the response of prices and wage rates; they recommended patience and a continuation of restrictive policies. By the beginning of 1971, however, wage rate increases had actually accelerated slightly despite high unemployment; and, once excess inventories had been disposed of, the rate of price increases also picked up.

The new element in the picture was the expansion of social welfare benefits, which undermined the historic relationship between unemployment and wages. It is not difficult to see how this happened. If the desperation of the unemployed is reduced by the availability of benefits, there is less pressure on them to take the first job they can find, something that economists quickly realized. As Robert Havemen recently put it, the unemployed can now "prolong [their] job search . . . refuse to accept work except at higher offered wages or cease active labor market participation." Or, as Edgar R. Fiedler, Assistant Secretary of the Treasury for Economic Policy in the Ford Administration, explained.

> A change has taken place in the unemployment-inflation trade-off since the mid-1950s. . . . [One reason] is the unemployed today are subject to less economic pain than used to be the case, because of the development of more generous income-maintenance programs. . . . Consequently, most people who lose their jobs today are under less pressure to accept the first offer they get regardless of the pay and working conditions.

Slashing social programs will reinstate the terrors of being without a job. Unemployment benefits will be limited to twenty-six weeks unless joblessness reaches "catastrophic" levels nationwide; moreover, fewer of the unemployed will be eligible for either food stamps or medical benefits. Pressures on the unemployed will be enhanced by adding to their numbers. The dismantling of the jobs programs started under the Comprehensive Employment and Training Act added 350,000 people to the labor market. It has already been announced that 400,000 households receiving money under the Aid to Families with Dependent Children program will be declared ineligible. The Social Security Administration has accelerated a review, begun under the

Carter Administration, of Federal disability payments. Initial reports on 1,300 cases in New York State showed that 38 percent of the aid recipients were not entitled to benefits. The agency expects that 25 percent of the 500,000 cases reviewed nationwide during the next fiscal year will be found to be ineligible. And if the partial Social Security benefits at age 62 are reduced, or if the retirement age is raised to 68, millions of people will be compelled to remain in the labor force. The number of people looking for work will be further enlarged by reductions in housing subsidies, food stamps and Medicaid for the working poor.

Moreover, under the New Federalism, the Reagan Administration is moving to make many income-maintenance programs the responsibility of the states. Food stamp allotments are only the beginning. If this effort succeeds, it will eliminate the equalizing effect of national standards. Benefit levels will be driven down, since state governments are vulnerable to threats from industries to relocate to places where taxes and wages are lower. The decentralization of income-maintenance programs will also antagonize local taxpayers, especially the working poor, who bear the brunt of regressive state sales taxes.

Reagan's "reforms" will thus exert a powerful pressure on people to undersell one another, to take any job at any wage and under any conditions. The effects will be felt by a broad spectrum of people, especially those in the rapidly expanding service sector. Three out of four of those losing benefits will be women, most of them unskilled. They will be hired by the fast-food chains, hotels and offices to cook, serve and clean in competition with the existing low-wage work force, which is already largely female.

At bottom, the Administration holds a two-class view of human nature; it assumes that the rich are very different from the poor and that they require different kinds of incentives. The rich exert themselves for rewards; increase profitability by lowering taxes, for example, and they will step up socially useful investment. The poor, on the other hand, respond to fear and punishment; they must be goaded by hunger, and economic misery makes them more industrious.

In simple and human terms, the welfare state has reduced some of the hardships generated by a market economy that sloughs off the people it no longer needs as it does any other surplus commodity. People have resisted being treated as commodities, believing they had a right to subsistence. And they sometimes fought for that right. The programs of the welfare state were the fruits of those struggles. Moreover, the programs did more than merely protect those with the least power. They grew to a point where they enabled workers to improve their bargaining power. And that is why they are the target of a concerted attack by the privileged and the powerful, with Ronald Reagan serving as chairman of the board.   focus

In conclusion, two points warrant repeating. First, the Reagan administration was successful in achieving a massive restructuring of our social welfare programs. This restructuring was characterized by a pattern of stricter eligibility requirements and lower benefit levels in most programs. Second, although these changes were greeted by widespread support initially, many are now questioning the true motives and the basic wisdom of these policy changes. These concerns seem to emanate from an increasingly broader segment of the population. As we will show in the next section, this same pattern of initial broad support followed by growing levels of criticism also characterizes the defense programs of the supply-siders.

Increasing Defense Expenditures

In absolute dollar terms, defense expenditures during fiscal year 1981 were quite large, totaling some $157 billion. When judged in relative terms, however, defense outlays have become increasingly less important. As a percent of the Federal unified budget, defense expenditures have fallen from 48 percent in fiscal year 1960 and 39 percent in fiscal year 1970, to 22 percent in fiscal year 1981. When judged against the total spending in the economy, defense outlays represented more than 9 percent of Gross National Product in fiscal year 1960, but by 1981 they represented less than 6 percent. (The preceding figures are taken from the *1982 Economic Report of the President.*)

This pattern of falling defense expenditures apparently concerned both Democrats and Republicans. Indeed, President Carter asked Congress to increase both the absolute and the relative importance of defense spending. He wanted defense spending to increase from $157 billion in fiscal year 1981 to $293 billion in fiscal year 1986. This amounted to a $136 billion, or 86 percent, increase. The much publicized Reagan administration increase, on the other hand, called for defense expenditures to rise to $336 billion in fiscal year 1986. This represented an increase of $179 billion or approximately 114 percent. (The figures in this and the following paragraph are taken from *Setting National Priorities: The 1982 Budget.*)

It must be remembered that these increases, in part, are simply necessary to offset the effect of anticipated inflation in the purchase price of military goods and services. Recalculating the outlay projections in constant prices (fiscal year 1982 prices), it is apparent the Carter proposal would have generated a 26 percent increase in real defense spending between fiscal years 1981 and 1986, while the Reagan program calls for an increase in real defense outlays of approximately 52 percent. Thus, in real terms, both Carter and Reagan asked for increases in military spending, but Reagan's request was substantially greater than Carter's. The Reagan proposals would not only increase the *absolute* importance of defense, but also its *relative* importance. Defense outlays as a percentage of total Federal government outlays would rise from 22 percent to approximately 35 percent of the budget by fiscal year 1986. This represents about 9 percent of Gross National Product in 1986, compared to the current 6 percent.

In the debate which enveloped the increase in defense spending, one point became obvious. There was sharp disagreement over whether or not the same level of deterrence—that is, the same level of military preparedness—could be achieved by spending less dollars than Reagan proposed. We open our discussion of this issue with a reading which supports the Reagan position. Commander James P. Mullins takes the position that: (i) the Soviet Union constitutes a real military threat to the U.S., and (ii) the U.S. must "sacrifice whatever it takes to pay the price of freedom."

THE PRICE OF FREEDOM

James P. Mullins, *Vital Speeches,* August 1982

It's a distinct privilege to be here in New York today—to be where a fiercely independent spirit and the unwavering love and support of freedom has existed since colonial times.

In fact, one of the first attempts in the New World to win the independence we enjoy today occurred here in New York. In 1688, a New Yorker named Jacob Leisler led an uprising against the Stuart regime. He had the backing of the common people, but his backing wasn't organized; and, unfortunately, he was hanged for his trouble.

Years later, however, one of the first real challenges to British rule would also come from New York, this time when your state assembly refused to provide quarters and supplies to the British Army—an Army headquartered here in New York. And as we all know, it was in the woods of upstate New York, at Oriskany and Saratoga, where this nation actually began to build the democracy it wanted, where it actually began to win the freedoms it sought.

Forty-two years ago, when those democratic freedoms were seriously threatened by Axis tyranny, it was a New Yorker, Franklin Delano Roosevelt, who provided the leadership that turned this nation into the world's arsenal of democracy. With that arsenal we ended that war, but we did not end all tyranny. In fact, today our freedoms are again in great jeopardy—and today we again need strong leadership to meet the new challenges.

Few would deny that the world today is becoming increasingly more dangerous—dangerous to you, your children, and the democracy and freedoms we all enjoy.

Since yesterday, the Soviet Union has built eight more warplanes, 144 new missiles, 48 more tanks or armored vehicles . . . and has produced enough new hand weapons to equip an additional 1,400 infantrymen.

One would think from this feverish pace, that the Soviets are "just catching up." The fact of the matter, unfortunately for us, is that they caught up years ago . . . during years when we argued incessantly about the value of national defense.

Today the Soviets have almost 1,400 ICBMs . . . we have just over 1,000. Today the Soviets have 1,000 sea-launched ballistic missiles . . . we have about 575. Today the Soviets have some 4.8 million people in uniform . . . we have just over 2 million.

But that's not all. They have more than 7,000 fighter aircraft . . . we have fewer than 4,000. They have 220 attack submarines . . . we have fewer than 100. And they have 46,000 tanks, while we have just 11,000.

One must ask, at this point, just what the Soviets have in mind? Why do they continue to build at such a rapid pace? Why do they continue to subordinate their hard-pressed economy to the acquisition of even more war-making capability?

Frankly, I don't think the Soviets are very fond of our democracy . . . because I think we're standing in the way of Soviet world domination. We're a very large thorn in their side . . . a thorn that, ultimately, they plan to remove!

Just during the time I am speaking with you today . . . just during these few minutes . . . the Soviets will build another two missiles . . . missiles I believe they will aim at our ultimate destruction.

Facing up to that threat will not be easy. In fact, if history is any guide, it will be very difficult for us even to admit to ourselves just how much trouble we're in—to admit that the threat is greater today than ever before in our history— and to admit that, because of past neglect, our arsenal isn't what it used to be.

Historically we've always denied the unpleasant—we've always looked the other way—and somehow we've pretended it didn't exist.

In 1921, President Woodrow Wilson left office a broken and unpopular president . . . not because of any scandal . . . not because of any incompetence . . . but because he dared to attack America's denial of reality.

He dared to chip away at the wall of isolation we were building . . . a wall designed to protect us from the world's unpleasantries. And he dared to look at what his country didn't want to see . . . yet he was utterly rejected by those he tried so desperately to help.

The dangers Wilson foresaw, of course, did not go away. In fact, a decade later, from the ruins of worldwide depression, the seeds of Nazi tyranny were planted . . . yet we still did not want to see. And as the tentacles of imperialism began spreading, there were cries of warning . . . yet we still did not want to hear.

On September 1st, 1939, Hitler started World War II by attacking Poland. Two days later, both Britain and France declared war on Germany. Yet we pretended it was not happening. By the end of the month, Poland had been crushed by the German blitzkrieg . . . and Nazi plans called for a systematic annihilation of Poles . . . an extermination of some 5 million lives. Yet, we said, "surely this can't be true," and we went about our business as usual.

On November 13, 1939, the first bombs fell on British soil. And within a few weeks, food rationing began in Great Britain. But we had all we wanted to eat . . . and no bombs seemed to threaten our serene lifestyle.

We just couldn't admit to ourselves that we were threatened . . . we just couldn't come to grips with the unpleasant reality we faced . . . the unpleasant truth of those cold December days in 1939.

But as we all know, not admitting this reality didn't make it go away—and for us, those days late in 1939 quickly turned into a December 7th day late in 1941—a day when we were taught a painful lesson about the realities of life— and about the realities of death. Fortunately, then, we had the industrial might—we had the time to rearm—and we were able to see the conflict through to victory.

During those terrible years, we all learned a valuable lesson—we all learned that you can't ignore a "1939"—and that if you do, it will quickly become a "1941." But apparently there are many who believe that, as in 1941, we'll have time to rearm America, because I see that same lack of preparedness, that same denial of reality throughout our country today as we saw in 1939. But the sad reality is we will not have time to get our act together—to mobilize and rearm. Modern weapons technology has seen to that.

One need only look at Czechoslovakia and Poland to see clear manifestations of tyranny's expansion. One need only consider the flagrant use of chemical and biological agents in Afghanistan, agents the Soviets have sworn never to use . . . agents that indiscriminately subject even the most innocent child to a cruel and inhumane death. . . .

One need only consider the Soviets' use of these weapons to correctly gauge the value of their assurances . . . the trustworthiness of their sworn oath . . . the hostile intent of their leadership.

Many in this country caution against overreacting to Soviet provocations . . . yet they somehow forget to condemn the provoker. Many are morally outraged that we spend what we do to maintain our nuclear arsenal . . . yet they accept without comment the Soviets' larger nuclear arsenal we must defend against. We need only open our eyes to see the reality we face.

For example, each year the Soviets produce more warplanes than we and all our allies have totally committed for the defense of Europe. Yet many argue about the cost of defending Europe . . . they argue whether such defenses are really needed . . . they argue whether the Soviets really have expansionist designs . . . they argue whether this is really any of our business . . . in fact, they argue and argue some more . . . yet they never face up to the unpleasantness they want so desperately to deny.

Just consider the tremendous concern today, both in government and private sectors, over the size of the federal budget . . . and in particular, the defense budget. Many condemn the increases in defense spending as the cause of our economic ills.

Yet they fail to look at the facts . . . they fail to see that until fiscal year 1982 defense spending, as a function of "real dollars" has been lower than 1962 levels. In fact, except for the Vietnam buildup and in spite of the increases in fiscal years 1981 and 1982, on the average the defense budget declined from 1962 to 1982.

Many look back at the "golden day" of the late Kennedy and early Johnson years, and yearn to go back . . . yearn to return to that time when, they believe, we had our priorities straight . . . when we had defense in its proper, subordinate place.

Well, I'd like to go back to those years too, because we spent a much greater share of our nation's resources for defense then than we do now. In fact, between 1964 and 1979 we reduced defense spending from 8 percent to 5 percent of our nation's GNP. During those same years, however, we increased our federal non-defense spending from 11 percent to 16 percent of GNP. In other words, while we were chopping away at our national security, we were funneling more and more money into non-defense programs.

The Soviets, of course, were not sitting idly by. They took advantage of our desire to deny the unpleasant . . . our fascination with only the nicer things in life . . . and they undertook an unprecedented buildup of war-making capability. During the decade of the '70s, the time when we were under-funding our defense programs, the Soviets were increasing their defense spending dramatically.

There were many weapons systems we didn't buy during that period . . . weapons we should have bought . . . weapons we must now buy at today's inflated prices. For example, we should have bought the B-1 then, but we didn't. Now we must rely on our fleet of aging B-52s, an airplane which, in many cases, is older than the crews who fly it.

It's going to take a great deal of time and money to replace just those B-52s, but we have no choice. Just as we did in the 1930's, we've ignored an unpleasant reality in the '70s. Now it's 1939 all over again . . . now it's time for us to pay the price while we still can afford to pay it!

The United States Air Force has an aging inventory of airplanes, an inventory where three-fourths of the fleet that must deter war . . . that must keep you free . . . three-fourths of that fleet is over nine years old. By contrast, 30 years ago, only 14 percent of our fleet was over nine years old.

But it's not only the fleet that has suffered. The cumulative decrease in military spending has directly impacted our ability to go to war—and thereby, our ability to deter war.

We haven't been able to give our aircrews the flying hours they should have had, we haven't been able to do much of the maintenance we should have done, and we haven't been able to purchase many of the munitions and spare parts we should have purchased.

Additionally, we've had to underfund some of our "people programs"— we've too often capped pay and removed benefits, and we've seen many of the well-publicized problems in morale and retention develop as a direct result.

The decade of neglect has also taken a terrible toll on our defense industry. We've starved out many of our most important suppliers, we've lost many of our most talented people, and we've allowed our industrial base to become outdated and less competitive. So we're in the unenviable position today of needing more, needing it quickly, but not having the capability to produce it.

Fortunately, with this administration's recognition of the problem, our industrial base is now beginning to show signs of recovery. And fortunately, with the real growth we've had in defense spending over the past two years, we've started the process of restoring strategic balance, restocking spares and munitions for readiness, and modernizing our aging forces.

But we must recognize that this will be a long-term effort, one requiring substantial sacrifice and resolve on the part of both the government and industry. For we're not actually increasing our forces yet—we must first catch up from past neglect before we can do that. In fact, our aircraft procurement programs remain well below levels needed to cope with greatly expanded Soviet capabilities. And it still takes years even to produce a few landing gear parts.

Now getting back on the right track is going to be expensive, but the point is that we can afford it. In reality, we'll spend more on alcoholic beverages today than we'll spend equipping and operating our Air Force. And Americans will spend more on recreational activities this year than we'll have in the entire Air Force budget.

Sometimes we just don't seem to function with good common sense—and I think one of those times is now. We don't argue about the cost or value of alcoholic beverages, and we don't argue about the cost or value of recreational activities. But we do constantly argue about the cost and value of defense. And we often defer long-term considerations to the myriad of short-term gains and comforts that tempt us.

Here's an example of what I mean. When we think of our defense budget, we often forget what it would cost us in dollars alone if we were unable to deter war. We're not even talking here about loss of life or loss of freedom. We're just talking about money.

In World War II, where our way of life was clearly threatened, we spent about 542 billion dollars to fight the war and survive. Now this includes 54 billion for veterans benefits which we're still paying today, and 200 billion for interest on war loans.

But have we considered what it would cost to fight that same war today? Assuming just a five percent inflation rate annually since World War II, one would find that the cost today would exceed four trillion dollars. That's almost 19 times the defense budget for FY 1982.

In fact, if you took out a mortgage today at 15 percent for 30 years on a four trillion dollar loan, your payments would be 50 billion 600 million per month. And you know, that's about how we'd have to finance such a war today. If we made the mistake of weakening our deterrence, and thereby could not avoid a war, we'd have to mortgage the future of our businesses and families to pay for it.

To deter war, we must have a military capability which can clearly deal with those who threaten us. Now therein lies our greatest challenge, yet therein also lies our greatest opportunity to preserve the peace. In 1939, after years of neglecting our defense industries, our enemies failed to gauge correctly the ability of America's private sector to produce war material. Had they known that in 44 months we could turn out 310,000 aircraft, 88,000 tanks, 27 aircraft carriers, 211 submarines, 358 destroyers, 900,000 military trucks, and 411,000 artillery pieces—had they known we had this capacity for productivity, World War II may have been avoided.

But our potential adversaries just didn't believe we had it in us—they were not deterred—and war became a reality. Now today, how do you suppose our potential adversaries gauge our defense industry's capability? How credible is that aspect of our deterrent? And how important is revitalizing our defense industry, even at the expense of other programs.

It's important to remember that defense, by keeping us out of world conflict, gives us the freedom and resources to do many other things. In this regard, defense is our greatest social program—for it has allowed us to even think about doing all those other "nice things" in life. But what good will our social programs be if we fail to deter war—or even worse, if we fail to keep this nation free? What good will urban development be if conquering armies are marching through our city streets?

These are questions we'd better start asking, because it's 1939 again. The threat to our way of life, to our own well-being and to the well-being of our future generations grows relentlessly around us, even as I talk with you now.

We've got to wake up, we've got to stop bickering among ourselves, we've got to get away from our nearsighted infatuation with short-term profit and comfort—and we've got to get on with the deadly serious business of deterring war with a strong defense. And nowadays, that means a defense that is substantially in being, with a back-up, long-term production capability if that is needed.

That also means spending what we need to spend—and it means producing what we're technologically capable of producing. The great arsenal of democracy is unique among many of the world's arsenals, because it's almost totally comprised of private industry. That has been our greatest strength, for it has made possible our unique diversity, and it has encouraged our "yankee ingenuity." This has allowed us to achieve what we have achieved. And I'm confident that in the future, this same strength will allow us to do what we need to do!

In conclusion, let me just say that it really doesn't matter how expensive an adequate defense will be—it's really not important how many short-term concerns we have to deter. In the final analysis, all that matters is that we do what needs to be done, that we sacrifice whatever it takes to pay the price of freedom. We must honor the obligation of being a free people, we must do for our future generations what prior generations have done for us.

For whatever the costs involved, whatever the price we pay, if we manage to meet the challenges we face, if we manage to keep this democracy intact, if we manage to keep this country free—then our defense will have been a bargain.

Thank you.

At first, it may not be obvious why the supply-side community must be aligned with efforts to increase that share of Gross National Product which goes to defense spending. However, because promoting individual freedom is their first priority, their position becomes clearer. What could challenge freedom more directly than a foreign power bent upon destroying the "free world"? How do we protect ourselves and our economic system which values freedom so highly? The answers to these questions seem obvious to the supply-siders.

Some critics of the supply-siders do not directly oppose an increase in defense spending. Rather, they argue that the Reagan supply-siders have gone too far too fast, and that the same level of deterrence can be achieved without such a rapid increase in defense spending. Of particular concern to these critics is Reagan's concentration on conventional forces. They consider this build-up to be "premature" or "excessive." Overall, the critics conclude that the Reagan administration has not justified its proposed increase in defense expenditures.

CAN WE REALLY DEFEND OUR DEFENSE BUDGET?

Setting National Priorities: The 1983 Budget

The Reagan defense plan has been criticized on a number of grounds. It is said to be unfair because its increases will be at the expense of major social programs. It is accused of being potentially inflationary because the defense goods and services required by it will, in the near term, exceed the ability of the economy to supply them. It is charged with being more generally counter-productive because it will continue to keep the federal deficit at an un-acceptably high level in the years ahead. However, all these sacrifices would probably be accepted if national security were considered to be in jeopardy. Thus the central issue is whether external threats justify as large an increase in defense spending as President Reagan has requested.

There are ample grounds for considering more modest rates of growth. The president and his advisers have expressed concern about windows of vulnerability and dangers in the immediate future, but they have not proposed funding the crash programs that would close the windows or meet the dangers. A reasonable inference to be drawn from the long-term nature of the programs being undertaken—most of which will not increase U.S. military capabilities before the late 1980s or early 1990s—is that the emphasis has been placed as much on escalating defense spending and satisfying traditional service preferences as on the acquisition of the military output needed to deal with major U.S. vulnerabilities.

There has been a remarkable continuity in what constitute the fundamental conditions of American security in the current age. For most of the years since World War II, the United States has followed a defense policy with two major

components: the deterrence of nuclear attack on the United States and its
allies by means of second-strike strategic and theater nuclear capabilities
designed to cover a wide range of military, economic, and urban targets
primarily in the Soviet Union; and the containment of Soviet and satellite
conventional power by means of U.S. and allied land, sea, and air forces with
the intercontinental mobility to deal with one major and one lesser attack,
wherever they might occur.

For all practical purposes, the administration has accepted this policy.
However, two modifications in it are being proposed. Whereas previous
administrations have concentrated on achieving the ability to outlast the
enemy in short conventional wars, the current objective seems to be to
prepare for nonnuclear conflicts of much longer duration. Furthermore, the
administration plans to acquire the additional capabilities required for what it
calls horizontal escalation. Thus any potential attacker must expect to be met
not only with a direct defense in a given theater, but also with U.S. assaults on
the attacker's own areas of vulnerability.

Despite the arguments about the relative strength of the U.S. and Soviet
nuclear forces, a nuclear stalemate exists and is likely to continue for the
foreseeable future. U.S. strategic nuclear bombs can deliver at least 3,000
warheads on targets in the Soviet Union at the present time, and that number
will rise as air-launched cruise missiles are deployed. However, the intercontinental ballistic missile leg of the strategic triad (whose three components
are bombers, ICBMs, and submarine-launched ballistic missiles) has become
vulnerable, and the ability of bombers to penetrate Soviet air defenses in the
late 1980s may become increasingly questionable.

The nonnuclear balance continues to be more precarious. Conventional
land forces in the continental United States are deficient in the intercontinental
mobility needed to deploy them to distant theaters in sufficient time to meet
realistic threats; they would also derive greater benefit from increased training
than from more modern equipment. Naval forces, while fully capable of
controlling essential sea lines of communication, are supported by an aging
fleet of auxiliary vessels and are deficient in the frigates and destroyers required
for convoy duty in a worldwide conflict. Should the Soviet Union engage in
slower but more powerful buildups in Europe and the Caucasus than are
currently anticipated, the United States and its allies could find themselves
deficient in the active-duty land and tactical air forces to counter-balance
these buildups.

The defense program of the Reagan administration only partly addresses
such problems. The deployment of mobile (MX) missiles, planned by the
Carter administration to reduce the vulnerability of the ICBM force, has been
canceled. The administration still proposes to fund as much as $20 billion for
the MX during the coming five years. But the deployment of the first forty
missiles will leave them as vulnerable as the existing ICBM force. Another $35
billion will probably be required for the acquisition of 100 B-1B bombers to

replace the B-52Hs, a substitution that will mean a small increase in the number of weapons that can be delivered to the Soviet Union on a second strike. Although it remains unclear what role continental air defenses should play beyond warning and peacetime surveillance, more than $5 billion is being programmed to modernize the existing system.

In fiscal 1983 alone, cancellations of some of the nuclear force programs (such as the B-1) and reductions in others (such as the MX and conventional air defense) would save about $3.5 billion in outlays. Total savings in outlays for the five-year plan could amount to as much as $42 billion in current dollars.

Nearly 90 percent of the resources the administration is programming for the conventional forces over the next five years are intended to modernize and increase the readiness and sustainability of existing capabilities. The remaining 10 percent, or approximately $115 billion, will go to six programs, of which the largest are the construction of thirty-six more ships for the Navy and the stockpiling of modern munitions for forty-five more days of intense combat.

Improvements in the baseline conventional forces of the United States— 19 divisions, 29 tactical air wings, and a general purpose fleet of 535 ships— have much to be said for them in principle. It remains questionable, however, whether the large and rapid investments that are being planned should be made simply because they are high on the services' list of priorities. Over five years, the savings of more than $20 billion from cancellations of or reductions in a number of such programs could be more productively used elsewhere. One possibility would be to improve the equipment and training of the National Guard and Reserve land and tactical air forces, for which more than $14 billion will be appropriated in 1983. In time, these forces could provide the capabilities needed to hedge against unanticipated Soviet deployments into Eastern Europe and on the border of Iran.

It is by no means clear that the increments to the baseline force proposed by the administration would be worth the cost. The expansion in conventional naval forces, centering on three carrier battle groups and a 35 percent increase in amphibious lift, is more a satisfaction of the Navy's desire for a 600-ship fleet than it is the creation of a powerful instrument for the dubious strategy of horizontal escalation. For the latter purpose, an even larger fleet and still other forces would almost certainly be required. By the same token, the proposed large investment in chemical bombs and projectiles can only be described as premature. And the rapid acquisition of sufficient "smart" munitions for several months of intense conventional combat seems an excessive hedge against future uncertainties about the nature and duration of nonnuclear conflict. Indeed, since haste does not seem to be of the essence, a more sustainable approach to the modernization, readiness, and expansion of the conventional forces has much to recommend it. Such an approach, while allowing for substantial increases in capability during the coming five years, would result in spending $86 billion less, in current dollars, than is being proposed by the administration.

The forces authorized in the mid-1970s to carry out the traditional U.S. nuclear and nonnuclear defense policy would require appropriations of almost $213 billion in fiscal 1983 and outlays of $197 billion. An intermediate defense budget designed to underwrite the same policy and also to take account of continued increases in the capability of the Soviet Union to execute certain specific attacks would increase appropriations to $226 billion and outlays to approximately $205 billion. The Reagan request, by contrast, proposes appropriations of $258 billion and outlays of $216 billion.

Realistically, defense outlays in the president's budget could be reduced by $11 billion in 1983, $28 billion in 1984, and $29 billion in 1985. Cumulative outlays from the intermediate defense option could amount to as much as $1.3 trillion by 1987, nearly $130 billion, or 10 percent, less than the cumulative outlays that would be incurred by the Reagan five-year defense plan. A serious and systematic case for going beyond a buildup of this magnitude remains to be made.   fOCUs

Conclusion

This chapter has examined the controversy surrounding the Reagan supply-side expenditure initiatives. As we have seen, the controversy has three parts. The first focuses upon general goals and objectives. The supply-side community applauds the slowdown in the growth of Federal government expenditures as a means of restoring economic freedom to the private sector, reducing inflation, and strengthening economic incentives. Opponents see these changes as unduly burdensome for the poor and unlikely to yield the predicted economic gains.

The second area of disagreement concerns the proposed reductions in social welfare-income maintenance programs. Supporters of the supply-side position offer the following arguments: the cost of being unemployed today is not the same as the costs of being unemployed in prior years, disability pensions have generated unwarranted increases in the number of people eligible for such pensions, and social welfare programs and income maintenance programs increase the number of people unemployed and living in poverty. The liberal opposition centers on two themes: (i) social welfare programs have not created a class of persons who are welfare-dependent, and (ii) the proposed changes are based on a romantic view of society which ignores the reality of poverty and, as such, represent nothing more than an attack upon the poor by the rich.

The third point of contention involves the one area of government spending scheduled for increased growth—military spending. The critics of the Reagan administration believe that the proposed levels of defense spending are excessive. They also maintain that the same level of military preparedness could be purchased with fewer dollars and over-expenditures could cause severe macroeconomic problems. Defenders of Reagan's defense budget respond that no price is too high to pay for freedom and that the potential macroeconomic problems are highly exaggerated.

CHAPTER 5

Budget Deficits and Monetary Policy

Introduction

The preceding chapters have examined the two sides of fiscal policy—taxes and expenditures—as separate elements. When considering these aspects of the economy, it is important to bear in mind that they are both affected by actions that the government may take in the area of monetary policy. The first section of this chapter is concerned with the impact that current fiscal policy has on the overall budget position of the federal government. This impact is reflected in deficits and surpluses and the overall level of national debt. The second section of this chapter examines the monetary policies that are implicit in supply-side economics.

Budget Deficits

It is ironic that a president and an administration concerned with the reduction and elimination of budget deficits should experience the largest deficits in the nation's history. Before examining why the Reagan administration found itself in this predicament, it is necessary to discuss the meaning of surpluses and deficits.

Whether a budget has a deficit or a surplus depends on the relationship between government revenues and government expenditures. If revenues exceed expenditures, there is a surplus; if revenues are less than expenditures, there is a deficit; and if revenues are equal to expenditures, the budget is said to be balanced. All this seems simple enough, but things are never as simple as they seem. Government revenues and expenditures can be calculated in different ways. An economist or politician may generate his or her estimates of revenues and expenditures assuming that new tax legislation will be enacted. Another government official may base his or her calculations on the assumption that economic conditions will reflect high employment. As a result, disagreement about the status of the government's budget can arise because those calculating the budget are using different concepts. In the following paragraphs we will define and describe several of these concepts.

The Unified Budget

The unified budget records the revenue the Federal government actually receives and spends over a certain period of time. As such, a surplus or deficit in the unified budget reflects two basic sets of factors. The first relates to existing legislation that determines, (among other things): tax rates, tax deductions, tax exemptions, tax credits, benefit levels of entitlement programs, eligibility requirements for entitlement programs, pay rates for Federal government employees, and defense expenditures. The second set of factors relates to economic conditions. For example, the higher the unemployment rate, the higher will be government spending for unemployment compensation and other income maintenance programs; the higher the interest rate, the greater will be the government's interest payments on the national debt; and the more depressed the economy, the lower will be the government's tax receipts.

The National Income Accounts Budget

A second budget—the national income accounts budget—is much like the unified budget in that it reflects both changes in legislative actions and changes in economic conditions. Two differences do, however, exist. The unified budget records those taxes actually paid by the taxpayer and does not distinguish between government expenditures which directly utilize resources and those that do not. The national income accounts budget records taxes during the period in which their economic impact is felt and includes expenditures which directly affect resources and incomes. Thus, it is possible for one of these budgets to indicate a surplus and the other a deficit—although the differences are not, in general, likely to be large.

The High Employment Budget

A third budget concept is substantially different from the unified and national income accounts budgets: the high employment budget. This budget's revenues and expenditures are affected by only one set of factors—legislative action. Thus, unlike the totals of the unified and national income accounts budgets, the outlays and receipts of the high employment budget are not affected by changes in economic conditions. This is because the latter estimates are based on a given economic condition, a state of high employment. Currently, the high employment budget estimates assume that 94.9 percent of the labor force is employed. If the economy is actually operating at high employment, there will be no difference between the unified or national income accounts and high employment budgets. If the economy goes into a recession, the expenditures and revenues for the high employment budget will remain unchanged but unified and national income accounts budget expenditures will rise and revenues will fall—reflecting a movement to smaller surpluses, from a surplus to a deficit or to increasing deficits.

The Current Services Budget

A fourth budget concept is the current services budget. This budget is somewhat like the high employment budget in that it estimates or reflects expenditures and receipts given no change in legislation and a set of assumed economic conditions. It differs from the high employment budget in that the assumed economic conditions may or may not be those of high employment. This budget is used as a baseline against which the impact of proposed legislation on expenditures and revenues can be assessed.

The last item to consider in this discussion is the notion of "off budget expenditures." This term refers to the borrowing and lending activities of various government agencies. These expenditures are important when the focus is on the total amount of borrowing undertaken by the Federal government. Total borrowing, as viewed by the Council of Economic Advisors in one of the selections in this chapter, is the national income accounts budget combined with off budget expenditures.

These budget concepts allow us to analyze the Reagan administration's proposed budgets, the controversy surrounding the consequences of budget deficits, and the advisability of a constitutional amendment calling for a balanced budget. We introduce this analysis with a statement from the 1980 Republican Party Platform. This is the platform, or statement of principles, adopted by the convention which selected Governor Ronald Reagan to represent the Republican Party as the candidate for the presidency in July, 1980.

Four points of the Republican platform should be underscored. First, the platform commits the Republican Party to a balanced budget which is to be achieved through the legislative process and not, at least initially, through the mandate of a constitutional amendment. Second, the platform asserts that it is not simply a question of balancing the budget, but a question of balancing the budget at levels which reduce the relative importance of government. The Republican Party believed it was desirable, indeed necessary, to reduce actual spending below 21 percent of Gross National Product. Third, the budget is to be brought into balance through tax cuts and a slower growth in government spending. Fourth, the platform maintains that the tax cuts, because they will stimulate the economy and increase aggregate supply, will "reduce the need for government spending on unemployment, welfare, and public job programs," and that government spending can be further reduced "by eliminating waste, fraud, and duplication."

REPUBLICAN PLATFORM POSITION

1980 Republican Platform Text

Taxes and Government Spending

Elsewhere in this platform, we have pledged for the sake of individual freedom and economic growth to cut personal income tax rates for all. Republicans believe that these tax rate reductions should be complemented by firm limitations on the growth of federal spending as provided by the Roth-Kemp Bill. The Republican Party therefore, pledges to place limits on federal spending as a percent of the Gross National Product. It is now over 21 percent. We pledge to reduce it. If federal spending is reduced as tax cuts are phased in, there will be sufficient budget surpluses to fund the tax cuts, and allow for reasonable growth in necessary program spending.

By increasing economic growth, tax rate reduction will reduce the need for government spending on unemployment, welfare, and public jobs programs. However, the Republican Party will also halt excessive government spending by eliminating waste, fraud, and duplication.

We believe that the Congressional budget process has failed to control federal spending. Indeed, because of its big spending bias, the budget process has actually contributed to higher levels of social spending, has prevented necessary growth in defense spending, and has been used to frustrate every Republican attempt to lower tax rates to promote economic growth.

The immediate burden of reducing federal spending rests on the shoulders of the President and the Congress. We believe a Republican President and a Republican Congress can balance the budget and reduce spending through legislative actions, eliminating the necessity for a Constitutional amendment to compel it. However, if necessary, the Republican Party will seek to adopt a Constitutional amendment to limit federal spending and balance the budget, except in time of national emergency as determined by a two-thirds vote of Congress.   focus

This economic blueprint, developed during the Republican Convention in Detroit, became reality when Congress passed the Economic Recovery Tax Act of 1981 and the Omnibus Budget Reconciliation Act. To underscore this achievement, President Reagan signed both into law on the same day, August 13, 1981. However, contrary to the grand plans and expectations of policy makers, as time passed, the Federal budget continued to reflect larger and larger deficits rather than the smaller deficits and surpluses which had been forecasted.

This miscalculation is well illustrated in the *1982 Economic Report of the President.* These calculations, which include on- and off-budget estimates, show a $73.8 billion deficit for fiscal year 1980, a $78.9 billion deficit for fiscal year 1981, and estimated budget deficits of $118.3 billion, $107.2 billion, and $97.2 billion for the fiscal years 1982, 1983, and 1984, respectively. Thus, the combined effects of the legislative actions taken in 1981 and the currently forecasted economic conditions have yielded higher budget deficits since President Ronald Reagan was elected than existed before he took office.

The initial reactions of the supply-side policy makers within the Reagan administration was to minimize the importance of these budget deficits. This was done in order to counter demands that taxes be increased in order to reduce the size of the projected deficits. In order to minimize the significance of the deficits, three lines of argument were employed by the Council of Economic Advisors. The first focused attention on the cause of the deficits. It highlighted the importance that economic conditions have on the government's budget position.

During the last year, better-than-expected progress on inflation has reduced taxable income, slowing the growth of revenues below earlier projections. The recession has temporarily slowed the growth of the tax base while increasing outlays for employment-related programs. In addition, the projected decline in inflation increases the projected deficit because the associated reduction in revenue growth precedes the later reduction in spending growth, largely as a result of the indexing of government programs.

The impact of economic conditions should not be, and cannot be ignored. This impact can be determined by comparing the budget totals of the national income accounts and high employment budgets. The national income accounts budget showed a budget deficit of $60 billion for calendar year 1981. If full employment could have been achieved, it would have generated an additional $50 billion in receipts and a $14 billion reduction in expenditures. In short, the presence of high employment would have turned a $60 billion deficit into a surplus of $4 billion. (These figures are taken from *Monetary Trends* prepared by the Federal Reserve Bank of St. Louis, September 23, 1982.)

Regardless of its cause, the budget deficit still exists, and the Council of Economic Advisors has used a second argument to minimize the deficit's importance. This argument concentrated on the relative, rather than the absolute, size of the deficits and stated that the projected deficits, although still substantial in relative terms, were "not unprecedented."

> The relative size of the deficit is far more important than the dollar magnitude. To the extent that deficits affect the economy, the effects of a given deficit will be relatively small in a large economy and large in a small economy. From an historical perspective, the projected deficits for fiscal years 1982-1984 are clearly substantial, yet they are not unprecedented when measured against the size of the economy.

On this point the Council's figures indicated that the Federal budget deficit, including on- and off-budget items—taken as a percent of Gross National Product—reached 4.5 percent in fiscal year 1976, while the projections for fiscal years 1982 through 1984 were 3.8, 3.1, and 2.6 percent, respectively. Thus, in these terms, the budget deficit was actually falling.

The third and last argument used by President Reagan's Council focused on the trend in the deficit. Here, the Council stated that a trend of declining deficits may be sufficient to achieve desired results.

> Perhaps the most useful and practical of these rules is the simplest rule: balance the budget. Even this needs to be seen as a long run rule, however, since the business cycle does cause variations that are difficult to calculate and offset. Furthermore, a strategy of reducing taxes in advance of spending cuts implies that it will take some time to achieve the desired level of deficits. Enforcing a trend toward a balanced budget would impose the fiscal discipline necessary to restrain the growth of government and send a message of government restraint to private individuals who can incorporate this essential information into their planning.

These efforts to minimize the importance of deficits—and, thereby, resist a retreat from the basic supply-side policy of tax and spending cuts established during 1981—fell on deaf ears. Some supply-side critics demanded that a portion of the remaining scheduled tax cuts contained in the Economic Tax Recovery Act of 1981 be postponed or even eliminated. Others, who predicted terrible consequences from these projected deficits, clamored for further substantial reductions in spending. Some conservative supply-siders went so far as to argue for cutbacks in the growth of defense spending. To quiet this rising chorus of criticism from both the right and the left, the Reagan administration was forced to take action. They were, however, very careful to choose a set of options which did not interfere with—that is, which did not compromise—the supply-side actions put in place during 1981. Essentially the Reagan problem was to reduce the current and projected deficits without reducing defense spending and without retreating from his basic supply-side economic incentive programs.

President Reagan's resolution to this problem is contained in the next selection. In a nationally televised address, the president outlined the benefits attained through his supply-side policies—lower inflation and lower interest rates. He then went on to declare that the new tax legislation he was supporting was not an abandonment of these supply-side policies. In his words, "it could be called the greatest tax reform in history," rather than tax increase legislation. Reagan claimed the new legislation, while still consistent with supply-side economics, will make the tax system fairer, reduce deficits, lower interest rates, and lead to a greater employment in the future.

THE 1982 TAX BILL

Ronald Reagan, *Vital Speeches,* September 1, 1982

I'm sure you've heard that "we're proposing the largest single tax increase in history." The truth is: We are proposing nothing of the kind. Then there is the one that "our economic recovery program has failed, so I've abandoned it and turned to increasing taxes instead of trying to reduce Federal spending." Well, don't you believe that one either.

Yes, there is a tax bill before the Congress tied to a program of further cuts in spending. It is not, however, "the greatest single tax increase in history." Possibly it could be called the greatest tax reform in history, but it absolutely does not represent any reversal of policy or philosophy on the part of this Administration (or this President). . . .

You will recall that when our Administration came into office a year ago last January, we announced a plan for economic recovery. Recovery from what? From a 1980 recession that saw inflation in double-digit figures for two years in a row. It was 12.4 percent when we arrived. Interest rates had gone into outer space. They were at the highest they'd been in a hundred years with a prime rate that hit 21½ percent. There were almost 8 million Americans out of work, and in several hard-hit industrial states there already were pockets of unemployment reaching figures of 15, 18, and even 20 percent. The cost of government was increasing at a rate of 17 percent a year.

Well, weeks and weeks of negotiations resulted in a Congressional Budget Resolution combining revenue increases and further spending reductions. Revenues would increase over a three-year period by about $99 billion, and outlays in the same period would be reduced by $280 billion. As you can see, that figures out to about a 3-to-1 ratio—$3 less in outlays for each $1 of increased revenue. This compromise adds up to total over three years of a $380 billion reduction in budget deficits. And remember, our original tax reduction remains in place, which means your taxes will still be cut $335 billion in these next three years. . . .

Within the new bill there has, of course, been disagreement over some of the specific provisions. For example, there is considerable confusion over the proposal to have withholding of tax due on interest and dividends, just as it is withheld now on wages and salaries. Many senior citizens have been led to believe this is a new tax added on top of the present income tax. There is no truth whatsoever to that.

We have found that, while the overwhelming majority of Americans faithfully reports income from interest and dividends and pays taxes on it, some do not. It is one of the significant areas of noncompliance (and is costing the Government $9 billion a year).

In the case of those over age 65, withholding will only apply to those with incomes of $14,450 and up per individual and $24,214 for couples filing a joint return. Low-income citizens below 65 will be exempt if their income is less than about $8,000 for an individual or $15,300 for those filing joint returns. And there will be an exemption for all interest payments of $150 or less. The only people whose taxes will be increased by this withholding are those who presently are evading their fair share of the tax burden. Once again, we are striving to see that all taxpayers are treated fairly.

This withholding will go into effect next July, not this January First, as was earlier reported.

There was little we could do about the budget already in place, but we could do something about the one that had been proposed for the fiscal year beginning in October of our first year.

I had campaigned on the belief that government costs should be reduced and that the percentage of the people's earnings taken by government in taxes should also be reduced. I also said that one area of government spending could not be reduced but must, instead, be increased. That was the spending necessary to restore our nation's defenses, which had been allowed to deteriorate to a dangerous degree in the preceding four years. . . .

It wasn't easy. We didn't get all the cuts we wanted, and we got some tax measures we didn't want. But we were charting a complete turnaround in Government policy, and we did get the major part of what we proposed. The Congress mandated spending cuts of $130 billion over three years and adopted the biggest tax cut in history. This, too, was to be implemented over a three-year period. It began with a 5 percent cut in the personal income tax beginning Oct. 1, 1981, then a 10 percent cut this last July and another scheduled for July 1, 1983. These will be followed by indexing of the tax brackets so workers getting cost-of-living pay raises won't be moved up into higher brackets. You have to realize inflation itself is a tax. Government has profited by inflation—and indexing will put a stop to that.

There were tax cuts for business and industry to help provide capital for modernization of plant and equipment, changes in the estate tax, capital gains tax and the marriage penalty tax. . . .

Our biggest problem—the last one to be solved in every recession—is unemployment. I understand how tough it is for those who are waiting for the jobs that come with recovery. We can have no rest until our neighbors, our fellow citizens who want to work are able, once again, to find jobs. Again, let me say, the main obstacle to their doing so is continued high interest rates. Those rates should be lower now than they are, with the success we've had in reducing inflation. Part of the problem is psychological—a pessimism in the money markets that we won't stay the course and continue lowering the cost of government. The projected increase in budget deficits has added to that pessimism and fear.

And this brings us back to that so called "greatest tax increase in history" and the budget proposals now before the Congress.

When I submitted the 1983 budget to the Congress in February, it contained very significant spending cuts on top of those we obtained last year. This time, however, we could not get the support we had last year. Some who had not been happy about the tax cuts then were now insisting we must have additional tax revenues.

In fact, they wanted to cancel the reduction scheduled for next July and the indexing of tax brackets. Others proposed tax increases amounting to about $150 billion over a three-year period. On top of this, there was resistance to the spending reductions we asked for and even attempts to eliminate some of last year's cuts so as to actually increase spending.

For many months now we've been working to get a compromise budget that would further reduce spending and, thus, reduce the deficits. We also have stood firm on retaining the tax cuts already in place, because, as I said, they are essential to restoring the economy.

We did, however, agree to limited revenue increases so long as they didn't harm the incentive features of our economic recovery program. We ourselves, last year, had called attention to the possibility of better compliance with the tax laws—collecting taxes legitimately owned but which were not being paid.

Back during the campaign, on Sept. 9, 1980, to be exact, I said my goal was to reduce by 1985 the share of gross national product taken by government in taxes to 20.5 percent. If we had done nothing, it would have risen to about 24.8 percent. But even after passage of this bill, the Federal Government will only be taking 19.6 percent of the G.N.P. by 1985.

Make no mistake about it—this is a compromise. I had to swallow hard to agree to any revenue increase. But there are two sides to a compromise. Those who supported the increased revenues swallowed hard to accept $280 billion in outlay cuts. Others have accepted specific provisions with regard to taxes or spending cuts which they opposed. . . .   fOCus

There should be no mistake about President Reagan's position with respect to the desirability of a balanced budget. Although his supply-side economics allowed for a deficit while the economic incentives generated by tax cuts, deregulation, and expenditure reductions worked their way through the economic system, Reagan began to speak out against deficits. Indeed, by the spring of 1982, he began to say that a balanced budget was of such high priority that it was necessary to go beyond the position taken by the Republican Party in its 1980 platform: he called for a constitutional amendment to balance the budget.

The American experiment with supply-side economics becomes somewhat ambiguous at this juncture. Only time will tell whether or not President Reagan's call for a constitutional amendment in the spring of 1982 was due to his doubt about the wisdom of supply-side budget deficits or was motivated by other considerations. We must remember that President Reagan's first budget, which was built upon the logic of the Laffer Curve, called for a deficit. But the supply-siders were confident that this deficit would be eliminated as "the powers of the marketplace were unleashed."

As this selection suggests, President Reagan has remained confident that the deficit will be eliminated. But if it is eliminated, it will presumably be the result of his supply-side deficits in fiscal 1982 and 1983. Why then would he deny future generations this powerful fiscal tool? Why would he make it, in effect, unconstitutional to ever use the tax cut aspects of supply-side economic policy again? His call for a constitutional amendment and the call for a tax increase may represent a break with the supply-side community. That is, it may indicate that the Reagan administration is becoming more "orthodox" and less "supply-side" in its conservative policy. It is clear, however, that Reagan was careful to protect the most fundamental part of the supply-side strategy—the reduction in marginal tax rates.

Let us now explore the consequences of budget deficits. The economic costs in terms of private capital formation that is " 'crowded out' by the rising claim of the deficit on a basically stable saving pool" is the subject of our next selection. Dr. Lora Collins, Director of Business Conditions Analysis for the Conference Board, maintains that government deficits, not government spending, is the major problem facing our economy during the 1980s. She argues that if the Federal government is going to maintain a high level of spending, whether that spending is for non-defense or defense purposes, it should be financed with taxes on consumption rather than by borrowing, which causes the government to compete with the private sector for the limited loanable funds available in the marketplace.

THE HARMFUL EFFECTS OF DEFICITS

Lora S. Collins, *Across the Board,* April 1982

The red ink in the President's budget message was barely dry before loud cries of dismay were heard. The financial community is dismayed because it identifies deficits with high interest rates, and high interest rates with trouble; the average citizen is upset because he identifies deficits with inflation. Congress is worried because the voters are worried. Is all this worry justified? Insofar as it relates to inflation and interest rate pressures beyond 1982, and to prospects for economic growth in the 1980s, the answer is Yes. For 1982, the fears are probably excessive: The deficit this year is not going to have much impact on interest rates or inflation. In a weak economy, the financing of even a large Federal deficit is unlikely to cause great strain, because during recessions the private sector tends to have a greater desire to save than to use the saved resources for investment. This argues against further upward pressure on interest rates as a consequence of the 1982 deficit. The recession is also the dominant influence in the inflation picture this year, and a moderating one.

However, the deficits projected beyond 1982 are a matter of real concern. The critical thing about Federal deficits is that they absorb real resources that would otherwise very probably go into building up the stock of productive capital. This is the effect whether the deficits are financed in an inflationary or a noninflationary way. The core issue is how we divide up the nation's total production. The things that worry Wall Street and the average voter—high interest rates and inflation—are closely related to this central issue. High rates are a market response to the pressures of the deficit, for it is in the financial markets that the deficit-driven competition for resources is waged. And inflation can result from economic policies that try to smooth over that competition and reduce its discomfort. The current political agonizing over spending and inflation will be useful if it focuses our attention on the key tenet of economics—that means are finite, choices must be made, and you have to pay for what you get.

The resources that Federal deficits absorb are the resources saved by other sectors. The lion's share of our economy's output is used up right away. That immediate use is what economists call "consumption." The output that is not "consumed" consists of goods that will yield benefits over a future time span. These are "investment" goods, and some part of a nation's output must consist of such goods if there is to be any growth in the stock of productive capital. In the United States, there is a striking degree of stability in the share of total output that is saved, provided that one averages out purely cyclical swings. However, Federal deficits have been absorbing a rising share of that savings pool. That is, the Federal government's spending exceeds its income and it thus absorbs resources saved by other sectors. Those are the nonconsumed resources that are available for capital formation, and their absorption by the Federal deficit has apparently had a negative impact on the growth of the capital stock and therefore on the economy's ability to grow. If the Federal deficit's claim on the savings pool rises further, it could seriously hinder capital formation. There may well be a problem for capital formation even if the government's claim on the savings pool simply holds at the present level. All of this is independent of inflation; that is, independent of whether the deficit does or does not lead to inflationary economic policy.

What is to be done? The possible courses are easily stated, though not easily achieved. We can live with deficits, and do so with or without inflationary economic policies, or we can balance the budget. With or without inflation, a Federal deficit is a preemptive claim on the savings pool. But deficits without inflation are a more attractive option, if we care about achieving adequate capital formation, because the national willingness to save is almost certainly greater in a noninflationary environment than in an inflationary one.

As to balancing the budget, the Administration argues that we must not balance it through higher taxes because that would constitute acceptance of an excessive spending level. However, while Federal spending has been rising faster over time than total economic activity, the margin of difference cannot be called dramatic: The ratio of Federal spending to GNP moved up about 3 percentage points from the mid-1950s to the late 1970s. The Administration is committed to a substantial increase in defense spending, but it seems unlikely that Americans want to pay for that increase with a major undoing of government's nondefense roles. Consequently tax increases have to be considered.

National Saving and Federal Deficits

. . . The Federal deficit has increased from 0.3 percent of the national output in the 1960s to 2.5 percent in the late 1970s, while other uses of national savings have undergone a relative shrinkage. We cannot say for sure what the causality is, since we do not know for sure how things would have looked in the absence of that burgeoning deficit. Conceivably, the share of national output saved in those circumstances might have been lower, and the share going into capital formation consequently no different from what it actually was. But it seems more probable that the deficit has been a moving force, and that capital formation has given ground—been "crowded out"—by the rising claim of the deficit on a basically stable savings pool.

A substantial increase in the national saving rate would obviously be a big help, as it would make room for both Federal deficits and increased capital formation. Stimulation of the saving rate is a prime goal of "supply-side" economic policy and was a major argument advanced for the Administration's tax cuts. This goal may be realized, but not with dramatic swiftness. And while we are waiting for a rise in our national willingness to save, we face deficits that put a large claim on the existing savings supply. Moreover, the remarkable stability of the average saving rate, in the 9½-11 percent range over the past three decades, suggests caution in projecting increases in the 1980s.

Deficits and Inflation

There is no reason, in principle, why the resources to cover a Federal deficit cannot be extracted from the other economic sectors without the accompaniment of inflation. If a deficit is inflationary, it is because it leads the monetary authorities to an inflationary policy, that is, to a policy allowing too-rapid growth of money and credit. Although deficits need not have this effect, they often do. When the Federal government spends more than its revenues, it must round up the necessary additional resources by borrowing. The government is always going to get what it wants: Federal borrowing is not deterred by interest-rate levels or any other constraint (other than a meaningless debt ceiling), and in this sense the Federal deficit is a preemptive claim on resources saved by other sectors.

This diversion of savings from other potential users can be painful, and that pain is felt as upward pressure on interest rates because financial markets are where the struggle for control over resources is played out. This is unpopular, and the response over the years has often been a monetary policy stance that seeks to ease the pain by fostering liberal expansion of credit. In effect, this means conducting monetary policy so that the financial system creates new dollars to absorb the prevailing demand for credit and avoids an escalation of interest rates in the short run. Unfortunately, the cumulative result is that the total dollar volume of spending in the system grows faster than total real output—which is the definition of inflation. . . .

A Balanced Budget

Federal spending can be paid for entirely with taxes or partly with taxes and partly wih borrowing. These are simply alternative ways of rounding up the resources needed for government programs. Suppose the budget had been balanced during the past two decades through higher taxes, with Federal spending the same as it actually was. In such circumstances, it is conceivable that capital formation would have been no greater than it actually was. This would be the result if the higher taxes had caused private saving to be lower than it actually was, so that no greater amount of saving was available to support capital formation even though no saving was being absorbed by a Federal deficit. This says that the higher taxes would have fallen on saving, not consumption. The generally proconsumption bias of the American tax structure gives plausibility to such an argument. Unfortunately, we can't resolve the matter, because we can't test the alternatives with all other things held constant. What seems most probable, however, is that the higher taxes would have been paid only partly with reduced saving and partly with reduced consumption. This would have resulted in a national saving rate somewhat lower than actually recorded; but with no deficit to be financed, that saving rate would have supported a somewhat higher rate of capital formation than we actually had.

Now, suppose we raise taxes enough to balance the budget in the 1980s, at least on a "full employment" basis (that means that deficits would occur only as the result of recessions, when the private sector's claim on national saving is weakened and covering the deficit is not a serious problem). Would such a tax-financing strategy hold down savings and thus repress capital formation, leaving things no better than in the deficit-financing case? There is a strong belief to that effect in the Administration. A variant of that belief is that Federal spending has become too large, that it is a burden that must be lightened, and that raising taxes would be wrong because it would legitimize and confirm this burden. This is a popular view and it has some truth, but the popular perception sees a graver situation than actually exists. • • •

It is said that to close the budget gap with higher taxes means accepting an intolerable level of spending. Some perspective is needed, and one thing worth noting is that the American ratio of public spending to overall economic activity is hardly outrageous in comparison with other countries. To make such a comparison, it is necessary to lump Federal, state and local spending together, since the distribution of responsibilities among levels of government differs a lot from country to country. Thus aggregated, the U.S. spending ratio is well below the European standard; and while the U.S. ratio is well above the Japanese, ours hasn't been rising as fast as theirs.

The current focus on cutting Federal spending probably does reflect a deep-seated sentiment that we have permitted Federal activity to grow faster and to become larger than we really want. But we should not think that we cannot afford all of the Federal spending that we really do want, for both defense and nondefense programs. And we must seriously consider paying for it through taxes on consumption if we are serious about fostering adequate capital formation.   focus

Thus, for business economist Collins, a deficit constitutes a burden because it absorbs resources that would otherwise have been available for capital formation. The loss of these funds to the government sector reduces the private economy's "ability to grow," whether or not the deficit is inflationary. Inflation, in turn, depends on whether the money supply is increased in order to finance the deficit. Finally, it is argued that if the deficit is to be financed through taxation (as opposed to an increase in the money supply, which would generate inflation, or to a larger national debt, which reduces investment and economic growth), the choice of taxes is very important. In order to avoid a reduction in investment, which might occur if increased taxes reduced savings, new taxes must be levied on consumption.

But not everyone agrees with these conclusions. In an article which appeared in *Across the Board,* in May of 1982, Conference Board Chief Economist, Albert Sommers maintains that before meaningful budget discussion can take place "it is desperately important for us to rationalize the criteria by which we appraise the course of Federal spending. . . ." In developing this theme, he emphasized three points (i) a conventional balanced budget will not necessarily lead to full employment (ii) a conventional balanced budget would place an unfair burden on businesses who have planned on the basis of long-term spending projections and (iii) government, like businesses, should distinguish between capital expenditures and outlays to finance on-going operations.

These points deserve elaboration. The Federal government, in preparing its budget from year to year makes no distinction between one-time expenditures for capital projects, such as roads, bridges, or railroads, and payments for continuous programs such as food stamps or medicare. Since many of the programs are governed by legislation, there is little freedom to cut expenditures in those areas. In order to balance the budget, as called for by the Reagan Administration, some of the capital projects would have to be curtailed or cancelled. This would result, according to Sommer's view, in a decrease in employment, rather than the increase projected by those in favor of a balanced budget. Many businesses would also suffer, since they plan their spending on capital projects over several years. With these issues in mind we turn to an examination of the argument concerning a constitutional amendment requiring a balanced budget.

Our final selection in this section on budget deficits directly addresses President Reagan's call for a balanced budget constitutional amendment. In this short selection, Yale University professor William Nordhaus raises four reasons why we should not pass such an amendment: (i) economic policy should not be embodied in the Constitution; (ii) there is no objective basis for evaluating the claim that Federal spending is excessive; (iii) it would complicate economic management; and (iv) the amendment, even if passed, can be voided by a number of Congressional actions.

AGAINST THE BALANCED BUDGET CONSTITUTIONAL AMENDMENT

William Nordhaus, *New York Times,* September 5, 1982

On Aug. 4, 1982, the Senate approved by a vote of 69 to 31 a constitutional amendment altering the process of fiscal policy making. If successful, this amendment would revolutionize economic policy more than any step since the introduction of Federal budgeting or central banking more than six decades ago.*

The proposal contains two sets of requirements—one for planning purposes and the other for actual fiscal operations. In all cases, Congress may override these requirements by specific votes of "supermajoritarian" exception—a vote requiring more than a simple majority, such as three-fifths of all members.

The first two sections of the bill contain the planning requirements. First, Congress must adopt a planned balanced budget. Second, there is a requirement that planned revenues, i.e. taxes, grow no faster than actual national income.

In addition to these constitutional pieties, there are two action-forcing clauses. The expenditure limitation clause of Section 1 requires that actual outlays, i.e. expenditures, do not exceed planned outlays.

But the amendment requires that planned outlays cannot exceed planned revenues, which cannot grow faster than national income. Taken together these imply that actual spending cannot grow faster than national income. Thus, the budget contains a hidden constraint on the growth in Government spending.

*The resolution was subsequently defeated in the House—Eds.

The second action-forcing feature, Section 6, is a technique for enforcing the balanced budget amendment. This section allows an increase in the debt limit only when a supermajority approves. The provision is a key because an increase in the net Federal debt of, for example, $100 billion, arises automatically from a Federal deficit of $100 billion.

Thus, while the planned budget balance may be evaded by disingenuous forecasting, in the end, the requirement to raise the debt limit cannot be side-stepped when a deficit occurs.

On close scrutiny, the intellectual basis for the new procedures is that there is thought to be a fundamental bias in the legislative process. In their quest for re-election, members of Congress are driven to satisfy the desires of their constituents, which generally means higher expenditures.

But why a constitutional amendment? The current crop of Congressional conservatives appears unwilling to continue the hard work of changing statutes through the legislative process, and looks rather for quick relief from a constitutional mandate.

The logic behind the amendment—that Congress must change its own procedures because it mistrusts itself—resembles an alcoholic's sobriety campaign. In an attempt to curb excesses, he changes the rules by locking up the bottles and hiding the key on top of the refrigerator. If desperate, he ends up supporting prohibition.

In examining the proposal, the following four points are central.

The first involves the wisdom of embedding economic policies in the Constitution. Is it sensible to elevate current economic dogmas, especially those as poorly grounded as budget-balancing doctrines, into the fundamental document of the Republic? As Justice Oliver Wendell Holmes cautioned, the "Constitution is not intended to embody a particular economic theory."

The next question is whether the amendment represents sensible economic policy. The expenditure limitation provisions are the outgrowth of a political belief, particularly fashionable since the 1980 election, that Federal spending is excessive.

This conviction becomes steadily less convincing as we see the poverty lines and potholes get larger each day. It has no basis in modern political science. In any case, it seems a strange belief to embody in a framework for governments.

Third, by contrast there is no rationale whatever for the budget-balancing provisions. At best the budget-balancing rule is irrelevant. It is a delusion to believe that there is no logical connection between the deficit or surplus of the Government in any major economic variable—inflation, unemployment, productivity or growth.

At worst the rule could complicate economic management, forcing Congress to cut spending during a recession. Like a dog chasing its tail, Congress must increase taxes only to find that this depresses the economy further and still leaves a gaping deficit.

Requiring a budget in constant balance is no more sensible than requiring a driver to keep his foot halfway down on the accelerator at all times. Such a rule might be reasonable on the desert, but it would look silly going up a steep hill and be disastrous going down an icy road.

Fourth, perhaps the most troubling is, will the amendment work or will it be evaded? Will the Congress become a budgetary teetotaler, or like the well-meaning alcoholic, will it remember that the key is hidden on top of the refrigerator and unlock the evil spirits of deficit spending? On this issue one fact is absolutely clear: If Congress wishes to evade the amendment, there are countless gimmicks that will reduce outlays or deficits on paper because of the primitive nature of Federal accounting concepts.

Equipment can be rented rather than bought. Expenditures can be put off budget. Program expenditures can be replaced by tax credits. Loan guarantees can replace purchases. It is estimated that a $100 billion national health insurance plan could be implemented by regulation without adding a penny to Federal expenditures.

It is impossible to predict the outcome. But we must weigh the possibility that, at some point in the future when political sentiments have changed, widespread evasion will make a mockery of this amendment.

In weighing the cost, risk and benefits, the case against it is persuasive. The amendment begins a risky and virtually irreversible experiment by changing the fundamental governing rules of our republic, using faulty economic reasoning and untried parliamentary requirements, in terms that are easily evaded, all in the pursuit of an ill-conceived objective.

If the amendment is so flawed, how could 69 Senators support it? Perhaps Bernard Baruch had the appropriate insight in his forward to MacKay's "Extraordinary Popular Delusions." "Anyone taken as an individual is tolerably sensible and reasonable—as a member of a crowd he at once becomes a blockhead." focus

This section of the chapter has attempted to provide an understanding of the position of the Reagan administration on the issue of budget deficits as well as the arguments—pro and con—of the consequences of deficits and the impact of a balanced budget constitutional amendment. We now turn to the related topic of monetary policy.

Monetary Policy

The agency of the Federal government responsible for the conduct of monetary policy is the Federal Reserve System, more popularly known as the FED. By statutory provision the FED is independent from Congress and the president. This division is designed to free monetary policy from partisan politics. This does not mean that the president is prohibited from exerting pressure on the FED to pursue policies the administration favors. What it does mean is that the president has no direct control over the FED. Congress may also try to pressure the FED, but, short of legislative action, Congress is unable to directly control monetary policy. When the FED was created at the turn of the century, it was believed that control of the money supply was too important to be influenced by the transitory political considerations that can frequently determine the actions of both the executive and congressional branches of government.

The FED's power is concentrated in the hands of the seven individuals who comprise the Board of Governors. Most visible among these seven is the chairman, a position currently held by Paul Volcker. He was appointed to the board and selected as chairman during the Carter administration. Therefore, when evaluating monetary policy, it is necessary to separate those policies proposed by the supply-siders inside the Reagan administration and those policies that are actually initiated by the independent FED.

A second point which merits special attention is the sharp disagreement which surrounds the "appropriate conduct of monetary policy." One group of economists, appropriately grouped under the name "monetarists," believes the FED should focus its efforts on controlling the size of monetary aggregates (various measures of the money supply). Another group, which includes both liberals and non-monetarist conservatives, believes the FED should concentrate its attention on controlling interest rates. In October 1979, the FED shifted from a focus on interest rates to a focus on monetary aggregates. As will be seen in several of the next selections, there are those who feel that this switch from an interest-rate target to a monetary-aggregate target was a mistake. Our concern, however, is the impact of this shift on the implementation of supply-side economics.

Thus, we will begin our discussion of monetary policy within the context of Reagan's supply-side economics. On this issue, it is best to underscore the basic agreement between the FED and the Reagan administration. Both believe the growth rate of the money supply is the major determinant of the rate of inflation; therefore, both believe that to lower rates of inflation we must slow the growth of the money supply. The Reagan administration's position is clearly stated in the *1982 Economic Report of the President:*

> A slow and steady rate of monetary growth is one of the four basic elements of the administration's economic recovery program. While the formulation and implementation of monetary policy is the responsibility of the Federal Reserve, the administration believes the announced policy of the Federal Reserve is consistent with the economic recovery program. Thus, the administration expects that the Federal Reserve will achieve an orderly reduction in the trend of monetary growth to a noninflationary rate.

But to say that there is a basic agreement between the FED and the Reagan administration is not to say that there are no areas of disagreement regarding the conduct of monetary policy. The following selection isolates two basic differences. The first is a disagreement regarding the importance of budget deficits. Here the administration takes the position, as indicated earlier in this chapter, that economic recovery and less inflation can be achieved even with budget deficits. The FED maintains that deficits must be reduced and eventually eliminated. The second disagreement concerns monetary management. The administration has called for a slower growth in the money supply and has demanded that it be achieved smoothly. The FED, on the other hand, believes that smoothness should not be achieved at "any cost." Kemper Financial Services analyst, David Eastburn, examines these questions.

WHERE REAGAN AND VOLCKER DIFFER

David P. Eastburn, *Forbes,* March 13, 1982

At the moment, Administration officials are being circumspect about their relations with Paul Volcker and the Federal Reserve, at least as these relations appear to the public. But let the money supply surge unexpectedly and disconcertingly, as it did in January, or sag suddenly, and Treasury Secretary Regan or the President himself may complain about the Fed's inability to keep things under orderly control. In a press conference President Reagan complained that the spurt in the money supply was sending out wrong signals. So the present lull in the verbal exchanges is somewhat deceptive and may have conveyed the false impression that the differences are highly technical and meaningful only to experts. Such is not the case. The differences are fundamental. The Administration believes that the economy can recover and inflation can be reduced in an environment of both huge deficits and tight money. The Fed believes the projected deficits are fundamentally incompatible with healthy economic growth because they involve high interest rates.

A second difference of opinion is over how to manage the money supply. The Administration is now committed to monetarism. Its officials believe it vital to get the growth rate of money down and to do so smoothly. The Fed also believes the growth rate of money should gradually be reduced, but it is not committed to smoothness at any cost.

To understand this difference, let's back up a bit. In October 1979 the Fed decided on a basic change in its procedure. Instead of continuing to try to influence the economy by closely controlling short-term interest rates, it began to focus directly on the money supply by feeding a supply of reserves into banks at the necessary rate. This change delighted the monetarists, who had been saying all along that the Fed was on the wrong tack in mothering interest rates. But monetarists have been unhappy with the results. Interest rates have indeed fluctuated much more widely than before, as everyone expected. Unfortunately, the rate of growth of money has fluctuated as well.

Milton Friedman, the grand guru of monetarism, has complained that, since October of 1979, money growth has moved in a "yo-yo pattern," from a 13% decline (annual rate) between November 1980 and February 1981 to a 25% increase between October 1981 and January 1982, with somewhat lesser volatility in other periods. The Administration seems to share Professor Friedman's unhappiness.

The matter is confusing and deceptive because there are many technical issues involved. But at the core is a fundamental matter of monetary philosophy. . . .

The Administration and monetarists have good intentions. They want to make people less uncertain by reducing the number of surprises from sharp jumps and drops in money growth. But they underestimate the complexity of the world and their solution is oversimplistic. The economy and financial markets are complex organisms in any case, but given the shocks they have experienced in recent years, they are even more skittery and hard to manage today. Big jumps and drops in money growth undoubtedly make the problem worse. They contribute to higher and more volatile interest rates. How interest rates behave also influences how much money people want to hold and, in turn, the rate of money growth. The interrelationships are close and unpredictable.

Those close to the White House and elsewhere who press the Fed to iron out fluctuations in the money-supply figures should keep this in mind: If the Fed were to try to get smooth money growth in short periods, it undoubtedly would provoke even greater gyrations in interest rates than it has since October 1979. This is not, as Milton Friedman asserts, because the Open Market Committee is made up of "unreconstructed Keynesians" (this from an unreconstructed monetarist). It is because Fed officials believe it is necessary to weigh the costs and advantages of what happens to money growth against what happens to interest rates. It will not try to get smooth money growth at any price. This is the basic difference between the Federal Reserve and the monetarists in the Administration. It is a matter of fundamental monetary philosophy, not just technique.

The argument will not go away. In the meantime, markets are worried sick about a concern greatly transcending the fluctuations in money growth—the horrendous deficits looming ahead. Until that problem is tackled, market participants will remain edgy and nervous, building risk premiums into interest rates, being reluctant to make commitments and reacting excessively to short-run surprises. This kind of financial market is hardly conducive to the increased volume of investment the Administration is trying to stimulate through its supply-side policy. And it is hardly an environment conducive to more precise control of the money supply.

The Administration would be well advised to advertise what the Fed has accomplished in the longer run. Money growth in the past four years looks like this (M1B annual averages):

1978—8.2%
1979—7.7%
1980—5.9%
1981—4.7%

Because of shifts among the Ms these figures may not completely reflect the degree of progress.* But even with allowance for the possibility, the rate of money growth is being brought down, as both the Administration and the Fed want. Confidence could be enhanced if the Administration were to make

*Ms refers to different measures of the money supply—Eds.

more of this desirable trend instead of caviling so much about movement around it. Everyone would be better off if the Administration would cease picking on the Fed and concentrate on what really is shaking up the markets, namely those frightening budget deficits.   **focus**

The next selection also concentrates on the differences between the FED and two sets of Federal Reserve critics. One set of critics is the monetarists, led by the most famous monetarist of all, Milton Friedman. These critics agree with Reagan's charge that the monetary authority has not lived up to its full responsibilities. The monetarists argue that even though the FED may have announced a shift in policy from controlling interest rates to controlling monetary aggregates, the FED has not practiced monetarism—at least not Friedman's brand of monetarism. Friedman maintains that monetarism demands a "stable pattern of monetary growth" and the FED has been allowing erratic variations in the money supply. The second set of critics is the non-monetarists, who maintain that the FED *is following monetarist doctrine.* According to these critics, who include such luminaries as former presidential advisor, Walter Heller and Wall Street economist Henry Kaufman, monetarist doctrine is wrong. They say that monetary policy would be more effective if the FED concentrated on controlling interest rates instead of the monetary aggregates. Marilyn Wilson, Princeton Fellow and senior editor of *Dun's Business Review,* summarizes these criticisms.

IS THE FED MONETARIST?

Marilyn Wilson, *Dun's Business Month,* May 1982

Most of the economic experts cheered when in October 1979 the Federal Reserve Board decided to abandon its time-honored focus on interest rates and instead gear policy to controlling money supply growth. After years of runaway inflation, there was widespread agreement that it was time to uncork Dr. Milton Friedman's all-purpose prescription for noninflationary prosperity. "At that point, we were all monetarists," says economist Ben Laden of T. Rowe Price Associates.

Today, this consensus is collapsing under the weight of recession and high interest rates. Some Wall Street economists, most notably Henry Kaufman of Salomon Brothers Inc, say monetarism is poisoning, not curing, the economy. Friedman and other true believers, frustrated and on the defensive, say the problem is that the Fed is not practicing monetarism at all. Both factions are putting pressure on the central bank to change its ways—while those in the middle warn that the financial community will react badly to *any* shift in monetary policy.

The debate is complicated by the fact that the critics have different ideas of what "monetarism" means. Most economists who endorse the basic theory simply believe there is a distinct relationship between the growth rate of the money supply and the rate of inflation and economic activity. "We say it's essential to control money, but we don't think it's a perfect cure-all," argues Laden.

Friedman and his disciples, however, preach that strict control of the money supply is all that's needed to solve the nation's economic woes—if the job is done right. Many of these devout purists, including Treasury Under Secretary Beryl Sprinkel and White House economic adviser Jerry Jordan, hold high posts in the Reagan Administration, so monetarism is now being linked with the alleged failure of supply-side economics, the latest brand of the free-market viewpoint. "A lot of the criticism about monetarism has little to do with monetary policy," says monetarist Leif H. Olsen, chief economist of Citibank.

Supply-Side Monetarism?

Is the Federal Reserve Board actually practicing monetarism? And if so, is the theory failing its real-life test?

Milton Friedman's answer to both questions is "no." So far, in his opinion, the Fed has paid only lip service to the goal of a stable pattern of monetary growth. "My complaint about monetary policy is not that it has been persistently 'too tight' or persistently 'too easy,' but that it has alternated erratically between the one and the other," he says.

The Fed's major sin, in the eyes of the strict monetarists, is that it is still trying to control interest rates instead of the money supply. The board's refusal to adopt their methods of money control also outrages the Friedmanites, who believe the job is simple if the right techniques are used. For example, they believe banks should be required to hold reserves that are in line with current deposits. Currently, a two-week lag is allowed.

The purists were somewhat mollified when the Fed recently said it would stop issuing the weekly, seasonally-adjusted money supply numbers that are so closely watched by the markets. Instead, every week it will report an unadjusted four-week moving average of the money supply. "Everybody knows the adjusted numbers are terrible and highly destabilizing," says monetarist Allan Meltzer of Carnegie-Mellon University.

The ongoing criticism both amuses and worries many moderate economists, who believe the Fed is indeed on a monetarist path. "The high priests also accuse [Prime Minister] Margaret Thatcher of not following the religion either, but she certainly thinks she is," says University of Minnesota economist Walter Heller, who was chairman of the Council of Economic Advisers under President John F. Kennedy. U.S. Trust Co. economist James J. O'Leary is concerned that the monetarist catcalls will undermine public confidence. "Here the Fed is doing for the first time what the monetarists have always wanted, but they're leading the sniping pack," he says.

The infighting doesn't bother consulting economist Joel Popkin, who dismisses it as "academic arrogance" from monetarists who never had to put their policies into real-world action, as does Fed Chairman Paul Volcker. The hardest bricks are being thrown at the theory itself, the Washington-based consultant points out. "Monetarism is under attack because it doesn't provide a cure for inflation at a modest price," he says. "We always knew that; the only thing is, we've never tried it before."

Precisely because the price is so high, Henry Kaufman thinks it's time to stop trying. The Wall Street analyst predicts "unacceptable economic and financial violence" if the Fed continues to target the money supply. "Under monetarism, there are no restraints other than those produced by interest rates", he says, which means gyrations in both short- and long-term rates, high real interest rates and massive changes in the nation's credit structure—among other problems.

Many experts scoff at the dire predictions—and a few wonder about Kaufman's motives. "Some people in the financial market are blaming monetarism for everything but the floods in the Middle West," says Citibank's Olsen. "The truth is that they don't like change, because they've built inflation into their planning. Now monetarism comes along and starts to bring inflation down, so they're complaining." Edward Guay, chief economist at Connecticut General Life Insurance Co., agrees that monetary policy "just about destroyed Henry Kaufman's assumptions about the 1982 economy." Investors who based their strategies on predictions of unabated inflation are starting to ask questions, he adds.

An Imperfect Test

Olsen, who claims Kaufman both "misunderstands and misinterprets" monetarism, believes critics of the theory are saying in a roundabout way that they are in favor of government intervention in the financial markets. "Monetarists are just as concerned about having lower and stable interest rates as everybody else," he says. "The point is that we long ago identified excessive growth of money as the ultimate source of instability."

Monetarist or not, the majority of economists believes the Fed is giving monetarism an imperfect test—but one that is clearly not a complete failure. "The bottom line is that we have had slower growth in M-1 [cash in circulation plus demand deposits, the most widely accepted measure of money] in the last couple of years and the rate of inflation is down dramatically," says Rudolph G. Penner of the American Enterprise Institute. "That's all anyone said would ever happen."

Given the handicaps the Fed faced when it embarked on a monetarist policy, many analysts feel this success is remarkable. "A forgotten, but crucial problem was the initial condition of the economy," says Jason Benderly of Washington Analysis Corp., a Bache Group subsidiary. Things could hardly have been worse, he recalls. Paul Volcker had to try and reverse thirty years of accelerating inflation, fifteen years of slowing productivity growth and ten years of sluggish real economic growth. "The worse the disease, the longer it takes for the cure to work—no matter how potentially successful," he concludes.

In Benderly's estimate, real growth (which was down 0.3% in 1980 and up only 0.9% in 1981) will rise 1.5% this year and 2.5% in 1983. Inflation (which ran 10%-to-12% in 1980 and 8%-to-9% in 1981) will be up 6.5% this year and only 5% in 1983. "The numbers are moving in the right direction," he notes.

Both the critics and the fans of the Fed see plenty of room for improvement in monetary policy, however. The high-church monetarists want Volcker to do it their way, Kaufman thinks the growth of credit should be targeted instead of money, while others say the central bank should simply set the federal funds rate at three percentage points above the inflation rate. Benderly says the Fed is already experimenting with a new index that measures the liquidity of various new types of financial assets. He contends this "Divisia Index" will vastly improve the Fed's ability to track movements in the markets.

Walter Heller believes monetary policy should be geared to overall conditions in the economy. In his opinion, the rate of inflation, the rate of unemployment and the rate of growth should all be targeted along with interest rates.

Given the current economic malaise, Heller maintains that the Fed is keeping far too tight a grip on the money supply."Without any help from fiscal policy, Volcker could afford to ease up on monetary policy now, for the simple reason that there's an enormous amount of slack in the economy," he says. For the first time since the Great Depression, Heller points out, the nation has experienced three years of no real growth in Gross National Product.

Catch-22 for all of these suggested changes is that the Fed may not be in a position to shift gears—even if it wanted to. U.S. Trust's O'Leary calls it the "trap of government policy": "The Fed is under pressure to be purer than Caeser's wife because of the huge federal deficit and fears of resurging inflation," he says.

O'Leary acknowledges that there are many things the Fed should do in order to improve operations in the open market, modify the lags in money supply reporting and update the measures of money. "But they can't do it now because that would be seen as a change in their hard-nosed position," he says. "The only thing that's holding interest rates where they are is the Fed's credibility—almost any move they make would send rates right through the roof."

No Alternative

Even monetarists like Meltzer concede that there are signs that the credibility of the central bank has increased. "The gyrations continue, but the market reacts less. People believe the targets are working," he says. For this reason alone, O'Leary contends, the Fed has absolutely no alternative but to stay the course—even though he fears the likely upshot will be high unemployment and low growth for the foreseeable future.

If O'Leary is right, even bigger bricks will be thrown at monetarism and even louder complaints about the Fed's techniques will be voiced by true-blue monetarists. It's possible, of course, that by this fall the budget worries will be over, the economy will have picked up and both inflation and interest rates will be down. In that case, Dr. Friedman is sure to step forward and take a bow. **fᴏ©ᴜs**

It is important to recognize that not all conservatives are monetarists (both Friedman and Kaufman are conservatives, but Kaufman is certainly no monetarist). Indeed, there is a clear and distinct possibility of conflict between supply-siders and monetarists. For example, the supply-siders would rely primarily on cuts in tax rates and government spending as a means of restoring the economy's health, while the monetarist camp would maintain a stable growth in the money supply in order to generate sustained economic growth. The point of confusion is the fact that there is no unanimity within the Reagan administration. The administration includes both supply-siders and monetarists. Our next selection takes up this question. It suggests that there is a consistent monetary and fiscal policy within the Reagan administration and denies that there is any substantial conflict between the monetarists and the supply-siders. Under secretary of the treasury, Beryl Sprinkel argues that tax cuts will stimulate savings and that the path to lower interest rates is through tight money, not smaller budget deficits. That is, tight money will end inflation, and once inflation is controlled, interest rates will fall. Finally, Sprinkel asserts that monetarism and supply-side economics have common foundations: "both theories argue that government policies can be a significant detriment to private initiative and both seek to reduce these government influences."

THERE'S NO CONFLICT BETWEEN MONETARISTS AND SUPPLY-SIDERS

Beryl W. Sprinkel, *Challenge*, July/August 1982

It is reported that when Samuel Johnson was asked why he defined "pastern" as the knee of a horse, he replied, "Ignorance, madam, pure ignorance." In looking over some of the public discussion of the administration's economic policy, citing alleged shortcomings or failures of Reaganomics, monetarism, or supply-side economics, I often wish that some of the critics would be as candid as Mr. Johnson in explaining the source of their views.

I mention this by way of introduction because I believe that what often appear to be major differences in perceptions of national economic conditions and policy options actually reflect primarily a failure to agree on definitional terms. For example, as one who considers himself a monetarist of sorts, I often have trouble reconciling my views with those that some people attribute to "monetarists." Implementation of sound and sustainable economic policy requires public debate which involves the issues, not exercises in setting up straw men labeled monetarism, supply-side economics, or whatever, in order to knock them down with great flourish and indignation.

For example, frequent reference is made, both here and abroad, to an alleged inconsistency between our current monetary and fiscal policies. Often this perceived imbalance has been treated as a clash between "monetarism" and "supply-side economics."

I'd like to discuss some critical points regarding the matter of the *consistency* of the economic recovery program.

Is Our Fiscal Policy Too Loose?

The President thinks so and thus continues to recommend further cuts in the growth of spending. His critics apparently agree with him on the question of looseness but they would like to correct the situation by raising revenues. These are questions falling as much within the domain of one's political philosophy as within that of economic theory. We have to be honest about the terms of the ongoing discourse. The issue is how much the government should spend and how that spending should be financed. Federal spending rose from slightly more than 20 percent of GNP in 1970 to almost 24 percent in 1981. The President would like to slow the growth of government spending enough to drop this share back to 20 percent or less by 1984. That was the target of a year ago and it remains. The cut of four percentage points would take a major chunk out of the deficits which are currently projected for the out-years.

On the other side of the issue are taxes. As I suggested earlier, the deficit is a complex issue. Obviously, government borrowing absorbs saving and *ceteris paribus* raises the real cost of credit to the private sector. Also, projections of continuing deficits and their implications for government actions in the future can have a significant negative effect on expectations. Important as these issues are, however, they must be weighed against the cost of raising various taxes. The relevant question is which approach has the smaller detrimental effect on the prospects for stimulating the long-run productive potential of the economy. The administration believes that the tax system has been a major force in constraining growth of income and economic opportunity. Modest progress has been made in correcting that problem and a lot of thought should be given to the costs of reversing that progress simply to balance the budget. Furthermore, the historical record leads us to the conclusion that increases in taxes are more likely to stimulate government spending than to reduce the deficit.

Is Our Monetary Policy Too Tight?

By choosing criteria creatively one can always show this to be the case. Some critics would point toward high inflation-adjusted short-term interest rates; others—toward the so-called overvaluation of the dollar relative to other major currencies; others still would invoke the drop in real economic activity; while yet another group of critics would look at the rate of growth of total credit rather than a narrow measure of money.

Personally, I think that as long as the rate of growth of M1 exceeds the trend rate of growth of total output, the case for monetary policy's being too *tight* cannot be convincingly made. Essentially, the argument comes down to the question of what the optimal path of disinflation is. Even the most severe critics acknowledge a remarkable reduction in the rate of inflation. No one would deny that this disinflation of the economy resulted in considerable discomfort to millions of individuals. Would a somewhat more accommodating monetary policy result, to get fancy, in a smaller net present discounted value of aggregate pain over time? I say "no" and can safely challenge anyone to prove me wrong—anyone, that is, who objectively assesses the long-term costs and distortion of inflation. Once again I would appeal to both critics and supporters of this administration's policies to discriminate between points of economic analysis and value judgments.

A Credible Economic Program

Let us turn to another critical issue: an economic program, even if consistent, must also be credible. It is important to distinguish between the credibility of intent and the credibility of outcome, the former being necessary but, of course, not sufficient for the latter.

Even granting that I am not an unbiased judge of this administration's determination to stick to its announced economic policies, I wonder, given our record, what it takes to earn one's badge of trustworthiness. As promised, we reduced the growth of hundreds of government spending programs well beyond what was universally considered politically possible before November 4, 1980; we eliminated a great many regulations and restructured others; we ended regular intervention in foreign exchange markets; we haven't resorted to bailouts of shaky enterprises; we didn't buckle under the threat of a potentially crippling strike by a public employees' union; and so on, and so on. Most symptomatic, in the midst of a rather severe recession in a mid-term election year, we have not attempted to pressure the Federal Reserve to expand the money supply more rapidly. Can there still be any doubt regarding this administration's commitment to its economic policies? I think not.

I do recognize, however, that even among those people who believe in the Reagan administration's ability to persevere in pursuing its policies, many doubt that these policies will yield the promised results. This is what I call the credibility of income. The expressed doubts, as we all know, center around the presumed crowding-out phenomenon during the recovery phase. As the story goes, the high real cost of credit will discourage investment and nip the recovery in the bud. In order to stave off this calamity, a reduction in the government borrowing requirement by means of raising taxes is being suggested; and since the administration is demonstrably resistant to the idea of raising taxes, it is alleged that the economic forecast of resumed sustainable growth is not to be believed.

Neither the scenario of continued sluggishness in the economy nor the cure proposed by the administration critics is self-evident. First, the odds are overwhelming that inflation-adjusted long-term interest rates will come down substantially; their present level simply cannot be sustained at current and prospective inflation rates. Granted, a *ceteris paribus* reduction in the government deficit would depress those long-term rates even further. But how relevant is this observation if the reduction is to be achieved by a tax increase which induces a decline in the private sector's willingness to save? When the *ceteris paribus* does not hold, is it clear that the proposed cure is better than the alleged disease? Tax and tax and spend and spend is not our hallmark. If the President is correct (and I believe there is not the slightest doubt that he is) that higher tax revenues mean more government spending, then one must pause before advocating raising taxes. If government expenditures increase to the full extent of the incremental tax increase, the case against this course of action is clearcut and requires no further elaboration. But even if every additional dollar in tax increases were to generate, say, only 50 cents in additional spending, still the government would be preempting a larger share of the nation's resources than under present proposals. I doubt this would stimulate a burst of economic activity.

Furthermore, I do not share the confidence that a reduction in federal deficits by means of raising taxes would translate to any appreciable extent into lower real long-term interest rates. In fact, rescinding the scheduled cut in marginal income taxes would probably have the opposite effect. It is worth pointing out, it seems, that a marginal propensity to save of less than one is a necessary, *not* a sufficient, condition for reducing the supply of private credit by less than the reduction in the government demand for credit due to higher tax revenues. Should the 10 percent reduction in personal income tax rates scheduled for 1983 be repealed, I would not have to stretch my imagination to conceive that a combination of reduced incentives to work and an incremental increase in government spending would probably lead to higher, not lower, real long-term interest rates.

In addition, maintaining moderate money growth—"tight money," to some—is a certain method for improving the condition of credit markets. The combination of inflation, the tax system, and regulations on financial markets has encouraged a great deal of private borrowing to purchase real assets. These efforts to protect wealth have been quite evident in the housing boom of the 1970s. Monetary discipline would greatly reduce this drain on credit, encouraging a shift back to holding of financial assets. The result is downward pressure on real rates of interest.

Finally, I cannot suppress the urge to remind our critics that the interest rate, or cost of capital services, is not the only argument in a standard investment function. In case they have forgotten, expected demand for output figures in this quite prominently. Increasing people's taxes cannot but depress the expected level of sales and, consequently, depress today's demand for investment goods.

No Conflict

For those who still think there is some kind of conflict between supply-side and monetarist economics, perhaps it is useful to think of the situation this way. Monetary and supply-side economics are based on the proposition that private initiative is the source of wealth and higher standards of living. Both theories argue that government policies *can* be a significant detriment to private initiative and both seek to reduce this perverse government influence.

What has been characterized as the supply side of our economic policy deals with the effect of government spending and financing on the willingness and ability of individuals to take a chance on productive ventures. The monetarist component deals with money in the belief that high and variable inflation is detrimental to work, savings, and investment—and that inflation is a monetary phenomenon. The goal of the supply-side and monetary elements of our policy is the same: to increase the productive potential of the economy. The only difference is that they focus on different aspects of government behavior.

Reaganomics is carefully designed to rid us of stagflation by limiting money growth and inflation, while increasing incentives to produce more real goods and services. I am convinced it is working.   focus

Sprinkel's contention that there is unanimity within the Reagan administration is not surprising—in as much as he is one of the members of that administration. However, the view from outside the Reagan administration is somewhat different. Outsiders find many differences between the monetarists and the supply-siders, especially when the supply-side community is extended to include important persons outside the Reagan administration. This was the position taken in a recent article in *Business Week*. This essay suggests several differences between monetarists and supply-siders: (i) supply-siders believe that growth and disinflation (lowering the rate of inflation) can be achieved simultaneously, monetarists do not; (ii) supply-siders believe that a return to the gold standard is necessary for control of the money supply, monetarists do not; and (iii) supply-siders believe that budget deficits must be reduced before interest rates will fall, monetarists do not.

THE CLASH BETWEEN SUPPLY-SIDERS AND MONETARISTS

Business Week, August 24, 1981

Now that the Reagan Administration has engineered the most dramatic shift in government spending and tax policy since the New Deal days of Franklin D. Roosevelt, the burning question is whether it will work to stimulate the economy and contain inflation. Followers of traditional Keynesian economics, who have advocated stimulating demand to make the economy grow, have said all along it would not. On Wall Street, doubt that the new program will work is reflected in stock prices that refuse to go up and interest rates that refuse to go down. Even more significant, supply-side economists who supplied the intellectual force behind the Reagan program have turned skeptical.

In the past month, the apostles of supply-side economics, notably Jude Wanniski head of Polyconomics Inc., a political consulting firm, and Arthur B. Laffer have both attacked the Reagan Administration for backsliding. They fear that Reagan's mind has been taken over by monetarist economists in the Treasury who are trying to control the economy by regulating the money supply, mainly M-1B, the measure of cash, demand deposits, and NOW accounts. They are predicting that Reagan's program will founder in a collision between fiscal stimulation, caused by the tax cut, and the Federal Reserve monetary policy. What Laffer and Wanniski argue for is a return to a gold standard as a base for the currency.

The debate between the supply siders and the monetarists is more than an intellectual exercise. At stake is U.S. fiscal and monetary policy and the level of interest rates. The original supply siders have joined other doubters of the Administration's program in predicting that interest rates will stay high, choking off both the boom in private investment and the era of strong economic growth promised by Reagan.

Gold Convertibility

Alone among economists, supply siders have long argued that the Administration could reach its main goals—lowered inflation and strong growth—at the same time. But this would require a return to the gold standard, which was formally abandoned by former President Nixon in 1971, in addition to the massive tax cuts that have been passed. "The government should guarantee the purchasing power of the U.S. currency by making it convertible into gold," says Arthur B. Laffer, a chief architect of the supply-side doctrine. "Until that is done, we do not have a serious anti-inflation policy."

Monetarists have consistently disagreed with the supply siders that strong growth and a lasting deceleration of inflation can be achieved simultaneously in the short run. They have argued that interest rates will decline as the economy softens for a short time in response to a consistently tight monetary policy. If interest rates come down soon, the monetarists, who now have the dominant position in the Administration, will be proved correct. Then the voices of the supply siders will be muted, along with those of other skeptics. But if interest rates stay high, then the supply siders' drive to make the U.S. dollar convertible into gold—the missing element of the complete supply-side program—has a good chance of succeeding.

For the moment at least, the failure of interest rates to decline, as the monetarists have been predicting since early this year, has helped the supply siders' cause. Seizing on this failure, the supply siders' exuberant zealot, Wanniski, a longtime economic adviser to Representative Jack Kemp (R-N.Y.), recently launched a new drive for the gold standard. In a July 27 letter to *The Washington Post*, Wanniski argued that monetarism would doom the U.S. economy to recession, and he personally attacked President Reagan's monetarist friend, Nobel laureate Milton Friedman, whose monetarism, he said, would be "buried." Other supply siders take exception to Wanniski's attack on Friedman. "I wish that my friends wouldn't imply that I would join in an attack on the man that I consider the best economist in the country," says Laffer.

'The Wraps are Off'

But there is also no doubt that Wanniski is speaking for the supply siders on the substantive issue of a return to gold. "Until the U.S. returns to gold, interest rates will continue to be volatile, and the economy will continue to be sluggish," says Lewis Lehrman, head of Lehrman Corp. and a leading supply sider.

The supply siders had muted their criticism of monetary policy during the fight for tax cuts, partly because their political leader, Representative Kemp, wanted it that way. "He asked me to cool it," says Wanniski, "but now the wraps are off." Indeed, having extolled the virtues of tax cuts up and down the land, Laffer is now downplaying their relative importance in a total economic package. "If spending cuts are 1 and tax cuts are 10, then monetary policy is 100," he now says, adding that he is completely convinced that the monetary policy now being followed by the Federal Reserve Board is "terrible."

The supply siders will drive for gold on these fronts:
■ Continued drumfire from Wanniski, Laffer, and their supply-side colleagues outside the Administration.
■ A political campaign by Kemp, who will make the restoration of gold convertibility his No. 1 priority.
■ An effort to influence the report of the Gold Commission, which is scheduled to report on Oct. 6 of this year. The commission, created by legislation sponsored by Senator Jesse A. Helms (R.-N.C.) and Representative Ronald E. Paul (R-Tex.), is regarded by the supply siders as a key forum for advancing their views. Says Lehrman, a member of the commission: "The Administration's views on gold are agnostic but not hostile" to those of the supply siders.

So far, the Administration, although studying gold, is hewing firmly to monetarism. As a consequence, the main effect of the supply-side attack to date is to enrage the monetarists, both inside and outside the Administration. "That Laffer sure is a dancer," says Carnegie-Mellon economist Allen H. Meltzer, chairman of the Shadow Open Market Committee, a bastion of monetarism that had counted both Treasury Undersecretary for Monetary Affairs Beryl W. Sprinkel and Council of Economic Advisers member Jerry Jordan among its members until they became the leading monetarists inside the Administration.

What is critical—but perhaps not widely understood—is that the battle between the monetarists and the supply siders is not between supporters and critics of the Federal Reserve. The monetarists are generally satisfied with current Fed policy, but their basic antipathy toward the institution is well-known. The supply siders are, if anything, even more hostile. They would like to see the Administration curb Fed power to create money by making the quantity of money depend not on whims but on the quantity of gold.

A paradox of the current debate is that the supply siders also call themselves monetarists. This is obviously true about Laffer, in the sense that he believes that monetary policy is far more important than fiscal policy. But the brand of monetarism espoused by those who would return to the gold standard is so different from conventional monetarist policy that is now in place as to make it a totally different doctrine. This can most easily be seen in the vastly different ways in which the two groups answer the key questions about monetary policy.

Can the Federal Reserve Control the Quantity of Money?

The answer of such conventional monetarists as Meltzer, Sprinkel, and Jordan, as well as their mentor, Friedman, is an unequivocal "yes." They argue that they can point to mountains of evidence spanning many countries and many decades that if central banks focus on controlling bank reserves or the monetary base—the raw material out of which banks create money—

governments can exert enough control over business to bring about both price stability and satisfactory economic growth.

Quantity control is impossible to achieve, say the supply siders, because banks, individuals, and corporations so ingeniously invent new monetary and credit instruments to serve as money that what the monetarists call money is impossible even to define, let alone control. Says Alan Reynolds, formerly an economist at First National Bank of Chicago and now working with Wanniski at Polyconomics: "The Fed, by placing a limit on the checking and time deposits that are included in the monetary aggregate that it is trying to control—M-1B—is causing the kinds of money not included in that aggregate, like money market funds and overnight corporate repos, to grow extremely rapidly." Reynolds, in fact, believes that the rapid growth of such things as money market funds and corporate repos means that money is not nearly as tight now as the monetarists, who look mainly at narrower definitions of money, think it is.

Should the Federal Reserve Try to Control the Quantity of Money?

To conventional monetarists, such control is the key to everything else. But the supply siders believe that control of the quantity of money is an inappropriate goal of policy. Laffer argues that never in the history of banking has any institution provided a guarantee of the quantity of its assets or the quantity of its liabilities (which include the bank deposits that make up most of the nation's money supply). Rather, they have always guaranteed their "quality." And, he says, what is true of commercial banks should also be true of central banks. Laffer believes that this quality control can only be guaranteed by gold.

"The only thing government should do is produce a quality product—the money supply—as opposed to regulating the quantity of money in the marketplace," says Laffer, who clearly believes that he is currently the true defender of the monetarist faith. Laffer says, for example, that he has no quarrel with the results of the massive statistical studies by Friedman and Anna J. Schwartz, who is serving as the executive director of the Gold Commission. He believes that the relationship between the growth rate of narrowly defined money and the monetary base, which was demonstrated in the monetary history of the U.S. and which forms the basis for conventional monetarism, is correct. The trouble, he says, is that this monetarist bible was published in the early 1960s and covers a period "when the U.S. dollar was convertible into gold."

The link between the dollar and gold was finally severed with the closing of the gold window almost 10 years ago. Laffer argues that his forecasts have been far better than those of conventional monetarists since then.

"Soon after the gold window was closed," he says correctly, "I published an article predicting that inflation would move into the double-digit range and that interest rates would soar. The prediction," he says, again accurately, "was ridiculed by everyone, including the Friedmanians. But events since then show that my model was better."

Will the Current Monetary Policy Bring Down Interest Rates?

To this question, the supply-side answer is a resounding "No." Although Lehrman, who has been placing more emphasis on the need for further spending cuts than most other supply-siders, believes that there will be interest-rate volatility in the short run, with some dips, he thinks a sustained move toward lower rates will only occur with a move toward gold. Only then, he says, "will individuals have enough confidence in the long-term inflation outlook to be willing to hold a 30-year bond at lower rates."

Monetarists hold that there is conclusive evidence of a strong linkage between money growth and inflation and interest rates. And they further believe that there is no systematic evidence that credit demand has any sustained effect on inflation, interest rates, or real growth. "We can have lower interest rates and lower inflation if credit is growing rapidly or slowly. Credit conditions are determined by savings and the productivity of capital," says Meltzer, citing a strong investment boom in Japan, despite the fact that inflation is running at some 4% to 5% and interest rates are less than half the U.S. level. What Japan has done is to control money growth.

Monetarists do see the short-term threats to their program. Although they are generally satisfied with the Fed's performance, they worry over seeing inability or unwillingness to prevent short-term lurches in money growth. They note that interest rates were coming down nicely from December of last year to March of this year, when the Fed seemed to have money under control. But then the money supply lurched in April, bringing another rise in rates.

Monetarist economists hope—but are not certain—that the Federal Reserve will avoid policy lurches from now on. That explains the heat that such Administration monetarists as Sprinkel put on the Fed when it seems to be deviating from its targets, even though they know that the heat will lead Fed officials to go complaining to the White House.

What Would Be the Consequences of Going Back to Gold?

The supply siders believe that by severely limiting the Fed's power to manipulate money, a gold standard would not only produce price stability and lower interest rates but also allow the tax cut to work its magic. "The tax bill is marvelous, wonderful," says supply-sider Laffer. "It has improved incentives even more than did the Kennedy tax cut of the 1960s. It creates the conditions of a boom that will make those of the 1920s and 1960s look pale by comparison."

The monetarists are not so sure. They argue that a country that links its currency to gold makes itself vulnerable to severe business cycles. When the world is on a gold standard, they say, fast-growing countries experience an increase in income and prices that leads to balance-of-payments deficits. Those deficits drive gold out of the country, pushing money supply down and threatening recession.

Monetarists argue that it was this kind of instability that drove most countries off gold in the 1920s and 1930s. "The supply siders have a romantic view of the gold standard," says Meltzer. "What they forget is how much countries cheated on its basic rules to insulate themselves from recession."

The supply siders are hopeful that the Gold Commission will lead the way back to the gold standard. Lehrman, the supply siders' point man on the Gold Commission, has a specific plan. The government, he says, should announce that on some date—say, Jan. 1, 1982—it will fix the weight of gold represented by each dollar two years later, say on Jan. 1, 1984. It should also say that the dollar price of gold shall be fixed, based on market conditions, 90 days prior to the scheduled convertibility date, say on Sept. 1, 1984. The Administration should then send legislation to Congress defining the gold content of the dollar.

A return to gold may seem remote in Washington, where a triumphant Administration is now mainly focusing on vacations. But then, so did massive supply-side tax cuts at the time that Ronald Reagan won the election. **fOCus**

The *Business Week* article raises some interesting points, the most interesting of which is how the supply-siders within the Reagan administration view these issues. That is, do Reagan's supply-side policy makers agree with supply-siders Laffer, Wanniski, and Lehrman on the need to return to the gold standard? If we assume that the *1982 Economic Report of the President* represents the last word of the administration on this issue, the answer to this question is "no"; that is, the administration sides with monetarists in rejecting a call for reinstitution of the gold standard. Their position is reached after examination of prior experience with the gold standard as well as the possibility of developing a "better" gold standard.

AGAINST THE GOLD STANDARD

"Gold Standard," Council of Economic Advisors,
Economic Report of the President, 1982

The evidence presented indicates that previous gold-standard periods were characterized by: (1) lower *average* inflation and money supply growth;

(2) greater *fluctuations* in inflation, money supply growth, and output growth; and (3) higher unemployment rates than in the period 1946 to 1979. Although comparisons across time periods are difficult to make because of the difficulty of controlling for differences, including the effects of wars, droughts, and other shocks to the economy, it is far from clear that gold standards produced better overall results than those produced during the post-World War II period.

Could the United States forge a better gold standard now? There are two options: restore some form of gold cover requirement without convertibility or restore a gold cover requirement with convertibility; either with partial or full gold backing. The first option prevailed from 1934 until 1968, a period during which Federal Reserve Banks were required to keep a minimum of legal value gold certificates (valued at $35 an ounce) behind each $1 of their note liabilities. A more structured variant would be to restrain money creation by linking the central bank's ability to create liabilities to a legislated schedule of changes in the official price of gold and changes in the amount of gold reserves required for each dollar of central bank liabilities. Central to such a proposal would be a requirement that the actual gold stock remain fixed in size and that changes in its value occur only through variations in the official or bookkeeping price of gold. Not only would there be no requirement to buy and sell gold at the official price, the Treasury would be prohibited from doing so. In other words, there would be a gold reserve requirement for the money supply, but no convertibility regardless of whether the official price of gold was below, at, or above the market price. In sum, this option would essentially constrain the annual growth of the monetary base.

Under the second option the United States would fix permanently the dollar price of gold—that is, make the dollar convertible into gold—without concern for whether or not other countries would follow our example. The difference between a partial and a full backing would be that, whereas full backing would establish a one-to-one link between the gold stock and the money stock, partial backing would not. But in both cases, random shocks in the gold markets would create serious problems in controlling monetary aggregates and hence the general price level. . . .   **fOCUs**

Thus, there is much disagreement regarding the conduct of monetary policy. Even though the Reagan administration supports, in general, the FED's efforts to reduce the growth rate of the money supply, this can not be taken as grounds for complete agreement. The disagreements are many and varied, with attacks on the FED from both monetarist conservatives, nonmonetarist conservatives, and liberals. Important also are the disagreements between monetarists and supply-siders as well as some supply-siders and the administration.

Conclusion

This chapter has taken up issues regarding budget deficits and monetary policy. It has established that the basic position of the supply-siders in the Reagan administration was one of opposition to budget deficits and that this was a position based on principle. Indeed, when faced with growing budget deficits, the Reagan administration has argued that its supply-side tax initiatives have to be sacrificed in order to reduce budget deficits. This position, based on principle, has hardened, and now the Reagan administration supports a constitutional amendment which guarantees a balanced budget.

With respect to monetary policy, the supply-siders within the Reagan administration seem to support the monetarist notion that to eliminate inflation there must be a smooth and steady decline in the rate of growth of the money supply. This position has brought the Reagan administration into conflict not only with the FED, but also with liberals and some conservatives. Yet is has not aligned them with the "radical right" supply-siders who maintain that it is necessary to return to a gold standard.

CHAPTER 6

The New Federalism

Introduction

This chapter examines the debate which surrounds an often overlooked extension of the theory and philosophy of supply-side economics: "New Federalism." The proponents of New Federalism view this program as yet another part of their free market-oriented public policies. They argue that if the prejudicial impact of the Federal government on important economic decisions is to be reduced and someday eliminated, some of the Federal government's power must be transferred to lower levels of government which are "closer to the people." President Reagan's New Federalism is, consequently, an attempt to identify those functions best handled by the Federal government and those best handled by smaller, more localized governmental units, and to distribute these responsibilities accordingly.

This goal is totally consistent with other supply-side policy objectives. As we have learned in the preceding chapters, the controversy which surrounds supply-side public policy often focuses upon the degree of power which is to be assigned to our national government. That is, how much influence (power) over our lives should the Federal government have? This is the real question which separates liberals and conservatives. Supply-siders and other conservatives portray the Federal government as a bloated, ineffectual, non-productive entity which has absorbed too much power in the economic arena. They maintain that this concentration of power has seriously infringed upon the rights of individuals to act as they see fit and at times forces these individuals to act against their own best interests. One solution to this problem offered by the conservative community is to limit the growth of this economic power by curtailing the spending of the Federal government. They say a government that has less to spend in the marketplace, will exercise less coercive power over important economic decisions. A second solution, which is usually joined to this plea for reduced government spending, is a reduction in taxes and regulation. A reduction in taxes and regulation will not only leave more revenues in the private sector, but will eliminate many of the disincentives that are present in the system. Thus, a reduction in taxes and government regulation enhance the power of the private sector. New Federalism represents a third broad policy. Its proponents contend that shifting some of the powers of the Federal government to state and local governments will further reduce the influence of government in our economy. The impact of this program—just like the impact of reduced government spending, taxes, or regulation—is intended to unleash the power of free market forces.

The supply-side logic is straightforward. If the activities of "Big Government" distort the efficient allocation of scarce resources in the economy, then one obvious solution to this problem is to transfer the power of the one big government to a host of smaller, less influential governments. Fifty state governments acting in their own self-interests will have less coercive force than one Federal government. Two thousand local governments will have even less coercive force. Indeed, the larger the number of decision-making units and the smaller their size, the more government will mimic the marketplace.

Supply-side advocates of New Federalism contend that two major advantages can arise from this transfer of power. The first is an efficient allocation of scarce public resources. Government, if it is to be efficient, must satisfy the needs of its constituents. A government whose power extends over a vast number of different people with different needs will necessarily find itself at the mercy of numerous special interest groups, each trying to satisfy its specific demands. These groups are often successful because those unaffected by the special interest group's program find the proposed costs to be minimal. Consequently, unless people are directly affected by a given special interest program, they will not find it in their immediate interest to oppose it. Thus, big government—in the face of the demands of a number of special interest parties—will find itself supporting a substantial number of these groups. In some cases, it may find itself supporting programs that are diametrically opposed to one another.* This can only result in gross government overspending. That is, this promotes a situation where government is inefficiently allocating scarce public resources among competing claims. On the other hand, smaller governmental units, which represent less diversified groups of people, are not as susceptible to this problem. These smaller governments represent relatively small groups of people who are more likely to share the same needs and the same values. If special interest groups do arise, the costs of responding to them will no longer be ignored since the costs must be borne by a small group of taxpayers. Thus, special interest programs and conflicting programs are less likely to arise. As a result, smaller, more localized governments will better recognize the real problems faced by their constituencies, and can allocate their scarce resources more efficiently.

To repeat, smaller governmental units are "closer to the people" and, as a result, they are more likely to respond to the legitimate demands of their communities. They are less apt to be susceptible to a host of competing self-interests and can better allocate their scarce public resources to provide for the true concerns of the communities they are meant to serve. If expenditure responsibilities are diverted to these local governments, the end result will be a decentralized government whose influence in the marketplace is minimal. Such a decentralized government would satisfy the qualifications of a good government by efficiently allocating scarce resources. Thus, for its supporters, New Federalism represents the best of all possible worlds.

A second major advantage of transferring some economic power from our large, centralized Federal government to smaller state and local governments, is to better align elected officials with the constituencies which should be their legitimate concern. Proponents of President Reagan's New Federalism find it absurd and indefensible for a legislator from New Mexico to vote on funds to upgrade the transportation system of New York City. They maintain that Federal legislators should concentrate on national problems and leave state and local problems to those levels of government. Thus, supporters of the New Federalism argue that this new delineation of power would increase the efficiency of the decision-making process used by government.

In short, this reshuffling of the balance of power between the Federal government and the state or local governments will limit the impact of government activity in the economic arena, provide for a more efficient allocation of scarce public resources while satisfying the legitimate needs of our people, and (as President Reagan said in his 1982 State of the

---

*For example, it is often noted with some sarcasm that, while government spends millions of dollars yearly advising us of the ill effects of smoking, it is at the same time spending millions of dollars yearly subsidizing the production of tobacco.—Eds.

Union address) "make government again accountable to the people, . . . make our system of federalism work again."

These themes are echoed in the first three selections in this chapter. The authors of these articles ask us to look to and learn from history. They ask us to be sensible and logical. They are convinced that if we learn the lessons taught by the historian and the logician, we will recast our system and, in the process, return government to the people.

The Conservative/Supply-Side Economics Case for a New Federalism

Our first selection presents a detailed view of the historical and philosophical underpinnings of New Federalism. This article argues that if we are to judge New Federalism, we must first understand "Old Federalism," and the role it played for our founding fathers; we must become aware of the major changes that have occurred which warrant a cry for a New Federalism.

William Schambra, the author of this essay, argues that our form of government represents an attempt to "forcibly reconcile two theoretically irreconcilable systems." That is, our founding fathers proposed to let two opposing philosophies of popular government exist at the same time. Each philosophy had its own view of man and its own view of how best to govern man. Up until the time of our nation's founding, each philosophy was seen as a separate and distinct option for efficiently governing a society. Schambra contends that our founding fathers wisely decided to allow both philosophies to peacefully co-exist in our society, hoping to reap the best of both, and at the same time, to limit the worst of both.

Schambra maintains that the problem of inefficient and ineffective government has grown out of a liberal 20th century utopian dream to merge these two philosophical traditions "into one coherent doctrine." As Schambra notes, "liberalism promises to create the sense of community thought possible by the Anti-Federalists only in a small republic, on a national scale, through the energetic government established by the Federalists." In Schambra's view, the efforts of the 20th century liberals to achieve this "sense of community" has been disastrous for our nation and our economy.

Constitutional scholar Schambra's solution to the problems created by this liberal experiment is for "both traditions (to) be resurrected and restored to their appropriate spheres." In other words, his solution is to restore the Old Federalism of our forefathers. Under such a system, the Federalist and Anti-Federalist philosophies "function as they functioned prior to the New Deal: together, yet in tension, one correcting and moderating the excesses that follow from the other."

THE ROOTS OF FEDERALISM—OLD AND NEW

William A. Schambra, *Public Interest,* Spring 1982

. . . Two traditions of American political thought grew out of a quarrel at the time of the Founding in 1787. The Federalists, led by Alexander Hamilton and James Madison, and the Anti-Federalists, including such people as Patrick Henry, Richard Henry Lee, Mercy Warren, and Melancton Smith, disagreed about how best to constitute popular government. Madison and Hamilton—principal authors of *The Federalist* essays defending the proposed Constitution—argued, contrary to centuries of political teaching, that an energetic national government was compatible with, indeed essential to, popular government. The national government described in *The Federalist* would have, for its "first object," the protection of the "diversity in the faculties of men, from which the rights of property originate." . . .

The Federalists understood that there was a certain unloveliness about the commercial republic. It relied upon and encouraged the vigorous pursuit of wealth—not always a pleasant spectacle. But "multiplying the means of gratification" and "promoting the introduction and circulation of the precious metals, those darling objects of human avarice and enterprise" was the only way to "vivify the channels of industry and . . . make them flow with greater activity and copiousness"; that is, it was the only way to promote the "prosperity of commerce" which had become the "primary object" of "all enlightened statesmen." National prosperity would only be assured if there were adequate economic incentives for the self-interested individual; Hamilton's *Report on Manufactures* was a blueprint for the creation of such incentives.

The Founders also realized that the pursuit of wealth would result in inequalities among men, given the "different, and unequal faculties of acquiring property." But, as Hamilton argued, inequality followed inevitably from the freedom that the large commercial republic made possible: "an inequality would exist as long as liberty existed . . . it would inevitably result from that liberty itself." Inequality was a small price to pay for liberty, according to the Federalists.

This Federalist "package" of principles—an energetic national government administering a large territory, commerce, national diversity, individual self-interest, and inequality, all in the name of prosperity and liberty—forms one great tradition of American political thought. It is certainly the primary tradition given the success of the Federalists in incorporating their principles into the Constitution. But it is by no means the only tradition of American political thought, as the late Herbert Storing reminded us. The Federalists were challenged at the time of the Founding by what came to be called Anti-Federalism. Professor Storing was the first to make clear that the Anti-Federalists were *for* something, and what they were for had a powerful appeal in 1787, and continued to have a powerful appeal throughout American history. The Founding did not settle everything, according to Storing: "it did not finish the task of making the American polity. The political life of the community continues to be a dialogue, in which the Anti-Federalist concerns and principles still play an important part." In fact, "the Anti-Federalists are entitled . . . to be counted among the Founding Fathers."[1]

The Anti-Federalists

The Anti-Federalists shared with the Federalists a commitment to popular government and liberty. This fundamental consensus made possible the Founding, and gave the ratification debates the air of a quarrel within the family, rather than of a civil war. But the Anti-Federalists dissented from the view that popular government or republicanism was possible in a vast extent of territory, and under an energetic central government. The main reason for the Anti-Federalists' dissent was their belief, taken from Montesquieu, that republicanism was possible only with public-spirited or virtuous citizens. Republican citizens had to be imbued with the "love of the laws and of our country"; they must exhibit a "constant preference of public to private interest." Only an alert, public-spirited citizenry, they believed, would give that amount of attention to public affairs that self-government or republicanism truly requires. . . .

It was not only necessary that wealth be roughly equally distributed, but also that there not be too much of it. Too much wealth tended to draw attention away from public things, and to corrupt republican morality. Thus, frugality or austerity was important for the Anti-Federalists, who agreed with John Adams that "frugality is a great revenue, besides curing us of vanities, levities, and fopperies, which are real antidotes to all great, manly, and warlike virtues."

Finally—and we come to the specific point of dissent from the Federalists' large republic—all these rigorous conditions for community could be had only in a small republic. Here again, the Anti-Federalists claimed as their authority Montesquieu, who argued that "It is natural for a republic to have only a small territory," because in "an extensive republic, the public good is sacrificed to a thousand private views." In a small republic, the "interest of the public is more obvious, better understood, and more within the reach of every citizen"; thus, public affairs will command sustained public attention. That is the reason the Anti-Federalists championed a modified confederal form of government for the new nation, in which primary political responsibility was left to the "small republics" in the states.

To the Federalists' strong national government over an extensive territory, the Anti-Federalists preferred a weak national government, with primary political power left to the states. That was because the Anti-Federalists preferred a republic animated by civic virtue or public-spiritedness to one animated by commerce and individual self-interest; a republic resembling a homogeneous community to one characterized by diversity, or a multiplicity of interests; a republic that insured a general equality to one that tolerated the inequalities that spring from liberty; and a republic with an austere, frugal—what we would call "no-growth"—economy to one that encouraged prosperity, growth, and luxury.

It is impossible to survey the principles of Anti-Federalism without acknowledging their appeal, or sensing the power of their dissent from the Federalist position. And it would be regrettable if we, as a nation, had to accept one "package" of principles to the utter exclusion of the other. Fortunately, Americans are not faced by that unhappy choice. For the Federalists, while writing into the Constitution most of their principles and thus giving us the large commercial republic, did not have it all their own way in 1787. . . .

No one understood better than Alexis de Tocqueville the complex coexistence of Federalist large republicanism and Anti-Federalist small republicanism in American life. According to Tocqueville, Americans had "forcibly reconciled" those "two theoretically irreconcilable systems." There was no name for the government that resulted; it was a kind of "incomplete national government," which combined "the various advantages of large and small size for nations."

America was so prosperous, Tocqueville understood, because it was a large, commercial republic; it had given "free scope to the unguided strength and common sense of individuals." There were dangers in the individualistic pursuit of wealth, however, since it is "always an effort" for commercial men "to tear themselves away from their private affairs and pay attention to those of the community; the natural inclination is to leave the only visible and permanent representative of collective interests, that is to say, the state, to look after them." That was, of course, the ideal condition for tyranny. Furthermore, commerce could be dehumanizing, since "love of comfort" introduces the individual to "petty aims, but the soul clings to them; it dwells on them every day . . . in the end they shut out the rest of the world and sometimes come between the soul and God."

Countering these tendencies, Tocqueville argued, were the American traditions of local self-government and private association—traditions kept alive by the decentralizing impulse of federalism. American law-givers had wisely given "each part of the land its own political life so that there would be an infinite number of occasions for the citizens to act together and so that every day they should feel they depended on one another." Private voluntary associations of all kinds similarly served to draw men upward from mere self-interest into public life, combating the dehumanizing effects of individualism. Citizens acting together and depending on one another come to form a genuine community; a certain public-spiritedness or civic virtue is generated by local self-government, and men come to love their "little republic." Such public-spirited citizens, Tocqueville noted, will not be likely to surrender control of public life to the state.

For Tocqueville, then, the "forceable reconciliation" of "two theoretically irreconcilable systems" was absolutely central to the survival of American liberty. When he inquired into the "main causes tending to maintain a democratic republic in the United States," the first cause was "the federal form . . . which allows the Union to enjoy the power of a great republic and the security of a small one." The two systems or principles would always be in tension, according to Tocqueville, each threatening to consume the other. For instance, in Tocqueville's time, the states were powerful enough to challenge the existence of the union. The real danger, however, lay in the future, when a centralized national government would threaten to swallow up the local institutions so important for liberty. . . .

The New Deal Synthesis

The central claim of modern liberalism—or at least of that strain that runs from Theodore Roosevelt's "New Nationalism" to Franklin D. Roosevelt's "New Deal"—is that it could resolve the tension between these two principles, collapsing them into one coherent doctrine and giving us the best of each. That is, liberalism promises to create the sense of community thought possible by the Anti-Federalists only in the small republic, on a national scale, through the energetic government established by the Federalists.

Essential to the creation of the "Great Community" (John Dewey's description of the liberal goal) is the reduction, by a powerful central government, of those community-disrupting inequalities that spring from modern industrialism. According to Theodore Roosevelt, "The people . . . have but one instrument which they can efficiently use against the colossal combinations of business—and that instrument is the government of the United States." Modern liberalism, in Herbert Croly's famous formulation, would fulfill the "promise of American life" by marrying Jeffersonian democracy—characterized by the "good fellowship" that comes from "life in a self-governing community"—to Hamiltonian nationalism. This promise to combine into one coherent whole what had theretofore been considered rival political traditions would give the New Deal public philosophy an overwhelming moral and political appeal.

A comprehensive account of the liberal idea would have to begin with the appearance of Croly's *The Promise of American Life* in 1909, where the marriage of principles was first described, and continue through Theodore Roosevelt's presidential campaign of 1912, when this new brand of liberalism was injected into American political life, to Franklin Roosevelt's "New Deal," the apotheosis of modern liberalism. Here, however, we will consider primarily the mature form of liberalism, the New Deal public philosophy.

The New Deal public philosophy, according to Samuel Beer, had two characteristic elements: centralization and egalitarianism. Centralization meant that the national government—as opposed to the state governments that traditionally had been central to Democratic Party doctrine—would now do what needed to be done to meet the crisis of the Great Depression. This was far more than a doctrine of administrative centralization; in fact FDR hoped to create a true sense of national community—characterized by public-spiritedness, discipline, and self-sacrifice—in the face of national problems. In his first Inaugural Address, Roosevelt urged us to "move as a trained and loyal army willing to sacrifice for the goal of a common discipline . . ." We had to be prepared to "submit our lives and property to such discipline," and to exhibit "a unity of duty hitherto evoked only in time of armed strife."

Essential to the task of creating national unity, according to FDR, was the amelioration of extreme inequalities of wealth or power that make community difficult—as the Anti-Federalists had noted a century and a half before. Hence, the second theme of the New Deal: egalitarianism. Some of FDR's programs, such as the social security system, involved a mild degree of wealth redistribution. Other measures, such as the National Labor Relations Act of 1935, served to reduce differences in power and influence between the corporations and unions.

An energetic central government, fostering equality by reducing disparities of wealth and power, and cultivating in the people a certain public-spirited devotion to the general good, would, in Beer's words, further the "process of national integration" in which "the community . . . is made more of a community." That was the liberal promise: the creation of the small republic within the large republic, the marriage of Federalism and Anti-Federalism.

Community vs. Commerce

It would be more accurate, of course, to describe the promise of liberalism as the marriage of the *best* in Federalism with the *best* in Anti-Federalism. Like all proposed marriages of principles in which only the best elements of each are retained and the worst of each dropped, this proposed marriage was utopian.

Modern liberalism promised community—but now *without* the state, local, and private institutions that the Anti-Federalists had considered the very source of community. Liberals were, in fact, hostile to local institutions, as such institutions were notoriously backward and provincial. As Arthur Schlesinger, Jr. put it recently, "local government historically has been the . . . last refuge of reaction." It was no longer necessary to pay the price of provincialism for community, however; liberalism's "great community" would be drawn together by a powerful, progressive President, using his office as a "bully pulpit" to preach selfless devotion to the common national good.

Liberalism also promised to sustain the material abundance of the commercial republic—but this time *without* the unattractive self-interested individualism and inequality that the Federalists had considered the source of abundance. Those unsavory features of commerce would gradually be supplanted by community and public-spiritedness, apparently without harming commerce itself. In short, liberals promised prosperity, while harboring suppressed hostilities toward the traditional sources of prosperity. Liberals assumed that abundance was here to stay and that we could now get on with the task of assuring a more equitable distribution of abundance in the name of community. . . .

The utopianism implicit in the prospect of a great national community, which would combine sustained prosperity with widespread and increasing equality, became apparent in the 1960's and 1970's. In particular, equality became the consuming passion of liberalism, and, embodied in a growing central government, began to cut deeply into liberty and prosperity. Liberalism less and less successfully suppressed its hostility toward the necessary preconditions of growth. Anti-Federalist community began to devour Federalist commerce.

The growing liberal devotion to equality manifested itself primarily, of course, in a concern over the proper distribution of wealth. That concern had begun modestly enough as the desire to provide a floor for the least fortunate, and thereby bring them into the national community. The desire to provide a floor, however, swelled into a passion to eliminate all distinctions in the distribution of wealth—the assumption being that property was not private, but at the disposal of the community. Christopher Jencks would argue that "we need to establish the idea that the Federal government is responsible not only for the total amount of the national income, but for its distribution," and that we would have to "alter people's basic assumptions about the extent to which they are responsible for their neighbors and their neighbors for them." The assumption in John Rawls's *A Theory of Justice* was that everything— including an individual's talents and abilities—belonged to the community. The notion that the community was now responsible for the proper distribution of wealth was reflected in the proliferation of federal social welfare programs in the 1960's and 1970's, and in the national tax structure, which came to be seen as a device for income transfer as much as for collection of revenues.

As the community demanded a more equitable distribution of wealth, it also demanded tighter government supervision of the economy in general. In the "ferocious scrambling rush" of commerce, the public good all too often was sacrificed to a variety of private goods. The national government had to remedy this imbalance—and so, throughout the 1960's and 1970's, it became deeply involved in the regulation of commerce on behalf of "community values" like public safety and clean air and water. All these redistributive and regulatory projects, of course, meant bigger and bigger government. The second principle of the New Deal—centralization—assumed proportions unanticipated by liberalism's founders.

The single-minded pursuit of community and equality through heavy taxes, massive regulation, and social engineering recently began to take a toll on national economic performance. It became increasingly apparent that Anti-Federalist community and equality, and Federalist commercial prosperity, were *not* so easily reconciled. This, of course, was something that the Anti-Federalists had seen long ago, when they had argued that a simple economy, frugality, and austerity were the only routes to community. It is not surprising, then, that this Anti-Federalist idea found an echo in liberal pronouncements as the economy slowed down in the late 1970's. Liberals no longer even tried to suppress their hostility toward the preconditions of commerce. The very principles of prosperity and growth were questioned, and the virtues of austerity, frugality, and a no-growth economy endorsed. Even President Carter would say in his Inaugural Address that "we have learned that *more* is not necessarily *better.*"

The problem would have been seen clearly by Tocqueville. In his eyes, the American experiment was successful because we had kept the two great American traditions apart, each in its appropriate sphere, yet in a healthy tension. The effort to marry the principles, however, had joined centralization (now free of its vital counterweight of local government) to equality (now lacking its vital counterweight of individual liberty). Relieved of their ballasts, equality and centralization had moved toward their logical conclusions and became radicalized. The result was a doctrine that drove us toward "a great nation in which every citizen resembles one set type and is controlled by one single power."

Restoring the "Essential Tension"

If, in fact, the New Deal public philosophy is dead or dying, it is because the utopian character of the marriage of Federalism and Anti-Federalism has become clear, on a practical level, to the American people. They simply are not prepared to pay the price of a redistributive tax structure, massive welfare programs, a powerful and intrusive central government, and a no-growth economy, in order to achieve the liberal vision of the great national community.

Any public philosophy that would replace the New Deal, however, must return for its elements to the two American political traditions, for they both express immutable yearnings in the American soul. Neither tradition may be ignored. Contemporary conservatism (or, at any rate, libertarianism) and contemporary radical liberalism fail to understand this. Each of these strains of political thought does avoid the utopian excess of collapsing together the two political traditions. Each, however, commits the equally utopian excess of radicalizing one tradition at the expense of the other. Thus libertarianism (and its 19th century precursor, laissez-faire capitalism) makes the error of radicalizing the liberty, self-interest, and commerce of the Federalist tradition, while ignoring the equally legitimate impulse toward community and public-spiritedness. Conversely, the contemporary left embraces only the Anti-Federalist principles of community and equality—and, in some of its more exotic manifestations, even the Anti-Federalist "small sphere"—while despising the principles of self-interest and commerce.

America will be returned to political health only if we avoid these utopian errors and restore the Tocquevillian condition in America. Both traditions must be resurrected and restored to their appropriate spheres. They will then function as they functioned prior to the New Deal: together, yet in tension, one correcting and moderating the excesses that follow from the other.

The new terms of political discourse in Washington suggest an awareness of this need to restore the Tocquevillian condition. We seem to have rediscovered the Federalist idea that one of government's primary concerns is the provision of incentives for individual economic enterprise. Restoring the "prosperity of commerce" through the stimulation of individual self-interest has once again become the "primary object" of our statesmen, at least momentarily. Nor does this concern with reviving the economy signify an abandonment of the principle of community. Rather, we now look again— with the Anti-Federalists and Tocqueville—to state and local government and private associations to satisfy the American yearning for community. The new terms of political discourse indicate a sort of instinctive return to the healthy separateness and tension of the two American political traditions.

Whether these new terms of political discourse become the *permanent* terms remains to be seen. The supreme test will be whether a comprehensive, politically persuasive alternative to the utopian vision of the New Deal can be formed from the two American political traditions. To that end, this administration must make explicit what is already implicit in its programs of supply-side economics on the one hand, and the "new federalism" and private sector initiatives on the other.

This is by no means assured, of course, for the utopian vision of the great national community continues to have tremendous appeal in America. From the vantage of modern liberalism, supply-side economics appears to be simply a return to unrestrained individualism and mean-spirited self-aggrandizement. This economic program, by "taking from the poor and giving to the rich," can only compound the inequalities that liberalism has painstakingly ameliorated over the past five decades. Supply-side economics is, in short, a profound repudiation of the principle of community. The same may be said of the new concern with local and private institutions. Local and private communities are anachronistic, parochial "refuges of reaction"—mere mockeries of the great, progressive national community that, in liberalism's view, is the proper goal for America. In its struggle for survival, modern liberalism promises to take full advantage of the moral high ground that comes with the defense of the principle of community.

Contemporary American politics will be characterized for some time to come by the struggle between an as yet vaguely formulated Tocquevillian view of America, and a well formulated but politically exhausted liberal utopian view. However this contest is decided, it cannot be understood until we first understand its theoretical components—the two great traditions of American political thought.

Footnote

1 Herbert J. Storing, *What the Anti-Federalists Were For* (Chicago: University of Chicago Press, 1981), p. 3.

President Reagan's economic advisors echo Schambra's plea for the return to these two distinct governing philosophies. They, like Schambra, call for the re-emergence of the healthy tension within government that these conflicting philosophies foster. In the *1982 Economic Report of the President,* these advisors declare that we need to "use the level of government closest to the community involved for all the public functions it can handle."

Reagan's economic advisors have taken note of the explicit costs and benefits that would accompany a return to this "important principle." Equating efficiency with "good" government, they argue that efficiency demands that benefits accruing from a specific government program should be paid for by the recipients of those benefits. More specifically, communities that *benefit* from specific government programs—like subsidizing mass transit systems—should bear the *costs* of these programs. Adherence to this simple rule assures the residents of communities that their local governments will not make spurious demands on scarce public resources. In addition, this will help guarantee that constituents of local communities will only demand from their local governments those goods and services the communities truly need.

Another selection in support of the New Federalism takes the theoretical vision of its supporters and shows how the Reagan administration proposes to put this principle into practice. In the article the Office of Management and Budget (OMB) indicates the actual steps needed to implement the New Federalism program, explains the rationale behind its implementation, and addresses one of the major questions associated with this shift in the balance of power between the Federal government and state governments. That is, the OMB analyzes whether or not state governments are capable of assuming the larger fiscal role that will be delegated to them under the New Federalism program. Citing increases in black voter registration, more diversified and resilient revenue sources, and greater administrative expertise in state governments, OMB concludes that state governments are indeed capable of assuming the task.

THE NEW FEDERALISM INITIATIVE

OMB Major Themes and Additional Budget Debate, Fiscal Year 1983, 1982

President Reagan has a number of broad and fundamental goals for his presidency. One of the most important of these is to alter the relationship between the Federal and State and local governments by shifting decision-making and responsibilities for a variety of policy, budgetary, and regulatory matters to State and local governments.

"The New Federalism Initiative"

President Reagan's "New Federalism" is motivated by a number of factors:

• A desire to restore the Constitutional balance between the Federal

Government and State and local governments. Under the Constitution, the powers of the Federal Government are limited.

> "The powers not delegated to the United States by the Constitution nor prohibited by it to the States are reserved to the States respectively, or to the people."
> *Article 10 U.S. Constitution.*

- A need to reduce the growing number of categorical Federal grants, which are encumbered with too many conditions, regulations, and staffing requirements.
- A belief that State and local governments are more responsive to the needs of both benefit recipients and taxpayers. The quality of State government has increased dramatically over the past two decades, as have the resources available to States formerly regarded as impoverished.
- A recognition that dividing responsibility for a program between the Federal and other levels of government results in neither being responsible.

Effects on the Political Process

The President's proposal will increase the effectiveness of State and local governments by giving them more control over activities that are more appropriately conducted at those levels. The proposals will also free Congressional resources now focused on local problems to concentrate more on national needs and problems.

- State responsiveness to local fiscal needs has dramatically increased. Total State aid to localities funded from the States' own revenues grew nearly six-fold from 1965–1980, and now surpasses $60 billion a year.
- The proliferation of Federal programs has undermined the ability of elected officials to make policy. From 1964 to 1978, the number of roll call votes in the House rose from 232 to 1,540 and the number of committee and subcommittee meetings rose from 3,596 to 6,771.
- In 1965 Representatives reported that they spent an average of one day a week on legislative study. In 1977 the Obey Commission reported that Congressional study time had shrank to only 11 minutes per day. The role of unelected staff rose correspondingly: from 4,500 House staffers in the mid-1960's to 9,000 in 1979.
- Stimulated by Federal growth, lobbying is now the third largest industry in Washington, with an annual budget of $4 billion. Excluding privately retained law firms and lobbyists, Washington offices of States, cities, and related public groups currently employ at least 1,500 persons and consist of at least 72 special State and local interest groups, 32 States, 3 State legislatures, 20 cities and 10 counties. Mayors and governors now spend increasing portions of their time regularly travelling to Washington.

The Effectiveness of State Governments

One of the original arguments for Federal assumption of so many of the tasks that belonged to the States was that the State governments were not capable of administering the programs. That is certainly not true today.

- As the Advisory Commission on Intergovernmental Relations has concluded:

  "A largely unnoticed revolution has occurred in state government. The states have been transformed to a remarkable degree. The decades of the 1960s and 1970s witnessed changes in state government unparalleled since the post-Reconstruction period a century ago, generally in the direction advocated by reformers for 50 years."

- Twenty years ago, all but five State legislatures were badly malapportioned. Since *Baker vs. Carr* (1962), every State has apportioned its legislature on the basis of one person, one vote.
- Past regional differences in wealth have narrowed dramatically. In 1960, the per capita income in the wealthier regions, the Mideast and Far West, was 16% above the national average, compared with an income level in the Southeast that was 27% below the national average.
- By 1977, the relative disparity had been reduced by 40% with the wealthiest region, the Far West, having per capita income 11% above the national average and the poorest region, the Southeast, only 14% below. Moreover, all the States in the Southeast have experienced growth in per capita income since 1970 at rates exceeding the national average.
- Between 1960 and 1980 black voter registration in the eleven Southern States rose from 29.1% of the voting age population to 59.8%. Southern white registration during the same period rose only 4%—from 61.6% to 65.7%.
- One-party States have largely become a phenomenon of the past. Since 1968, no single party has held a monopoly on senatorial and gubernatorial positions in any State.
- Every State judicial system is now required to hear and remedy cases arising under constitutional and other Federal law. In addition, State courts have taken the lead in many instances in extending rights beyond those recognized in Federal law. State court systems in virtually every State have been dramatically reformed.
- The proportion of State civil servants covered by a merit system has increased from 50% in 1960 to 75% in 1980.
- State revenue sources have become significantly more diversified and resilient. 36 States now have a corporate and personal income tax, as well as a general sales tax, compared to only 19 in 1960.

- The diversity of interest groups active at the State level has increased significantly since the mid-1960s. Witness the growth of environmental, ethnic and racial minority, disadvantaged, tax reform, handicapped and other citizen lobbies in virtually every State capital.
- Executive power in State government has become more focused, more accountable, and more professional. 46 States now have four-year gubernatorial terms; 45 permit their governors to succeed themselves; virtually all governors now control a State planning unit. Between 1965 and 1980, all States undertook reorganizations of executive departments; 24 States reduced the number of independently elected administrative heads.
- Almost all State legislatures now meet every year in either regular or special session; professional staffs now provide technical support for the finance and appropriations committees or in a central legislative unit in every State on a year-round basis, compared to only a handful 20 years ago.

Proposal

To more clearly delineate between Federal and State responsibilities and to bring about a greater efficiency in both service and administration of government, the President proposes a major reshaping of the fiscal relationship between the Federal Government and the States. The details of the proposal follow. The plan offers significant advantages to both State and Federal Governments.

- Starting in fiscal year 1984, the Federal Government will assume the full cost of the rapidly growing Medicaid program, to go along with its existing responsibility for Medicare. This will save the States an estimated $19 billion in 1984, which would rise to $25 billion in 1987 under present trends.
- Also starting in 1984, the States will assume the full cost of the two major components of our welfare system—Food Stamps, which is now federally financed but administered by the States, and Aid to Families with Dependent Children (AFDC), the cost of which is now shared between the States and the Federal government.
- On a nationwide basis, the "swap" of Medicaid for Food Stamps and AFDC involves a net saving for the States of more than $2 billion in FY 84, an amount that will grow in later years because of the rapidly rising cost of Medicaid. This swap is not dependent on the new trust fund described in the following paragraphs.
- The Federal Government will earmark existing alcohol, tobacco and telephone excise taxes, $.02 of the gasoline tax and a portion of the oil windfall profits tax for a new $28 billion Federalism trust fund that will belong to the states.
- The share of each state in the trust fund will be based on its 1979–1981

share of specified Federal grants now slated for "turnback" with an adjustment for any gains or losses for individual states resulting from the Medicaid-welfare swap.
- During a transition period of four years, 1984–1987, the states can use their trust fund money in either of two ways. If they want to continue receiving some or all Federal grants that are designated for turnback, they can use their trust fund money to reimburse the Federal agencies that make those grants and abide by Federal conditions and rules. Or, to the extent they choose to forego the Federal grant programs, they can receive their trust fund money directly as super revenue sharing, to be used for these or other purposes. There will be a mandatory pass-through of part of the super revenue sharing funds to local governments.
- The size of the trust fund will nearly equal the size of the turnback programs, which will total about $30.2 billion in FY 84. Thus the states, counting their net savings from the Medicaid-welfare swap, will lose nothing in fiscal terms and, equally important, they will no longer have to be concerned about Federal budget reductions.
- Beginning in 1988, the more than 40 Federal turnback programs—which involved 124 separate grants in 1981—will cease to exist and the States will be in complete control of their own priorities.
- Also after four years, the Federal excise taxes will start to phase out, by 25 percent each year, and will disappear after 1991. The trust fund will go out of existence on the same schedule. The States will be able to impose the same excise taxes at their option to preserve their revenues, with no tax-raising effect on the items concerned. Or they can choose other revenues, or reduce program cost.
- During the period of operation of the trust fund, taking into account the Medicaid-welfare swap, the problem of "winners and losers" among the states is minimal.

Rationale

The plan represents a long-overdue effort to sort out responsibilities within the Federal system on the basis of principles and criteria. Apart from national functions such as defense, the Federal Government will retain and, in some cases, assume full responsibility for the most dramatically increasing domestic social needs.

Under the plan, the Federal Government will be responsible for health insurance and income maintenance programs for the elderly, including Social Security, and health insurance for the poor of all ages.

The States will assume responsibility for domestic needs that are growing much less rapidly, have in most cases historically been a state and local function, and which even now are administered and largely financed by the States despite the proliferation of Federal grants.

As Governor Babbitt of Arizona has said:

"Congress ought to be worrying about arms control and defense instead of potholes in the street. We might just have both an increased chance of survival and better streets.". . .   focus

In summary, the proponents of the New Federalism enumerate three significant advantages of their program: (i) government will be closer to its constituents and thus better able to interpret citizen needs; (ii) because only the real needs of its citizens will be met, society's scarce public resources will be efficiently allocated; and (iii) as a result of these first two advantages, society will be left with a government which truly is accountable to its constituents.

The Critics Reply

Critics of the New Federalism do not deny there are disadvantages to our present Federal system of government. It is the extreme view of New Federalism, with its close attachment to free market economics, that worries the critics.

Indeed, some critics believe that the New Federalism is nothing more than a transparent attempt by free market proponents to force a reduction of social spending at all levels of government. This, they argue, is not political Federalism but free market economics in sheep's clothing. As a result, these critics have been quick to respond to President Reagan's initiatives. They have noted that their reservations with New Federalism do not concern the philosophic foundations of a Federal system, rather they are concerned with the practical question of which level of government is best equipped to handle society's most pressing problems.

To fully appreciate this argument, we must consider yet another interpretation of our historical roots. Our first selection argues that the Federal government was not only given ultimate power over the states; it was given the *responsibility* of ensuring a decent life for all of the nation's inhabitants—especially for individuals who reside in states that are not able to guarantee this.

Political scientist, Samuel H. Beer challenges the basic premise of the New Federalists who assert that the power of the Federal government comes directly from the states. That is, he directly disagrees with one of President Reagan's favorite lines: "the Federal government did not create the states; the states created the Federal government."

Beer also quotes historical documents. He contends that based on these documents, it is apparent some of our greatest leaders have held an opposite point of view from Reagan's. For example, Daniel Webster argued that "the Constitution is not a compact between the states, or by the people of several states, but by the people of the United States in the aggregate." In other words, it is the people of all the collective states who are the ultimate source of power—not the individual states. If Beer's interpretation of history is accepted, we would conclude that the states did not create the Federal government.

Beer then turns to our first Republican president, Abraham Lincoln who, Beer maintains, made this point even more succinctly: "The Union is older than any of the states and, in fact, it created them as states." This quotation implies that the states weren't states until the Federal government was created to unify the inhabitants of those first thirteen colonies.

Beer then examines the responsibility of the Federal government to insure a decent life for all of our nation's inhabitants. He again quotes from the writings of Daniel Webster, who argued that the purpose of the Union (Federal government) was not to create "a temporary partnership. It is an association of people, under a constitution of government, *uniting their power*, joining together their highest interest, *cementing their present enjoyments,* and blending into one indivisible mass, all their hopes for the future. (Emphasis added.)"

In other words, this nation was formed to harness the strengths and capabilities of a united people to ensure a good life for all of those people. Thus, it seems safe to conclude that if Webster were alive today he would argue that poverty for some of the people is the responsibility of all of the people. That is, it is safe to conclude that Webster would find that the existence of *poverty is a national problem* and that the Federal government, since it represents all the people, has the responsibility to address this problem and to do everything in its power to overcome this problem.

Given this historical interpretation, Beer implores the New Federalists to "give up their diversionary rhetoric" and, instead, "advocate the national idea."

WHO HAS THE POWER?

Samuel H. Beer, *New Republic,* July 19 & 26, 1982

I have a difference of opinion with President Reagan. We have all heard of the President's new federalism and his proposals to cut back on the activities of the federal government by reducing or eliminating certain programs and transferring others to the states. He wishes to do this because he finds these activities to be inefficient and wasteful. He also claims that they are improper under the U.S. Constitution—not in the sense that the courts have found them to violate our fundamental law, but in the larger philosophical and historical sense that the present distribution of power between levels of government offends against the true meaning and intent of that document.

In justification of this conclusion, he has relied upon a certain view of the founding of the Republic. In his inaugural address he summarized its essentials when he said: "The federal government did not create the states; the states created the federal government." This allegation of historical fact did not pass without comment. Richard Morris of Columbia took issue with the President, called his view of the historical facts "a hoary myth about the origin of the Union," and went on to summarize the evidence showing that "the United States was created by the people in collectivity, not by the individual states." No less bluntly, Henry Steele Commager of Amherst said the President did not understand the Constitution, which in its own words asserts that it was ordained by "We, the People of the United States," not by the states severally.

We may smile at this exchange between the President and the professors. They are talking about something that happened a long time ago. To be sure, the conflict of ideas between them did inform the most serious crisis of our first century—the grim struggle that culminated in the Civil War. In that conflict, President Reagan's view—the compact theory of the Constitution—was championed by Jefferson Davis, the president of the seceding South. The first Republican President of the United States, on the other hand, espoused the national theory of the Constitution. "The Union," said Abraham Lincoln, "is older than any of the states and, in fact, it created them as States. . . . The Union and not the states separately produced their independence and their liberty. . . . The Union gave each of them whatever of independence and liberty it has."

As stated by President Lincoln, the national idea is a theory that ultimate authority lies in the United States. It identifies the whole people of the nation as the source of the legitimate power of both the federal government and the state governments.

The national idea, however, is not only a theory of authority but also a theory of purpose, a perspective on public policy, a guide to the ends for which power should be used. It invites us to ask ourselves what sort of a people we are, and whether we are a people, and what we wish to make of ourselves as a people. In this sense the national idea is as alive and contentious today as it was when Alexander Hamilton set the course of the first Administration of George Washington.

Like the other founders, Hamilton sought to establish a regime of republican liberty, that is, a system of government which would protect the individual's rights of person and property and which would be founded upon the consent of the governed. He was by no means satisfied with the legal framework produced by the Philadelphia convention. Fearing the states, he would have preferred a much stronger central authority, and, distrusting the common people, he would have set a greater distance between them and the exercise of power. He was less concerned, however, with the legal framework than with the use that would be made of it. He saw in the Constitution not only a regime of liberty but also, and especially, the promise of nationhood. . . .

Hamilton summarized his views in the farewell address he drafted for Washington in 1796. Its theme is the importance of union. But this union does not consist merely in a balance of groups or a consensus of values, and certainly not merely in a strong central government or a common framework of constitutional law. It is rather a condition of the people, uniting them by both sympathy and interest, but above all in "an indissoluble community of interest as *one nation*."

Hamilton's nationalism did not consist solely in his belief that the Americans were "one people" rather than thirteen separate peoples. The father of the compact theory himself, Thomas Jefferson, at times shared that opinion, to which he gave expression in the Declaration of Independence. The contrast with Jefferson lay in Hamilton's activism, his belief that this American people must make vigorous use of its central government for the task of nation-building. This difference between the two members of Washington's Cabinet, the great individualist and the great nationalist, achieved classic expression in their conflict over the proposed Bank of the United States. Jefferson feared that the bank would corrupt his cherished agrarian order and discovered no authority for it in the Constitution. Hamilton, believing that a central bank was necessary to sustain public credit, promote economic development, and—in his graphic phrase—"cement the union," found in a broad construction of the "necessary and proper" clause of Article I ample constitutional authorization. Looking back today and recognizing that the words of the Constitution can be fitted into either line of reasoning, we must sigh with relief that President Washington, and in later years the Supreme Court, preferred the Hamiltonian doctrine. . . .

[Hamilton was] an integrationist. I use that term expressly because of its current overtones, wishing to suggest Hamilton's perception of how diversity need not always be divisive, but may lead to mutual dependence and union. Here again he broke from Jefferson, who valued homogeneity. Hamilton, on the other hand, planned for active federal intervention to diversify the economy by the development of commerce and industry. His great report on manufactures is at once visionary and far-seeing—"the embryo of modern America," a recent writer terms it. . . .

His leading opponent, Daniel Webster, has been called the first great champion of the national theory of the union. . . .

Historians of political thought usually, and correctly, look first to his memorable debate with Senator Robert Hayne of South Carolina in January of 1830. Echoing Calhoun's deductions from the compact theory, Hayne had stated the doctrine of nullification. This doctrine would deny to the federal judiciary the right to draw the line between federal and state authority, leaving such questions of constitutionality to be decided—subject to various qualifications—by each state itself.

In reply Webster set forth with new boldness the national theory of authority. Asking what was the origin of "this general government," he concluded that the Constitution is not a compact between the states. It was not established by the governments of the several states, or by the people of the several states, but by "the people of the United States in the aggregate." In Lincolnian phrases, he called it "the people's Constitution, the people's government, made for the people, made by the people and answerable to the people," and clinched his argument for the dependence of popular government on nationhood with that memorable and sonorous code, "Liberty and union, one and inseparable, now and forever."

These later passages of his argument have almost monopolized the attention of historians of political thought. Yet it is in an earlier and longer part that he developed the Hamiltonian thrust, looking not to the origin but to the purpose of government. These initial passages of the debate had not yet focused on the problems of authority and nullification. The question was rather what to do with a great national resource—the public domain, already consisting of hundreds of millions of acres located in the states and territories and owned by the federal government. Large tracts had been used to finance internal improvements, such as roads, canals, and schools, as envisioned by Hamilton and ardently espoused by the previous President, John Quincy Adams.

When Webster defended such uses, citing the longstanding agreement that the public domain was for "the common benefit of all the States," Hayne made a revealing reply. If that was the rule, said he, how could one justify "voting away immense bodies of these lands—for canals in Indiana and Illinois, to the Louisville and Portland Canal, to Kenyon College in Ohio, to Schools for the Deaf and Dumb." "If grants of this character," he continued, "can fairly be considered as made for the common benefit of all the states, it can only be because all the states are interested in the welfare of each—a principle, which, carried to the full extent, destroys all distinction between local and national subjects."

Webster seized the objection and set out to answer it. His task was to show when a resource belonging to the whole country could legitimately be used to support works on "particular roads, particular canals, particular rivers, and particular institutions of education in the West." Calling this question "the real and wide difference in political opinion between the honorable gentleman and myself," he asserted that there was a "common good" distinguishable from "local goods," yet embracing such particular projects.

In these passages the rhetoric is suggestive, but one would like a more specific answer: what *is* the difference between a local and a general good? Suddenly Webster's discourse becomes quite concrete. His approach is to show what the federal government must do by demonstrating what the states cannot do. Using the development of transportation after the peace of 1815 for illustration, Webster shows why a particular project within a state, which also has substantial benefits for other states, will for that very reason probably not be undertaken by the state within which it is located. . . .

Like Hamilton, Webster sought to make the nation more of a nation. As he conceived this objective, however, he broke from the bleak eighteenth-century realism of Hamilton and turned his imagination toward the vistas of social possibility being opened up by the rising romantic movement of his day. By "consolidation" Webster did not mean merely attachment to the union arising from economic benefits. Indeed, he blamed Hayne for regarding the union "as a mere question of present and temporary expedience; nothing more than a mere matter of profit and loss . . . to be preserved, while it suits local and temporary purposes to preserve it; and to be sundered whenever it shall be found to thwart such purposes."

The language brings to mind the imagery of another romantic nationalist, Edmund Burke; in his famous assault upon the French Revolution and social contract theory, he proclaimed that "the state ought not to be considered as nothing better than a partnership agreement in a trade of pepper and coffee, calico or tobacco, or some other such low concern, to be taken up for a little temporary interest, and to be dissolved at the fancy of the parties," but rather as "a partnership in all science; a partnership in all art; a partnership in every virtue, and in all perfection."

A later formulation echoes Burke's words and phrasing even more exactly, as Webster sets forth the organic conception of the nation: "The Union," he said, "is not a temporary partnership of states. It is an association of people, under a constitution of government, uniting their power, joining together their highest interests, cementing their present enjoyments, and blending into one indivisible mass, all their hopes for the future."

Webster articulated this conception most vividly not in Congress or before the Supreme Court, but at public gatherings on patriotic occasions. There the constraints of a professional and adversarial audience upon his imagination were relaxed and his powers as myth-maker released. Consider what some call the finest of his occasional addresses, his speech at the laying of the cornerstone of the Bunker Hill Monument on June 17, 1825. As in his advocacy and in his debates, his theme was the union. What he did, however, was not to make an argument for the union, but to tell a story about it—a story about its past with a lesson for its future.

The plot was simple: how American union foiled the British oppressors in 1775. They had thought to divide and conquer, anticipating that the other colonies would be cowed by the severity of the punishment visited on Massachusetts and that the other seaports would be seduced by the prospect of gain from trade diverted from Boston. "How miserably such reasoners deceived themselves!" exclaimed the orator. "Everywhere the unworthy boon was rejected with scorn. The fortunate occasion was seized, everywhere, to show to the whole world that the Colonies were swayed by no local interest, no partial interest, no selfish interest." In the imagery of Webster, the battle of Bunker Hill was a metaphor of that united people. As Warren, Prescott, Putnam, and Stark had fought side by side; as the four colonies of New England had on that day stood together with "one cause, one country, one heart"; so also "the feeling of resistance . . . possessed the whole American people." So much for Calhoun and his "system."

From this myth of war Webster drew a lesson for peace. "In a day of peace, let us advance the arts of peace and the works of peace. . . . Let us develop the resources of our land, call forth its powers, build up its institutions, and see whether we also, in our day and generation, may not perform something worthy to be remembered." Then he concluded with abrupt and brutal rhetoric: "Let our object be: OUR COUNTRY, OUR WHOLE COUNTRY, AND NOTHING BUT OUR COUNTRY."

With his own matchless sensibility Abraham Lincoln deployed the doctrine and imagery of Webster to animate the North during the Civil War. Lincoln's nationalism, like Webster's, had a positive message for peacetime, and it was this message that set the course of the country's development for the next several generations. Much that he did derived from the original Hamiltonian program, which, long frustrated by the dominance of the compact theory, now burst forth in legislative and executive action. During the war years, not only was slavery given the death blow, but also an integrated program of positive federal involvement was put through in the fields of banking and currency, transportation, the tariff, land grants to homesteaders, and aid to higher education. In the following decades, an enormous expansion of the economy propelled the United States into the age of industrialism, which in due course engendered its typical problems of deprivation, inequality, and class conflict.

A Republican, Theodore Roosevelt, first attempted to cope with these problems in terms of the national idea. Throughout his public career, an associate has written, Roosevelt "kept one steady purpose, the solidarity, the essential unity of our country. . . . All the details of his action, the specific policies he stated, arise from his underlying purpose for the Union." Like other Progressives, Roosevelt was disturbed by the rising conflicts between groups and classes and sought to offset them by timely reform. In this sense integration was T. R.'s guiding aim, and he rightly christened his cause "The New Nationalism." Effective advocacy of this cause, however, fell to another Roosevelt a generation later, when the failings of industrialism were raising far greater dangers to the union. . . .

Franklin Roosevelt's nationalism was threefold. First it was a doctrine of federal centralization, and in his Administration, in peace as well as war, the balance of power in the federal system swung sharply toward Washington. Roosevelt called not only for a centralization of government, but also for a nationalization of politics. In these years a new kind of mass politics arose. The old rustic and sectional politics gave way to a new urban and class politics dividing electoral forces on a nationwide basis.

The third aspect of Roosevelt's nationalism was expressed in his policies. Those policies do not make a neat package and include many false starts and failures and ad hoc expedients. Yet in their overall impact one can detect the old purpose of "consolidation of the union." . . .

None of these conflicts in nation-building is ever wholly terminated. Sectionalism still flares up from time to time, as between frost belt and sun belt. So also does class struggle. Similarly today, the cleavages among ethnic groups that boiled up with a new bitterness in the 1960s are far from being resolved.

The issue is not just ethnicity, but race. To be sure, ethnic pluralism is a fact—there are said to be ninety-two ethnic groups in the New York area alone—but this broad focus obscures the burning issue, which is the coexistence of blacks and whites in large numbers on both sides. That question of numbers is crucial. In other times and places one can find instances of a small number of one race living in relative peace in a society composed overwhelmingly of the other race. "Tokenism" is viable. But the facts rule out that solution for the United States.

Another option is the model of "separate but equal." In some circumstances this option could be carried out on a decent and democratic basis. It is, for instance, the way the French-speaking citizens of Quebec would like to live in relation to Canada as a whole. And, commonly, Canadians contrast favorably what they call their "mosaic society" with the American "melting pot." But in the present crisis Americans have rejected this option in law and in opinion as segregation. American nationalism demands that diversity be dealt with not by separation, but by integration.

For John F. Kennedy and Lyndon Johnson, the question was, first of all, civil rights. This meant securing for blacks the legal and political rights that had been won for whites in other generations. But the problem of civil rights, which was mainly a problem of the South, merged with the problem of black deprivation, which was especially a problem of northern cities. Johnson's "war on poverty" characterized the main thrust of the Great Society measures which he built on the initiatives of Kennedy. To think of these measures as concerned simply with "the poor" is to miss the point. The actual incidence of poverty meant that their main concern would be with the living conditions and opportunities of blacks, and especially those who populated the decaying areas of the great urban centers swollen by migration from the South to the North during and after World War II.

These programs were based on the recognition that membership in one ethnic group rather than another can make a great difference to your life chances. In trying to make the opportunities somewhat less unequal, they sought to bring the individuals belonging to disadvantaged groups—as was often said—"into the mainstream of American life." The rhetoric of one of Johnson's most impassioned speeches echoes this purpose. Only a few days after a civil rights march led by Martin Luther King had been broken up by state troopers in full view of national television, he introduced the Voting Rights Act of 1965 into Congress. Calling upon the myths of former wars, like other nationalist orators before him, he harked back to Lexington and Concord and to Appomattox in his summons to national effort. "What happened in Selma," he continued, "is part of a larger movement which reaches into every section and state of America. It is the effort of American Negroes to secure for themselves the full blessings of American life. . . ." Then, declaring that "their cause must be our cause too," he closed with solemn echo of the song of the marchers: "And—we—shall—overcome."

Considering where we started from some thirty years ago, our progress has been substantial. Still, few will assert that our statecraft—from poverty programs to affirmative action to busing—has been adequate to the objective. This problem still awaits its Alexander Hamilton. We may take some comfort from the fact that it is continuous with his great work. The Founders confronted the task of founding a nation-state. Our present exercise in nation-building is no less challenging. What we are attempting has never before been attempted by any country at any time. It is to create within a liberal, democratic framework a society in which vast numbers of both black and white people live in free and equal intercourse—political, economic, and social. It is a unique, a stupendous, demand, but the national idea will let us be satisfied with nothing less.

The federal system that confronts Ronald Reagan is the outcome of these three great waves of centralization: the Lincolnian, the Rooseveltian, and the Johnsonian. By means of his new federalism President Reagan seeks radically to decentralize that system. Does the history of the national idea in American politics suggest any criticism or guidance?

I hope, at least, that it does something to undermine the appeal of compact theory rhetoric. Rhetoric is important. Words are the means through which politicians reach the motivations of voters and by which leaders may shape those motivations. Both the compact theory and the national theory touch nerves of the body politic. Each conveys a very different sense of nationhood—or the lack thereof. My theme has been the national theory, which envisions one people, at once sovereign and subject, source of authority and substance of history, asserting, through conflict and in diversity, our unity of origin and of destiny.

Such an image does not yield a rule for allocating functions between levels of government. That is for practical men, assisted no doubt by the policy sciences. But the imagery of the national idea can prepare the minds of practical men to recognize in the facts of our time the call for renewed effort to consolidate the union. The vice of the compact theory is that it obscures this issue, diverts attention from the facts, and muffles the call for action.

Today this issue is real. A destructive pluralism—sectional, economic, and ethnic—disrupts our common life. It is foolish to use the rhetoric of political discourse to divert attention from that fact. I would ask the new federalists not only to give up their diversionary rhetoric, but positively to advocate the national idea. This does not mean they must give up federal reform. A nationalist need not always be a centralizer. For philosophical and for pragmatic reasons he may prefer a less active federal government. The important thing is to keep alive in our speech and our intentions the move toward the consolidation of the union. People will differ on what and how much needs to be done. The common goal should not be denied. We may need a new federalism. We surely need a new nationalism. I plead with the new federalists: come out from behind that Jeffersonian verbiage, and take up the good old Hamiltonian cause.   focus

Historical facts aside, specific criticisms of the New Federalism are focused upon two major concerns. There is a concern that the New Federalism will assign the responsibility to deal with the important social issue of poverty to the wrong level of government. Additionally, there is a concern that state governments will not be able to maintain their "closeness" to the people, given the increased load and responsibility they will be forced to assume under the New Federalism.

The concern for the question of poverty springs from the notion that poverty is a national problem, not a state or local problem. Critics fear that poorer states and localities, with relatively few economic resources, will not be financially able to respond to the needs of the poor without some Federal government support. This lack of funds will encourage a migration of some low-income families to those states which have the fiscal capacity to adequately respond to the needs of the poor. These new arrivals will compete for a share of the limited economic resources of those states. The overall result will be what one critic calls "a prescription for abdicating our national commitment to meeting the most basic human needs of our poor, disabled, elderly citizens, and our children of tomorrow."

The critics are most concerned with the president's proposal to turn over to local authorities the responsibility for running the two major social welfare programs currently in existence: Aid to Families with Dependent Children (AFDC) and food stamps. They recognize that, if the president has his way, by 1987 the Federal government will be out of the "welfare" business. This means that the sole responsibility of providing for the basic needs of those facing financial stress will be in the hands of state and local officials. In other words, by 1987 individual states and local communities will have to decide if they have a "poverty problem" and, more importantly, what to do about it, should they decide to officially recognize it. Some states will do all in their power to help their poor, and other states will choose to ignore the poverty problem. Is it fair, the critics ask, to subject the poor to the political whimsy of state legislators? Might this be a free market economists' attempt to subject the poor to the "spur of poverty"?

This theme forms the basis for our next selection. This essay argues that the New Federalism, as proposed by Ronald Reagan, is not only a scheme to get government out of the "welfare business"; it is a scheme to permanently dismantle the welfare system. Nick Kotz presents an alternative view. He contends that supporters of the New Federalism know full well that by giving state and local governments the responsibility to fund critical social welfare programs, such as AFDC and food stamps, the added fiscal burden will break already strained state and local budgets. This can only result in fewer benefits for the recipients of these programs. Indeed, if President Reagan's New Federalism is implemented, welfare assistance will be so unattractive "that potential recipients will have no choice but to get by on whatever work is available at whatever wage," contends Kotz. Ronald Reagan has said, "if you start paying people to be poor, you are going to have a lot of poor people." As Kotz, author of *Let Them Eat Promises*, points out, if you don't pay people who are poor, they will either starve or take any job—no matter how degrading, poorly paid, or unsafe that job may be. In other words, if poor people have only the alternatives of starvation or work, they will work. Total output will go up, but there will be losers in this free market game, says Kotz. The losers, as usual, will be those who don't play the game well: the poor.

WANT IS MAKING A COMEBACK

Nick Kotz, *New Republic,* March 24, 1982

It sounded like a dry exercise in bookkeeping, a clerkly transfer of bureaucratic functions: "A financially equal swap." An exchange "with no winners and no losers." Those were the terms in which Ronald Reagan described to state legislators the centerpiece of his new federalism—a plan whereby the fifty states would take full responsibility for food stamps and welfare, and, in a fair exchange, Washington would take complete charge of Medicaid.

Similar assurances accompanied the proposed 1983 budget cuts in aid to the poor. "Don't be fooled by those who proclaim that spending cuts will deprive the elderly, the needy, the helpless," the President warned. What may appear to be budget reductions are really only part of "a slowdown in the rate of federal spending." In fact, he emphasized, the highest priority in his budget, along with national defense, is to redirect resources toward "a reliable safety net of social programs for those who have contributed and those who are in need."

However Mr. Reagan softens these two Presidential initiatives with his own aura of goodwill, one fact is still clear. Ronald Reagan's long-stated goal has been a dramatic dismantling of federal social welfare, shifting to the states the responsibility for the basic survival needs of the poor. And that is his aim, both in the 1983 budget cuts, and in his accompanying plan for turning Aid to Families with Dependent Children, food stamps, and dozens of other programs over to the states. To comprehend what the President is proposing, and to separate reality from rhetoric, one must focus on both the 1983 budget and the new federalism. Taken together, these Reagan proposals represent a radical revamping of national social policy. More than that, they represent an *abandonment* of the national social policy that has been evolving since the beginning of the New Deal half a century ago. As Senator Alan Cranston, Democrat of California, describes it, the Reagan program is "a prescription for abdicating our national commitment to meeting the most basic human needs of our poor, disabled, elderly citizens, and our children of tomorrow." . . .

The President's recommendations promise to have significant long-term consequences. If the budget cuts and social program transfers are adopted, if tax reductions go fully into effect as scheduled, and if the Pentagon budget increases are approved, it will take a generation to reorder sufficient taxes and revenues to return the nation to a more generous social policy. . . .

[Martin Anderson, chief domestic policy adviser, and Robert B. Carleson, now special assistant for policy development and formerly state welfare director in California, share] Reagan's view that programs which permit workers to receive welfare or food supplements are too expensive and philosophically unsound. Their approach is to make government assistance so scarce and so unattractive—low benefits and unpaid labor—that potential recipients will have no choice but to get by on whatever work is available at whatever wage. The President explained the idea recently: "If you start paying people to be poor, you are going to have a lot of poor people."

The new federalism represents an extension of the strategy of the budget cuts: shrink federal social welfare and then place responsibility with the states, where it is certain to shrink further. In addition to the swap—AFDC and food stamps to the states, Medicaid to the federal government—Washington would "turn back" to the states responsibility for forty federal programs in education, social services, community development, and transportation. To pay for them, the President would create a $28-billion "federalism trust fund," collected from federal excise taxes on alcohol, cigarettes, and telephone service, and one-half the federal tax on gasoline. When the trust fund and federal excise taxes are phased out in 1991, the states can enact their own excise taxes to pay for their new responsibilities. (Excise taxes, however, do not provide a reliable, growing source of revenue, since they are based on units sold, not cost. Such taxes are also far more regressive than the income tax, and they are hard for a state to enact—particularly if neighboring states do not.)

Under the sketchy proposal announced in the President's State of the Union message, and amplified somewhat since then, many crucial details are left unsettled. But the direction of the program is clear: welfare responsibilities would be given to the states to deal with as they see fit—if they see fit. As a practical matter, states would have great latitude in deciding the range of benefits, or whether to continue programs at all.

Reallocating government responsibilities within the federal system to achieve greater simplicity, efficiency, and accountability is an idea that has broad appeal. Disagreement arises over the all-important details. In President Reagan's view, the transfer of AFDC and welfare to the states "will make welfare less costly and more responsible to genuine need because it will be designed and administered closer to the grass roots and the people it serves." Governor Bruce Babbitt of Arizona, perhaps the most prominent Democratic advocate of giving the states wider latitude, disagrees. "These programs are properly a national responsibility," Mr. Babbitt says. "When the unemployment rate is 16 percent in Michigan, but only 5.5 percent in Texas, it is manifestly unfair to ask Michigan residents to shoulder welfare burdens created by national economic policies. The safety net ought to be fashioned as a matter of integrated national policy equally applicable to an elderly citizen or malnourished child whether he lives in Maine, Mississippi, or Arizona."

Philosophical differences aside, the evidence strongly suggests that the proposed exchange would not be a "financially equal swap with no winners and no losers." In theory, the federal government would be assuming about $16 billion of state Medicaid costs and the states would pick up a similar

amount of federal AFDC and food stamp costs. But the dynamics of the new
arrangement virtually guarantee that poor people will be losers. Both the state
and federal governments will be drawn irresistibly toward cutting the benefits
of all three programs now offered in most states. Any states that resist a
reduction of benefits to the poor would almost immediately face higher costs
than in the present arrangement.

The Reagan Administration has talked about "maintenance of effort" by
the states, requiring them for at least several years to spend as much on food
and welfare functions as was spent in the past. But this safeguard would offer
only limited protection to the poor. At present, food stamps is a national
program with uniform national standards, fully financed by the federal
government but administered locally by the states. AFDC is a cooperative
program, in which the individual states set their own entitlement standards,
but the federal government pays 50 to 70 percent of the costs. Medicaid is a
joint program, in which both the individual states and Washington have some
voice in setting entitlement standards, and the Federal government pays 50 to
70 percent of the costs. The key issue is what would happen to benefit levels
and costs when states assumed full responsibility for food stamps and AFDC,
and the federal government full responsibility for Medicaid.

With all its imperfections, the food stamp program today is the sturdiest
safety net available to all needy Americans. In contrast to Social Security,
AFDC, Medicaid, and veterans' benefits, the only qualification is need,
defined by the national poverty line ($8,450 annual income for a nonfarm
family of four, $5,690 for a couple). Benefits are available to the elderly, intact
families, single parents with children, single persons, and couples without
children. Uniform benefits are adjusted periodically to reflect the cost of living.
The 21 million participants represent a broad cross section of the poor. Food
stamp households have an average gross income of $325 a month; more than
half have no liquid assets and half do not own a car.

Food stamps were expanded into this uniform, national program specifically
because many states did not make the earlier program available to people in
obvious need. As late as the early 1970s, hundreds of counties, including ones
with the worst problems of poverty-related malnutrition, refused to operate
programs. Other states provided inadequate benefits to only a small percentage of their poor. It is difficult to imagine how any state today would run a
food stamp program on its own: printing and distributing its own stamps,
authorizing and policing food stores, safeguarding stamps from counterfeiting,
etc. For individual states to take on these responsibilities, now borne by the
federal government, would involve prohibitive administrative costs and
burdens. It seems inevitable that states would eliminate the food stamp
program, and increase welfare checks to offset at least partially the loss of food
stamps, for at least some of the present food stamp recipients. But then the
states would run into a whole new set of difficult issues involving costs and
welfare policy.

The vast majority of states, in their present AFDC welfare programs, exclude thousands of current food stamp recipients from eligibility. Half the states do not provide benefits to intact families, and none provides benefits to single people or childless couples. Furthermore, the AFDC benefit and eligibility levels in many states are far more restrictive than national standards of the food stamp program. A number of states provide benefits only to families at or below 50 percent of the poverty line. Unless states broadened their eligibility standards and raised their benefits, millions of persons now receiving food stamps would lose their food benefits and receive nothing in return.

According to President Reagan, the states are up to meeting this challenge, thanks to civil rights and reapportionment laws introduced over the past twenty years. Those laws have made profound differences, but a vast disparity remains between the national standards of food stamp aid, determined in the White House and Congress, and AFDC standards in the various states. In Mississippi, a mother and two children with no other income receive a maximum AFDC grant of $96 a month. In Texas, a family of four receives a maximum of $141—or $38 less than that oil-rich state paid in benefits 12 years ago. In Arizona, a family of four receives $244, based on a standard of need last updated 10 years ago. Twenty-two states provide maximum benefits of less than $285 a month (or less than 50 percent of the poverty line). Since 1970, only two states have increased benefits as much as the inflation rate, while more than half the states have failed to reflect even one half of the increase in the cost of living.

It is the food stamp program, with its single national standard of need and regular updating of benefits, which has helped ease the disparities among states. Since food stamp benefits are tied to income, recipients in states with low AFDC benefits—or low wage levels—receive more food stamps than do recipients in higher benefit states. To pick the most extreme example, in Mississippi, a family of four receives the rock-bottom AFDC payment of $120 a month, but gets $235 in food stamps. Beyond any question, the food stamp program has revolutionized the standard of living for the poorest people in that poorest of American states.

Even when the states are relieved of their Medicaid costs, there is little reason to suppose that many of them will extend welfare coverage or raise benefits and update them periodically to achieve the same level of coverage provided by a combination of AFDC and the federal food stamp program. In fact, the evidence suggests that the elimination of federal financial support will lead to a reduction in welfare benefits. At present, with Washington paying 50 to 70 percent of the costs, states have had some motivation to raise even the most inadequate AFDC benefits. With more popular and powerful constituencies competing for limited state resources, it is difficult to envision states raising benefits, which for the first time will be fully dependent on state funds.

Relinquishing the federal role in AFDC and food stamps could hurt the poor in other ways as well. The needy will lose federal procedural rights to apply for aid and to get a hearing before aid is cut off. These rights to benefits with a federal component have been developed painstakingly by Legal Services lawyers and advocates of the poor over the last twenty years. In the past, many states and local jurisdictions gave or withheld aid with little regard to fairness and few procedural safeguards for the poor.

The net effect of the AFDC and food stamp transfer to the states would likely be an evaporation of whatever semblance of national standards have been set by food stamps. More people will move from low-benefit states to those which provide more generously for the unemployed and the needy. President Reagan will have created a welfare system directly contrary to the system envisioned in the national welfare reform efforts of the Nixon Administration in the early 1970s. Back then, Ronald Reagan was one of the few governors who opposed national welfare reform; he was advocating the same states-centered approach he has introduced today.

Somewhat ironically, the federalization of Medicaid also is likely to result in a distinct pattern of "winners and losers." At present, Medicaid eligibility requirements and the level of services differ greatly among the states. Twenty states use their own widely varying AFDC eligibility standards for Medicaid as well. Thirty states permit participation by the "medically needy" who have slightly higher income. Some states provide for "optional services," such as prescription drugs, eyeglasses, and dental care, while others do not. If Medicaid is operated as an entirely federal program, it would seem inconceivable, and probably unconstitutional, for such differences to be permitted. The federal government could hardly operate a national program in which, as at present, a family of four in California can get Medicaid if its annual income is below $7,800, but a similar family in Arkansas qualifies only if its income is below $3,100.

If the federal government set national Medicaid eligibility standards and benefits at the level of the more generous states, such as California, New York, and Massachusetts, the total yearly cost of the program would rise by some $14 billion—an unlikely objective for the Reagan Administration. It is much more probable that some middling standard would be set, by which needy citizens would receive improved coverage in the most limited benefit states, but fewer benefits in the more generous states. If these higher-benefit states decided to supplement federal Medicaid, they might be big losers in the "financially equal swap."

In making his recommendations, the President invited his critics "to put up or shut up." The most logical response to his new federalism proposal would be a different kind of trade, one in which the federal government keeps food stamps and takes over Medicaid and/or AFDC, and the states assume responsibility for less basic kinds of aid. But this would not be an equal swap financially, nor would Mr. Reagan buy it. So the present prospect is for trench warfare over which budgets get cut how much, and how much of last year's tax bonanza stays on the books.

The biggest danger is that Mr. Reagan's planned destruction of basic support systems for the needy will be carried out in the same atmosphere of haste, public ignorance, lack of debate, and political expediency that surrounded last year's budget cuts. The poor no longer have a strong voice in Washington, as they did in the heyday of the civil rights and antipoverty movements. More than anything else, the poor need advocates who can effectively take their case to the public. As a recent Opinion Research Poll showed, 38 percent of the public puts a high priority on cutting "welfare," but only 9 percent would cut "aid to the needy."

In off-the-cuff remarks in recent weeks, Mr. Reagan has continued to evoke a cheerful mythology about the problems of being poor in America. People who want to work can find pages of job openings listed in the newspapers. The hungry can eat by gleaning leftovers from the fields. Donations from food manufacturers can fill the gap. Poverty can be ended if each church would adopt ten families. Ronald Reagan has been purveying this kind of mythology, along with stories about the welfare queen from Chicago (his current example: the pupil who receives a free lunch and whose parents earn $72,000 a year), since his 1950s stint as a goodwill speaker for General Electric. Myths persist because people find it useful or comforting to spread them and believe them.

President Reagan wants to have policies that make poor people suffer, but he also wants to maintain his good-guy image. That is why, one recent day, he phoned a television anchorman to find how the federal government might help an elderly couple who had been shown losing their home because of an unpaid tax assessment. As it happens, it was a lawyer from the Legal Services program who had brought the couple's plight to the public attention, and is now fighting to save their home.

In the real world, one thing the President might do is reconsider his commitment to abolish that program. As the lawyer said, "I'm gratified he called and has compassion for them, but I'd like him to come down here and see how much misery his policies have caused."   fo©us

In examining the issue of New Federalism, this chapter has considered the New Federalists' allegation that small governmental units are more efficient in identifying and responding to the needs of people. Supporters of a New Federalism argue that these smaller governmental units handle most of these problems better than the Federal government, even though the Federal government has long been responsible for solving these problems. On the other hand, critics of New Federalism argue that the demands placed upon state and local governments under the proposed plan will strip those governments of their unique "closeness" with their constituents. Furthermore, these critics argue that New Federalism may be just one more step by free market enthusiasts to reduce the amount of spending at all levels of government and, thereby, reduce the economic role of government in our society.

CHAPTER 7

International Experience With Supply-Side Economics

Introduction

The conservative/supply-side economic policies that have been adopted by the Reagan administration in the U.S. have also been experimented with by several other countries around the world. Strangely enough, these experiments have appeared in both developed and developing, rich and poor countries. These countries, like the U.S., are in search of a new approach to solve their economic woes. Whether these experiments are true supply-side ventures or just another application of traditional conservative economics is the subject of this chapter.

Broadening our view of supply-side economics to include international experiences is of value for several reasons. First, if we are to make sound judgments about this theory we must examine all of the available evidence. That is, if we argue that supply-side economic policies are the answer for an ailing U.S. economy, we should expect to find these policies have been successful in other economies where they have been put into effect. A second and closely related reason for examining international experience is because, in the case of England, this experiment began well before the U.S. experiences. England is a developed economy, which began its experiment with the election of Margaret Thatcher as Prime Minister in May, 1979. Since this is an example which pre-dates the U.S. venture, it should offer valuable insights into what we can expect from our recent flirtation with supply-side economics in terms of its eventual success, unanticipated problems, alternative policy variations, and the importance of timing.

The Case of England

Since the British experiment with conservative/supply-side economics is closely linked to Prime Minister Margaret Thatcher, this experiment has come to be known as "Thatcherism." Thatcherism—although rooted in the same conservative philosophy as President Reagan's program ("Reaganism")—is not, in reality, a strict application of supply-side principles. As this book has tried to underscore, supply-side economics is *a* conservative economic theory, but it is not *the* conservative economic theory. In other words, even though supply-siders and conservatives adopt the same philosophical perspective, they can—and do—differ in several important respects.

One critical difference concerns how each camp views the beneficial effects of a tax cut. Both supply-side economists and conservative economists argue that a tax cut will directly increase private sector incentives and thereby stimulate economic activity. It is this expected increase in productive activity, which in turn will lead to an increase in taxable income and an increase in tax receipts, that allows supply-siders to argue that the tax cuts "will pay for themselves." The conservative economists who guide British policy, on the other hand, are unwilling to accept this basic axiom of supply-side economics. They argue that although large tax cuts may be beneficial to the economy in the long run, in the short run they could lead to excessive government borrowing in order to "pay" for the loss of tax revenues. Consequently, the economics of Prime Minister Thatcher calls for a reduction in government expenditures which matches the reduction in taxes. This, she believes, will insure a balanced budget—a budget where government borrowing and spending does not crowd out more productive private sector borrowing and investment.

Given this reluctance to incur a budget deficit (even if that deficit was the result of tax cuts which increased incentives), it is apparent that Prime Minister Margaret Thatcher is more of a conservative than she is a supply-sider. Prime Minister Thatcher has not adopted the large tax cut schemes that are advocated by the supply-side community. In fact, she has actually increased taxes by increasing Britain's value-added tax, a type of national sales tax, while slashing the personal income taxes of high income earners. As will be explained in the following articles, she would ultimately like to lower taxes, but for now her main priority is to avoid increasing an already burgeoning government deficit.

Another important difference between Prime Minister Thatcher's conservative experiment and the supply-side economic experiment in the U.S. is her strong, almost religious, adherence to monetarism. Because of her steadfast belief in the monetarist philosophy that "inflation is always and everywhere a monetary phenomenon," Thatcher maintains that the only way to cure inflation is through a stringent control of the money supply. That is, the Thatcher government firmly believes that inflation can inflict the greatest harm upon an economy when it doesn't allow businesses to plan confidently for the future—thereby creating an aura of instability that permeates the entire economy. Therefore, Thatcher believes, if the economy is to grow inflation must be eliminated even if the cost of eliminating it is very high levels of unemployment. This policy is central to her whole program.

The Thatcher view is in contrast to the supply-side view which contends that there is no need for extremely tight monetary policy and the resulting high levels of unemployment. Supply-siders believe they have a more painless way to squeeze inflation out of the economy. They argue that if inflation is the result of too many dollars (in Britain's case British Pounds Sterling) "chasing" too few goods, then two options are available for controlling the rate of inflation. First, there is the monetarist approach. This approach reduces the number of dollars that chase these limited goods. The second option, less costly in terms of unemployment, is to increase the amount of goods that the dollars are chasing. According to supply-side advocates, this can be done by increasing the productivity of the inputs used to produce output. Tax cuts, since they leave workers with more money for themselves, induce workers to perform their jobs more productively, say supply-siders. By the same token, business tax cuts which leave businesses with more money to invest in their plants and machinery will also increase worker productivity. Thus, tax cuts which increase productivity will lead to an increase in the total output of the economy. This, in turn, will result in less inflationary pressures because more goods will be chased by the same number of dollars, and, as an added benefit, since output is increasing, unemployment should be falling.

Although Prime Minister Thatcher's policies place her in the middle of the conservative camp rather than in the supply-side corner, her basic philosophy is quite in concert with the supply-side community. That is, both Thatcher and the supply-side advocates see Big Government as the main cause of their ailing economies. Thus, the ultimate goal of both groups is to reduce the influence of this "monster" in their economy. Furthermore, both groups are confident that private initiative and the productive (supply) side of the economy can achieve all of the economic and social goals of society.

Our first essay takes a detailed look at the major differences between the conservative policies of Prime Minister Margaret Thatcher and the more supply-side-oriented policies of President Ronald Reagan. In addition to examining their different attitudes concerning tax cuts and monetary policy, financial analyst David Hale introduces several other important disagreements between the two factions. For example, he argues that significant economic and structural differences exist between the U.S. and England, and because of these differences, we should be careful in drawing conclusions from one experiment and applying them to the other.

REAGANISM VS THATCHERISM: THEIR SIMILARITIES AND THEIR DIFFERENCES

David Hale, *Across the Board,* December 1981

Both supporters and critics of the Reagan economic program have been trying to pin the label of Thatcherism on those with whom they disagree. The arguments make this a particularly confusing period for anyone in the United States trying to understand what is really happening in the British economy.

Critics of the Reagan program, such as Leonard Silk of the *New York Times,* contend that the severe recession in Britain since Margaret Thatcher became Prime Minister in May 1979 has been the inevitable by-product of an economic policy that combines dogmatic monetarism with supply-side economics. The United States, he argues, is headed down the same road because of Reagan economics, which includes loose fiscal policy and tight monetary policy.

Reaganites counter by attacking Mrs. Thatcher for failing to implement a proper supply-side strategy. Both the *Wall Street Journal* and Arthur Laffer put the blame for the current British recession on Mrs. Thatcher's failure to cut taxes, reduce public expenditures, and effectively manage the growth of the money supply.

Who is correct? Each side has evidence in its favor, but neither is telling the whole story of the recent British experience. There are four major faults with many of the recent American comparisons between Thatcher and Reagan.

First, however similar Reagan and Thatcher may appear to be in ideological terms, their economic programs differ significantly both in composition and priorities. The major objectives of Mrs. Thatcher's first budget were redistribution of the tax burden, lower Government spending, and strict control of the money supply in order to reduce inflation. There were no large tax cuts akin to those in the Reagan economic program. Instead, Mrs. Thatcher redistributed about 7 percent of Britain's tax burden by slashing income tax rates—and making up lost revenues by increasing consumption taxes. Income tax rates were cut from 83 percent to 60 percent at the top of the tax tables and from 33 percent to 30 percent at the bottom. The Value Added Tax, a kind of national sales tax, was hiked from 8 percent on most items and 12.5 percent on luxuries to a unified 15 percent. Mrs. Thatcher also continued the established practice of annually adjusting UK tax brackets for inflation.

Mrs. Thatcher wanted to reduce the work disincentives for executives and other salaried people, but she took a cautious approach to cutting the aggregate tax burden because the Government's budget deficit was already equal to about 5 percent of GNP. She had been strongly influenced by the teachings of Milton Friedman, and thus did not want to produce a budget deficit that would undermine her plan to gradually reduce the growth rate of the money supply.*

Like the Thatcher Government, Reagan's Administration is committed to cuts in Government spending and slower growth of the money supply. But the Reagan approach to taxation and the overall balance between fiscal and monetary policy is far less orthodox than anything ever proposed by Mrs. Thatcher. For the period 1981–86, the Reagan program, as amended by Congress, will reduce taxes by $750 billion and expenditures by $250 billion. The Administration initially defended such large tax cuts on the ground that they would pay for themselves through higher economic growth. It also has argued, in recent months, that big multi-year tax cuts will frighten Congress into approving further large reductions in Government spending.

Such a policy represents a very bold gamble, because the Administration's ambitious plans for defense spending mean that any future budget cuts will have to affect the big, politically sensitive transfer payment programs, such as Social Security and Medicare. Those programs now account for almost one half of the Federal budget, compared to less than 25 percent 20 years ago. The defense share, by contrast, has shrunk from 49 percent in 1960 to 24 percent in 1980. . . .

Whereas the Thatcher policy team was dominated by monetarists, the Reagan program is the product of two different and sometimes competing groups of economists. First are the so-called supply-side economists, who in many ways are really pre-Keynesian classical economists. The classical economists were interested primarily in the behavior of the firm and the individual, or what is now called microeconomics. Their major policy concern was the maintenance of an unfettered and efficient marketplace in which the economy would achieve prosperity on its own. They did not worry about

*It should be understood that Britain embraced money targets partly because of the breakdown of the fixed exchange-rate system in the early 1970s. Before the movement to floating exchange rates, the principal check on inflation in Britain had been concern about the external value of the pound. Economic policies, which were perceived by the markets to be too stimulative or too inflationary, typically led to a run on Sterling and forced the Government to change course. When the fixed-exchange system broke down, the UK authorities lost a critical policy anchor. They and the public no longer had a self-defining crisis to help them restrain inflation pressures before they got out of control. Money targets were invented in order to provide a new policy anchor.

meeting annual targets for such macroeconomic variables as gross national product or full employment. Indeed, those concepts did not even exist until the Great Depression and the Keynesian revolution caused governments to take a much more active role in short-term management of the economy.

Second are the monetarists, who share many of the same philosophical attitudes towards the marketplace and the role of government as the "supply-siders," but whose first priority is the creation of a stable, disinflationary economic environment through strict adherence to steady, well-defined targets for the growth of money.

The supply-siders have brought a refreshing change of priorities to Washington. Instead of trying to fine-tune GNP with carefully timed injections of nominal demand or loose money, they are trying to improve the whole tax and regulatory microeconomic framework for work, savings, and investment. There is no automatic reason why they and the monetarists should disagree. The problem is that they have embarked upon such an ambitious program of tax reform that it is potentially incompatible with the other elements of macroeconomic policy.

The tax cuts are so massive when compared with probable spending cuts and the rates of economic growth implicit in the Federal Reserve's money-growth targets that the arithmetic of the Reagan budget strategy simply falls apart. The Administration has yet to determine which of its objectives—economic growth, money-supply growth, inflation, military spending—should have first priority. In so ambitiously pursuing all of them, there is a high probability that it will achieve none of them.

The second major difference between the Thatcher and Reagan programs is the fact that they were introduced in radically different economic environments. Almost from the start, Mrs. Thatcher's approach was derailed by a combination of domestic and external inflation shocks. The previous Labor Government had stimulated the British economy in the run-up to the general election of May 1979. After three years of pay controls, wages in the private sector were accelerating at a 14 percent annual rate while workers in the public sector were demanding adjustments both for gains in the private sector and for previous years of austerity. And inflation pressures in the world economy were worsening rapidly because of the Iranian revolution and the consequent doubling of oil prices.

Mrs. Thatcher's big hike in Value Added Tax added to the wage push momentum already building up in the economy. By that autumn, wages were growing at a 21 percent rate compared to 1978 levels. Despite its plan to cut public expenditures, the new Conservative Government also agreed to accept the recommendations of the previous government's comparability commission on public sector pay. This produced earning increases for civil servants of 24 percent between the third quarter of 1979 and the third quarter of 1980.

The Government's unwillingness to resist huge public sector pay increases, on top of the external inflation shocks spreading through the economy, meant that Mrs. Thatcher could achieve her money-supply growth targets only by intensifying the financial squeeze on the private sector. In November 1979, interest rates were jacked up to a record high of 17 percent in order to discourage companies from making pay settlements as large as those in the Government sector. They had already been hiked from 12 percent to 14 percent at the time of the June budget. While high interest rates made monetary policy seem very tight, they did not produce a rapid braking effect on either money or credit for several reasons:

☐ Both corporations and Government had to borrow in order to finance inflationary pressures already in the system.

☐ The Bank of England was not following a strict reserve targeting rule similar to that which the Federal Reserve has been trying to adhere to since 1979. Although the Bank permitted interest rates to rise to record levels, it was actually supplying reserves in order to prevent market pressures from driving interest rates even higher.

☐ The Bank's own statistical definition of money had been distorted by a set of controls on bank lending introduced by the previous Labor Government and continued by Mrs. Thatcher. This "lending corset" shifted money growth outside of the banking system, and thus made it difficult for the authorities to know what was really happening to the money supply. . . .

Whereas Mrs. Thatcher had nothing but bad luck with inflation during her 12 months, Mr. Reagan has enjoyed relatively good luck. When he took office, the U.S. economy was in the third quarter of a modest recovery and inflation pressures were starting to unwind from the double-digit levels of 1979 and 1980. The world economy had entered a period of gradual disinflation as well.

The Carter Administration pursued stimulative policies during the six months before the November election, but the inflationary effects of those policies were cancelled out by a very tough Federal Reserve policy during the spring and early summer of 1981. The high interest rates resulting from the Fed's policy have had some of the same effects on the dollar as the Bank of England's high interest rates had on the pound. On a purchasing-power parity basis, the dollar is now overvalued by nearly 14 percent. Because of the dollar's sharp appreciation, U.S. exports are having a more difficult time competing in world markets, while U.S. manufacturing companies sensitive to import competition cannot raise prices as easily as before. Like the overvalued pound in 1979–80, the overvalued dollar is shifting income from corporations to consumers through a profit squeeze and lower inflation. Ultimately, this process may self-correct in new layoffs and a recession—but nothing on a scale comparable to that in Britain since 1979. Also, Reagan has had a much easier time controlling the public sector's wage demands. He has broken the air controllers' strike by using military personnel and the Post Office has accepted only a modest pay hike.

If the Reagan economic strategy gets into serious trouble during the next 12 months, it will not be as a result of exogenous inflation shocks. It will be because the conflict between fiscal and monetary policies in the United States resolves itself through high interest rates, a squeeze on the private sector, and recession. Many analysts will then compare the poor performance of the U.S. economy to the recent British experience, but the starting points will have been very different.

Another fault with the Thatcher-Reagan comparisons is the different magnitude of the structural challenges facing the U.S. and UK economies during recent years. All of the major industrial countries have had serious problems during the 1970s with inflation, unemployment, and loss of markets to the newly industrializing countries, but it is in Britain that these difficulties have been most severe. Indeed, the growth rate of the British economy during the 1970s was the lowest of any decade since the Industrial Revolution began 200 years ago.

Britain's industrial decline started long ago, but it has been greatly accelerated during the past few years, ironically enough, by the impact of North Sea oil on the value of the pound. Mrs. Thatcher probably made the adjustment to North Sea oil more rapid and painful than it would otherwise have been by jacking up interest rates and increasing the pound's appeal as a petro-currency, but North Sea oil would have caused an upheaval in British manufacturing industry during the early 1980s, whichever party controlled the Government.

Until the late 1970s, UK industry had been accustomed only to devaluations. When the pound moved dramatically in the opposite direction, British businessmen had to change the habits of a lifetime. It could be argued that this change was long overdue, and that it will encourage UK industry to move upstream to higher, value-added products that do not compete on the basis of price, but it will take time for this process to occur. So far, British industry has seen only the destructive side of North Sea oil.

The transition through which Britain is now passing would be a difficult one for any industrial society, but it is especially troublesome for Britain because of its historical difficulties with industry relations and economic adaptability. Britain has one of the highest levels of unionization of any industrial country. Thirty-five percent of its private sector work force belong to unions. Eighty-three percent of its public sector work force are union members. That second number is especially significant because the public sector, including nationalized industries, accounts for almost one half of the economy. Many of the industrial unions in the private sector are also based on pre-World War II craft functions and thus frequently tend to be hostile to economic change.

Over the past 20 years, the unions have had two very damaging effects on the British economy. First, they have tended to drive real wages to levels that were uncompetitive, and thus increased the economy's natural level of unemployment. Second, they have been very effective during the past decade at pushing the income losses from external inflation shocks, such as OPEC price changes, onto the corporate sector. The resulting deterioration in profitability has further worsened the British economy's ability to generate investment and create new jobs. The Government has also added to these structural distortions by providing generous social security benefits, which often encourage people not to work, and by pursuing housing policies that create labor immobility.

Previous attempts to reform the trade unions, either through incomes policies or actual legal restraints, under both Tory and Labor Governments, have failed. As a result, British governments over the course of the 1970s became increasingly more tolerant of high unemployment as a legitimate tool of anti-inflation policy. However much the coincidence of North Sea oil and high interest rates may have worsened the situation recently, the sharp increase in the level of unemployment under Mrs. Thatcher, from 1.5 million to 3 million (at 12.2 percent, it is now at a 50-year record), is merely an extension of a trend going back more than a decade. Indeed, one recent study by economists at Liverpool University estimated that nearly two thirds of Britain's unemployed were jobless because of structural economic rigidities, such as high real wages or geographic immobility, rather than just the recent recession.

In the past, Britain resolved the problem of unrealistic wage demands and structural inefficiency by letting inflation and currency depreciation reduce the real value of pay increases. If inflation is to be suppressed and no longer play its traditional role as a compromise solution to the struggle over income shares, unrealistic pay growth can only result in high unemployment. Mrs. Thatcher can be faulted for not doing enough to change trade union laws or to modify regulatory policies which have built employment-destroying biases into the UK economic system, but if she has done too little in this area it is largely because all of her predecessors have tried and failed.

The economy inherited by Mr. Reagan has some structural problems that bear a striking similarity to those of the United Kingdom. Wages have been rising three or four times as rapidly as productivity growth since the late 1960s. The auto, steel, and rubber industries have serious problems with foreign competition because of unrealistic wage rates and in some cases obsolete plants. Numerous Government regulations, such as the Davis-Bacon Act or the minimum-wage laws, have built inflation-generating and employment-destroying biases into the U.S. economic system.

Taken as a whole, though, the structural problems in the United States are not nearly as severe as those in the United Kingdom. The public sector represents less than one third of the American economy. Only about one fifth of the work force are union members. As the air controllers' strike illustrates, U.S. public sector workers also enjoy relatively little solidarity with other members of the labor movement. American unions are viewed strictly as pay-

bargaining agents, not as the Government's social partner in the determination of important policy questions.

The intellectual and social climate in the United States is also much more
conducive to economic adjustment than that in modern Britain. In promoting
his program, President Reagan has been able to invoke a well-established
American folklore about the frontier spirit and the great economic success
made possible by the capitalist ethic. British society contains many more
elements, on both the left and right of the political spectrum, with a deeply-
embedded hostility to capitalism.

The major structural challenge facing the Reagan Administration is not so
much the run-down condition of the U.S. economy as it is the run-down
condition of the U.S. military. The country has to shift a substantial amount of
real resources to the defense effort, it is argued, if the Russians are not to
achieve military supremacy. Such a defense buildup will require a diversion of
resources from other sectors. The Administration hopes to shift the burden of
adjustment in the Federal budget onto nondefense discretionary spending
programs. It is questionable, however, whether the President and Congress
can jointly find enough money in that portion of the budget to accomplish the
Reagan defense objectives without jeopardizing the tax cuts or the big,
politically-sensitive transfer-payment programs. If they cannot, the defense
buildup may eventually force the President to reshape other parts of his
program and accept a less robust economic recovery than he had hoped for.

The fourth major weakness in the Thatcher-Reagan comparisons is the
bland assumption by almost everyone writing on the subject that the Thatcher
experiment has completely failed. While no one could describe the Thatcher
strategy as successful, it has not been without certain beneficial consequences
that could be important to Britain during the next world economic recovery.
The consequences:

☐ The high rate of unemployment has permitted British companies to make
substantial changes in work practices, producing a surge in productivity even
with output stagnant.

☐ Some firms have taken advantage of the overvalued exchange rate to
import new capital equipment, which also will improve British competitiveness.

☐ The Government has produced a significant change in the rate of inflation
and in wage behavior without resorting to wage and price controls. British
businessmen and trade unions will therefore be much more respectful of the
Government's money-supply targets and inflation objectives than they were
previously.

In addition to these developments, North Sea oil will eventually give Mrs.
Thatcher a second chance to reduce taxes and promote economic growth.
The Government's revenues from oil are projected to grow from 2.2 billion
pounds in 1979–80 to 10 to 15 billion pounds by 1985. If the Conservative
Government can hold the line on spending, these tax receipts should give Mrs.

Thatcher a renewed opportunity to make new tax cuts while also reducing Government borrowing and interest rates. . . .

The important point to remember in any comparison between Reagan and Thatcher is that the Thatcher program has been fiercely and dogmatically imposed upon Britain as much because of the failure of the Heath Government as the Labor Government that followed. The Heath Government came into office with a manifesto every bit as free-market oriented and anti-inflationary as Mrs. Thatcher's, but it was abandoned after a year because of a deteriorating economy. Mrs. Thatcher, too, has been forced to make concessions, but so far they have been the minimum required to maintain the Government. Indeed, she permitted interest rates to rise during September in order to correct any impression that she was easing policy too much.

The Reagan Administration has done more to change the political and economic environment in the United States than practically anyone thought possible 12 months ago. Unlike the Labor Party in Britain, even the Democrats have moved to the right and accepted much of the Reagan program. But the Administration itself has still not been tested under conditions of adversity. It has, if anything, been remarkably lucky.

When that luck starts to turn, and the contradictions in the program become more apparent, the personal comparisons between Thatcher and Reagan will become much more interesting. Only then will we know whether Reagan is as tough and determined an inflation fighter as Thatcher or whether, like Edward Heath, he will have to bend under the pressure of events and accept unpalatable compromises with inflation, tax increases, or incomes policies in order to keep the United States on a dash for economic growth and rapid rearmament.   fu(Eus

How effective have the economic policies of Thatcher been? David Hale notes that "while no one could describe the Thatcher strategy as successful, it has not been without certain beneficial consequences." Hale also notes that the high unemployment has allowed companies to make "changes in the workplace," that over-valued exchange rates have led to the importation of "new capital equipment," and that the get-tough policies of Thatcher have made people respect "government money-supply targets." But Prime Minister Thatcher maintains that she has done more than this. She claims that her policies have led to a change in attitude among the British populace—from a situation where people looked to the government to solve all of their problems, to one where there is more self reliance. Thatcher also asserts that the presence of high levels of unemployment does not prove that her policies are failing. She argues that the high levels of unemployment are a direct result of some companies "overmanning." In other words, the economy, over the years, has been carrying too much "dead wood" in the form of unproductive workers. Now that the economy is being forced to operate more efficiently, this dead wood must be transformed into something more productive. In the meantime, industries such as the steel industry must rid themselves of this dead wood if they are to compete in a world market.

Thatcher is certain of the future. She contends that her policies will lead to a more productive economy which will operate in markets that are free of damaging inflation. Moreover, she says her policies will lead to a society in which people are more independent and more willing to take on the responsibility of guaranteeing their own security. In her words, these accomplishments will help to "disconnect Britain from socialism."

MARGARET THATCHER REFLECTS UPON HER FIRST YEAR

James Bishop, *Illustrated London News*, May 1980

James Bishop: *Prime Minister, we are approaching the end of your Government's first year in office. Reviewing this not uneventful year what would you say were the Government's main achievements?*

Prime Minister: I think the first thing is a very big change in attitudes. When we came to power people tended to look to Government to make every decision, to haul them out of every trouble and to solve every problem. That was thoroughly unhealthy. They really should look to their own efforts for their own standard of living, not expect a government to do things for them. They really must look to management and workforce to solve problems within an industry, and not go to Government. We cannot have a system under which Government could fix prices, incomes, dividends, and determine how much money went out of the country by exchange control, and still have a free society.

Now the most interesting thing of all is how quickly (because it is within a year) attitudes have changed. Companies aren't automatically coming along to Government and saying, "We're in difficulty, you must give us a subsidy." Many members of trade unions are not just coming out on strike when they are called out on strike. Some of them are having ballots, some of them are saying no, we want to stick to our job; we have a duty to support our own families, and that is a loyalty as well. Even the South Wales miners didn't come out to support the steel workers on strike.

There is somehow a realization that there aren't any easy options left for Britain. It's because we were casting all our cares on Government and not solving our problems ourselves, not making our own efforts, not facing the facts of the situation, that we got into the position of decline that we did. So that's one achievement—change of attitudes.

Second, I think people realize that we really have got a long-term policy for the future—long-term, and fundamental to get things right. They know it's not going to be easy, because after all if a family has been living beyond its means for years, and all of a sudden has to live within them, it's not easy and it takes time. But they know it has to be done, and they know they won't succeed unless it is done. If one changes the analogy, you can perhaps say that a little unpleasant medicine now will save a lot of major surgery later. And that's very important. So people know that we are on to a long-term programme.

Third, it is recognized that we are trying to cut direct taxation, to leave people with more of their own money made from their own efforts. Geoffrey Howe's first Budget was courageous because it really did that, and his second particularly helped small businesses. So we're starting the means of more wealth creation, making it worth while for people to stay here. If they can build themselves up new businesses and be really successful they don't have to go abroad, they can stay and do it here, and provide the income here.

And then the fourth achievement is that we're beginning to try to turn over to a capital-owning democracy. That's very important. We don't want to have people dependent on governments, we want people with more of their own means being more independent of governments. The first stage is council house sales, so that people can have the pleasure, the joy and the capital of owning their own homes. That's only a start. Eventually we hope that people will be able to save their own capital out of their own income, and we've improved profit-sharing schemes and share option schemes for people who work in industry. But it's all to make people more independent of Government; in other words you're looking not so much to state welfare as to the well-being of the people by their own efforts, the state coming in when people are very unfortunate and need help.

You said recently in a television broadcast, I think on the eve of the Southend by-election, that some things were going to get worse before they got better. I'm wondering what things are going to get worse?
One is inflation. There are still price increases in the pipeline to come through, and there is no way of stopping them. Not all of the oil price increases are through. Not all of last year's wage increases are through. We're going to have problems with the retail price index in the next few months because we had the Budget last year in June, so the increases came through in June, whereas this year it was in March, so the increases are coming through earlier. The March on March figures, year on year, are going to look bad. So the price index will go up, I'm afraid. And electricity and gas prices, and rates increases, are very bad. Moreover we are having to provide for the public sector pay increases awarded by Clegg—and remember we were left that by the last government. That government said, "All right, we'll give you 9 per cent now and then you can take your claim to Clegg," and Clegg has been coming through with increases varying from about 9 to 25 per cent, and those the taxpayer and ratepayer must pick up. Now those things are coming through, and there's nothing I can do to stop them. I do not think there will be a downturn in the rate of inflation until about July.

Unemployment I'm afraid will also rise. There is so much over-manning that we've become thoroughly uncompetitive. Steel is a typical example. We import steel because our steel was pricing itself out of the home market. People think over-manning saves jobs. It doesn't. It means that you lose business and people go elsewhere, whereas if you had kept economical and efficient in running your business the orders would have stayed and you would have kept more steel output here.

So inflation and unemployment really are the difficult ones in the coming months.

There is a suggestion in the Budget that real incomes are going to have to fall.
This depends very much on people themselves. You may average things out and sometimes things may not look as good as you wish. But a lot depends on people: if you give them the incentive, the chance; if you have had new enterprise venture schemes; if you say, work hard and you'll keep more of your own money; and, with the kind of market we have here, where we have been importing things we could well produce ourselves, if manufacturers, managers and workforces really get stuck in they can earn more by recapturing our own markets. Now that's up to them. We can give them the incentives. They have got to take advantage of them.

What about investment?
This has been a good year for investment, and there will continue to be investment in some successful industries—in North Sea oil, the pharmaceutical industry, the chemical industry—and in some of the successful small businesses. I think as a whole we shall not get so much investment in the coming year, but that ought not to affect our output, because it's well understood that if we really used all our equipment and machinery to the limit we'd produce a lot more. But steel again is a classic example. They've got all this new equipment and machinery, but they will not use it as efficiently as it should be used.

Is there anything more that the Government wants to do, or could do to stimulate productivity in British industry?
We're constantly pointing out that there is no more money for more pay unless it's earned by more productivity. It is ironic that this fundamental rule—that if you take more out you've go to put in more effort or more efficiency—is so difficult to explain. If people demand more wages without becoming more efficient there are only two places those extra wages can come from: either by Government printing the money, which is inflation (and which is what has been happening), or by taking it from someone else, because he hasn't got the industrial muscle (which is almost a form of coercion). But you know how we're tackling it. We are saying we're not going to print the money, and that means that those who've got industrial muscle really must not use it to deprive others

of reasonable pay for the effort they put in. But it's not governments that pay wages, it's customers.

There's some concern, I think probably strengthened by what the Chancellor said in the Budget, that the revenues from North Sea oil, which are not inexhaustible, will be going into the general Exchequer funds to support current spending, rather than being used for specific investment, perhaps to find new sources of energy. Isn't there a case for using the money from North Sea oil in this way?
North Sea money should go to building up investments to take the place of North Sea oil when it's gone. Now how do you do that? There are several ways. First, the traditional way for this country would be to build up quite a bit of investment overseas, so that we had income always coming in from overseas. We need it. You'll remember that in pre-war days that was part of the explanation of our standard of living. We need it now first, because we need the income, but second, because a lot of people have invested in Britain and we have to pay interest out, so we must have interest and dividends coming in to cover this. And this is one reason why it was so important to release exchange control, so that companies here could set up subsidiaries overseas, so that people can invest overseas, so that we can earn income. These investments will replace the North Sea oil.

I agree that we have to replace the sources of energy. But after all it is Government or the taxpayer that finances investment in the electricity supply industry. We are building new power stations, and new nuclear power stations, so in a way you can say that money coming into the general Exchequer also goes out for that purpose. Some of the money the taxpayer pays out to the nationalized industries is to cover losses, but some of it is investment. I think you'll find that the financing going out to the nationalized industries next year will be a net £2,200 million.

Will you want to see a stepping-up in the nuclear power programme?
More nuclear power stations are being built, and I'm a great believer in nuclear energy in the longer run—although we still have a problem to solve with nuclear waste. But at the moment our problem is that we've got as much generating capacity as we're going to need within the next few years, and we have got more nuclear power stations coming on stream.

Can we look at one of the objectives that was in your party's manifesto for the last election, the objective of supporting family life? Cuts in public spending, the rising cost of mortgages and exceptionally high interest rates seem to be working against that objective—largely because the cuts seem to be hitting services rather than bureaucracy and waste.
The cuts aren't falling nearly heavily enough on bureaucracy and waste, I entirely agree. We are constantly on about this, and it happens both in local

authorities and central government, and central government's record on this in the last year is actually better than the local authorities'. But I think one must never equate family life with more state handouts. The family must look to their parents for their basic standard of living, and what Government has to do is to give families the opportunities to do things they would never be able to do otherwise. One is house purchase—council houses. The other is mortgages, which is also house purchase.

The worst thing I have had to do is to let interest rates rise, and it did affect mortgages. But even so the 15 per cent interest rate on mortgages is still below the current rate of inflation, and houses are going up in value I think faster than the mortgage rate. I am the first to know that it caused very difficult problems. I believe they are temporary. These are among the things we have to do that are temporarily painful, but they are to secure better things in the long run. And the reason why mortgage rates went up was because Government was spending too much. Its spending was not all covered by taxation, so Government had to borrow, and when governments borrow they are competing with building societies and manufacturing industries for money, so there are more people borrowing than saving, and the price goes up. The best thing we can do to help the person on a mortgage is to reduce Government spending and therefore to borrow less and thus relieve the pressure on the pool of savings and to get the interest rate down.

Now you'll be thinking in terms of things like school meals. There is still more than £200 million subsidy on school meals even after the economies. We're still spending more per child on education. We have kept up the spending on the health service, although we are putting up prescription charges. Can I just make a couple of points there? When prescription charges go up to £1 the actual cost of that prescription, which has to be met by the taxpayer, is £2.90. Second, a lot of people don't have to pay prescription charges—elderly folk, children, expectant mothers. In fact the exempt groups amount to 66 per cent of the prescriptions issued.

Can I just say one more thing on the family, where I think we really have helped? I feel very strongly that if a person is not a big income earner but nevertheless does a job which attracts a wage, a wage that is not very large, it's far better for him to work than to say, "I'll go on the dole and draw more money." First, it's far better to be occupied. Second, you get the respect of your family, because basically you are keeping them. Third, it brings up the children in the right way—to look to parents and not to the state. So we were careful to put up the supplement that goes to the wages of those in work, so if you have a comparatively low wage and are in work you do get this extra. And this year in this Budget we have put it up by 33⅓ per cent. This is because even in areas where wages aren't high we would rather people worked, and had the dignity and respect of working and got something extra from the taxpayer. And that is a positive real help to the family.

If I understood you rightly you are expecting inflation to peak at about mid-year. Would you think that interest rates will start to come down at about the same time?
If we're successful in curbing spending, in practice not on paper, I would certainly expect interest rates to be falling. That is our objective. It is still a question of trying to live within one's means, and not spending money before you've got it. If manufacturing industry is still borrowing very heavily then that will keep the rate up. But manufacturing industry should start to liquidate its stocks. The stocks are very high. They'll be selling them off and won't replace, so they will have more of their own cash, and I hope won't have to borrow as much as they've been doing in the past. The steel strike also has caused a lot of people to borrow to get them through; they've had to get stock from wherever they could.

In the manifesto you also spoke of trying to strike a balance between the rights and duties of the trade union movement. Do you think that the current proposed legislation is sufficient to redress that balance?
Not wholly. It's a start, and we recognize that it's a start. There are basically two things in the pipeline now. One is the Employment Bill, and the two very important things on that at the moment are confining picketing to one's place of work and some vital clauses on the closed shop which give individual members of unions far more rights than they have had for a long time against their union if they are wrongfully expelled. We are introducing more clauses to limit blacking. That is one whole area of trade union law.

The second thing is that we are saying to trade unionists if you really care about your members, if you are going to deprive them of their livelihood by calling them out on strike, you must see that they have some income out of union funds. After all, they have paid into trade union funds for years. It's a kind of insurance premium. If you call them out on strike, particularly if you call them out on strike without a ballot, they are entitled to look to you for strike pay during that time. We are going to assume, as you know, that members of unions have some strike pay during that time, and will therefore reduce the supplementary benefits accordingly.

In addition there is provision for postal ballots, so that any union can have a postal ballot on something major, for electing union officers or for a major strike, without it costing the union funds anything, and I hope that will induce members of trade unions to demand a ballot. . . .

A few years ago some people described Britain as ungovernable. Does your first year as the country's chief executive incline you to that view?
Very far from it. It really goes back to what I was saying about a change in attitudes. If you go back to the winter before last, when we were having strike after strike after strike in really fundamental services, this was because people had begun to think that they could demand things which would be auto-

matically forthcoming. That was something I had to get away from. If you demand things you've got to satisfy those demands by your own efforts.

I don't think the country is ungovernable. The country is responding to a government which says, "You've got to discipline yourself. You've got to start solving your own problems." And when people try, first they find that they can, and second they feel very much more self-respect. How can I put steel right if the managers and workforce can't, and why should they expect me to? Now it's required an iron nerve to do it, and a great deal of worry, but I am sure we were right to stand absolutely firm during the steel strike, and I'm sure it's very much better that we should have made them get together than just come along to 10 Downing Street and say, "Solve our problems for us."

In 1973, when you were Secretary of State for Education, you gave an interview to The Illustrated London News *during the course of which you were asked whether you wanted to be this country's first woman Prime Minister. You said you didn't, and you added, and I quote, "I think the first woman Prime Minister in this country will have quite a difficult time. I don't wish to be that person, and I don't think there is any chance of it." Well, circumstances obviously have changed. No doubt you are having quite a difficult time, but you seem also to be enjoying the experience. Is that a fair assumption?*

I remember saying that, but I had no idea that things would move as fast as they did. But the great thing in life when an opportunity comes is to seize it, because if you don't it will never come again. So when the opportunity opened up, I just put my name in. I didn't know what would happen. As you know, it's brought me all the way to Number 10. But it really was after 20 years in politics, 20 years of climbing up a ladder, step by step, one step at a time, always being certain that you had mastered one step before you took another. And so, when the opportunity came to go two rungs up, I was able to do it.

Now I am here, and from the day that I came I have felt perfectly right here. I didn't feel strange at all. I felt I could get to grips with the problem, and we did. I think we formed a government faster than one has ever been formed before—completely in two days—and we just got on with the job. I didn't set out to do a tremendous lot in 100 days, or in 200 days, or in 300 days. We have as it happens done a tremendous amount, we've even started de-nationalization. But I set out in the way I've always set out, to make the best use of each day as it comes, and that I think is the only way to do it.

You asked me if I enjoy it. Yes, I love it. I know that I have to take some hard decisions, and there are times when I think, "My goodness, people will think I'm very hard." And I'm not, in any way. It is just that there are times when you do have to be extremely firm, otherwise you are not going to get through. The easy way isn't always the best way, and therefore there are times when you have to be very firm and not flinch from it. But it's right for me, and I hope people feel that it's right for them. Because we are trying to be fair, fair to people who are unfortunate, who haven't got very much, fair also to people who are full of talent and ability, because they deserve fairness as well, they deserve a fair return for the tremendous effort they put in, and upon which we all rely. You will not do better for the less well off unless the talented and able can use their talents to their full extent and ability, and benefit from it themselves as well as benefitting others. Pennies don't come from heaven, they have to be earned here on earth.

What we have really been doing during this first year is that we have disconnected Britain from socialism, and from socialist attitudes.

We've been reviewing the past year. In conclusion, may we just look at the year ahead, and your priorities for this, the second year of your Administration?
If we're going to get things right we've got to do the three things. First we must get the rate of inflation down. Second we must steadily improve incentives, so that people have a reason for expanding, for building new businesses and creating new jobs. And third we must try to get people more independent, which means building their own security for themselves, their own homes, their own savings, their own lives. These three things must be done together and that's what we shall be doing.   **focus**

After two years of "Thatcherism" the British economy still seemed to be staggering. The attempt to decrease the growth rate of the money supply did not stem the tide of rising prices. Indeed, inflation was higher after two years than it was when Thatcher assumed the reins of power. In addition, unemployment reached record highs, and government deficits continued to increase even though Thatcher did all in her power to tighten the purse strings attached to government spending. What went wrong? Why didn't the British economy respond to this policy? Did her conservative/supply-side economic theories fail her?

In the next selection, two Nobel Prize Laureates present the conservative view of why Thatcher's economic policies failed. Milton Friedman argues that the major obstacle encountered by Thatcher's conservative economic policies was her inability "to get government spending under control." This, he asserts, was not entirely Thatcher's fault. In the U.K., the public sector accounts for a much larger part of economic activity than it does in the U.S. economy. Furthermore, public sector trade unions are much more powerful in the U.K. than they are in the U.S. As a result, the whole burden of implementing these policies has been placed on the shoulders of the private sector, a portion of the economy which is much smaller in Britain than it is in the U.S. Thus, the effect on the economy has been worse than had been expected. But, Friedman still contends that in the long run this will be beneficial to the British economy. That is, carrying this burden has forced the private sector to become leaner and more efficient. Consequently, he says, the aftermath of this process will be a more competitive British economy.

Frederick Von Hayek, on the other hand, contends that high rates of unemployment are unavoidable and necessary if we are to eliminate the evils of inflation. If anything, he believes the Thatcher government should strive for higher rates of unemployment in their attempts to bring down the rate of inflation. He maintains that "people will stand for over 20 percent unemployment for six months but will not stand for 10 percent for three years." In other words, Hayek believes that the "gradualism" which characterizes the policies of the Thatcher government will prove fatal. He concludes that "things have gone much more slowly than I hoped and thought was necessary to give Mrs. Thatcher a chance to succeed."

MILTON FRIEDMAN AND FREDERICK VON HAYEK REFLECT UPON TWO YEARS OF THATCHERISM

David Dimbleby, *Across the Board,* July/August, 1981

None of the figures looks encouraging. All of them show unemployment rising steadily to 3 million, or 3.5 million, or nearly 4 million by 1984, and output recovering painfully slowly. On the face of it, the prospects for the Conservatives in a 1984 election do not look too good.

And that raises the fascinating political question: Will the lady turn? Or has she already turned? The evidence varies, depending on whom you talk to. Her staunchest supporters say she was always a pragmatist, never inflexible, but will resist a panic rush for growth. However bad the election prospects are, bringing down inflation remains the priority. The money-supply targets cannot be abandoned. They may vary a bit from the medium-term plan, but monetary constraint must stay.

But some others think they see the end of the monetarist experiment, and are relieved. A severe recession, with social-service spending high, the tax-take falling, companies borrowing to avoid bankruptcy, has made the attempt to restrain monetary growth impossible, except at rates of interest that would guarantee Britain's final collapse. Interest rates can now be allowed to fall with a clear conscience and, fingers crossed, that will lead to sufficient recovery to start the economy on the path of growth and to start to bring unemployment down well before polling day.

It seemed instructive, at a time of such universal disillusion, to go back to the source of the theories the government embraced so enthusiastically only two years ago: Professors Hayek and Friedman, the two Nobel Prize winners, who were most influential in forming the policies prepared by Sir Keith Joseph and Mrs. Thatcher at the Centre for Policy Studies after the Conservative defeat of 1974. They do not have identical views, but both shared the aspirations of Mrs. Thatcher when she came to power and believed that she offered Britain the hope of radical reform. What do they think after nearly two years of Thatcherism? Is she still on course, or will she have to abandon the monetarist experiment?

"The record of the first two years," Friedman says, "has unfortunately been mixed. Many of the fine objectives that Margaret Thatcher proclaimed have not been carried out—and I don't blame Margaret Thatcher. I think she is a remarkable woman and I give her very high marks for what she has been trying to do, but she has unfortunately been obstructed by resistance from the bureaucracy, the Civil Service, and by resistance from within her own party. She does not, as it appears to me from far away, lead a truly united party. The major problems, in my opinion, arise out of her failure to get government spending under control . . . Instead of government spending going down as a fraction of income, it has, as I understand it, gone up. Unless that can be corrected, the prospects are not very good.

"That is the major failure which is at the bottom of some of the other failures. For example, monetary policy has not been steady. At times the growth in the quantity of money has greatly exceeded the target set by the Chancellor.

"The recession is much more severe than I anticipated and I believe it is more severe than would have been necessary had you been able promptly to get government spending down and to stay on a steady monetary course.

"I do not believe that the kind of shock policy that some people propose is desirable or necessary in a country in Britain's situation. There are some times when you have to have a shock situation. If you take some of the countries that have experienced inflation rates of 100, 200 or 1,000 percent, you cannot possibly follow a gradualistic policy, but in Britain's position I think a gradualist policy was the right thing. I don't think the mistake was that the cuts weren't deep enough. I think that the mistakes were that certain components of the policy were not carried out, in particular cutting government spending. I come back to that because I think that's the key problem."

But on the control of inflation Friedman and Hayek disagree. Friedman believes in a gradual decline. Hayek favors much more severe action, and regrets that it was not taken.

Hayek: "Unemployment is the necessary effect of stopping inflation dead. I would take any amount of unemployment which is necessary for this purpose, because that is the only way of bringing Britain back on a self-maintaining order and standard where it can in future begin a new growth. I'm not saying unemployment is a means of stopping inflation. It is an inevitable consequence. The conditions which make unemployment inevitable were laid during the previous inflation period. One point which you must stress is that you must get it over very quickly. It's an inevitable pain which you have to go through, but no political body can stand this for a very long period. I believe people will stand for over 20 percent unemployment for six months but will not stand for 10 percent for three years. From that point of view my proposal is politically more possible than Friedman's.

"It is not enough to reduce inflation. Inflation must be stopped dead, because in the long run a little inflation is quite as bad as a big inflation. In fact, as long as you retain a little inflation as part of the driving force you tend to increase it all the time. So long as a government says 'We have reduced inflation' it doesn't impress me at all. Once they tell me they have stopped inflation, I embrace them."

Hayek would also expect tougher measures to lead to a greater number of bankruptcies, and would not regret it: "I have, incidentally, often regretted that there haven't been more bankruptcies in the past; the British economy would be in a better position now if more firms had been eliminated and not kept artificially alive. I see the inevitability that a great many firms that ought not to exist, which ought to have disappeared long ago, should not be kept alive by artificial injections but should disappear as rapidly as possible. I always must emphasize—and to an economist it's obvious, of course—that the disappearance of a firm does not mean the disappearance of its productive equipment. It just means that one management takes over, which can make better use of the resources."

But Hayek's greatest worry about the state of Britain is not the failure to control government spending, or control the supply of money, so much as the failure, as he sees it, to introduce an adequate reform of the trade unions: "Trade union reform is basic for any chance of England to maintain the present standard of living. Unless Britain is enabled to compete effectively on the world industrial market, the country is in for continuous decline, certainly in her wealth if not in her absolute position.

"Essentially, all the privileges which have been granted by law to the trade unions, and the trade unions only, for 75 years must be rescinded. The trade unions have been explicitly granted by the law to do things which no other organization is allowed to do: breaking contracts without being responsible for the damage that has been done; using more or less disguised force for preventing people from doing what they regard as *their* exclusive rights, both on a large scale and in detail, in connection with the craft union systems or the demarcation problems; preventing other people from working altogether, by intimidation through what is called unviolent picketing, which, of course, is always a threat of violence. But I think the whole trade union legislation, at least for these last 75 years, has not only given them powers, it has created a mentality in England which is completely contrary to that required for a market economy.

"I'm greatly alarmed. Time is running short, and in this very crucial direction very little advance has yet been made. I'm quite sure that the Prime Minister aims in the right direction. I can't judge what prevents her from acting faster. But I am getting alarmed that the movement is too slow. The Minister in charge of it is not in favor of radical alteration. I have no hope that so long as the matter is in his hands the necessary things will be done."

Friedman concedes the importance of modifying trade union power, but believes it will only come about by reducing public-sector spending. If that happens, trade unions will automatically lose their influence: "In my opinion the trade union problem in Britain is almost entirely concentrated in the nationalized industries in the public sector. If Mrs. Thatcher or successive governments are successful in reducing the size of the public sector, I think you will simultaneously, without very great difficulty, reduce the trade union problem that you face.

"If you look at the places where you have been having strikes and difficulties, if you look at the relative behavior of wages, wage agreements in the private sector have been rather moderate; the major strikes and the major trade union problems have been in the public sector. The coal mines are not privately owned. It's been the industries or the companies which have been subsidized by the government, the automobile companies for example, where you have been having trade union problems."

Neither Friedman nor Hayek was as concerned with the depth of the British recession as with the failure to control public spending or to introduce major trade union reform. But on their view of the future they differed: Hayek gloomy, Friedman more cheerful.

Hayek: "Things have gone much more slowly than I both hoped and thought was necessary to give Mrs. Thatcher a chance to succeed, certainly within one term of government and possibly even if we count in terms of an eight-year period. I think the movement has been too slow. I don't think It is Mrs. Thatcher's fault. My impression is just more resistance in the circle of the government than perhaps she expected, more than she has been able to overcome.

"The attempt has to be made, and if it fails this time it just means that the decline will go on and people will still have to learn the lesson and be prepared to do what they are not prepared to do now. Nobody can judge. I don't think that any politician can be certain what he can do and not do. I regard it as my task to make politically possible what is said to be politically impossible. Whether it is politically impossible, I cannot judge. It has to be made politically possible by changing opinion."

Friedman: "I think she deserves credit for the strength of her views and her willingness to stick to her guns. I am a great admirer of Margaret Thatcher.

"The story isn't over. We have only seen the first stages of the battle. I think the battle goes on and I have considerable confidence that you have much better prospects in the next couple of years than you did for the past couple. I think the early stages are always the most difficult, when you have to counter set ideas and trends that are under way. So I don't despair that in two or three years from now the situation in Britain will look vastly better than it looks now. Inflation is falling, and as inflation falls, and as people come to recognize and take into account the falling of inflation, you will have the groundwork laid for a very strong boom in the British economy. Part of the process, part of the difficulty you have been going through, has also been laying the groundwork for strength. The problem is that the whole burden has fallen on the private sector because the public sector has not been cut, but one of the consequences of that is that the private sector is leaner and stronger and more efficient and ready to take advantage of the first opportunity to expand, to increase productivity and output, so that I don't believe one wants to look only backwards. You know, there is the old saying: 'It is always darkest just before the dawn.' "   focus

Critics of Margaret Thatcher's conservative economic policies reject the Friedman/ Hayek contention that conservative policies have not yet been fully implemented and that truly conservative policies have not been used to correct the failing British economy. These critics argue that Britain's stagnating economy is a direct result of implementing bankrupt conservative policies.

British economist Terry Ward explicitly challenges the Friedman/Hayek view of Thatcherism. He argues that their concern with British monetary policy, government spending, and employment policy is ill-founded. Ward finds that Margaret Thatcher's alleged loyalty to the monetarist explanation of inflation is not confirmed in her monetary policy. That is, while Thatcher claims to have pursued a restrictive monetary policy, in reality the money supply increased very rapidly in 1980. This rapid expansion of the money supply is a bit "embarrassing" for the monetarist camp, contends Ward. It should have resulted in an increase in inflation, but instead it was accompanied by a fall in prices. Ward pounces upon this apparent inconsistency. First, he claims that this demonstrates that there is no relationship between "monetary aggregates" (money supply—M3) and rates of inflation. Next, he argues that this is proof that control of the money supply is very difficult; a difficulty which, in part, can be traced to the existence of lags and imprecise definitions of money. Finally, he asserts that the recent reductions in the money supply, coupled with reductions in expenditures, have had their greatest impact in cutting back real output and employment rather than in lowering the rate of inflation.

Ward then addresses the Friedman/Hayek concern with Thatcher's inability to control the growth of government spending. Friedman/Hayek argued that this inability was directly linked to the increasing deficits that have occurred under her administration. Ward asks his readers to remember the implications of a high or full employment budget. As we explained in Chapter 5 of this book, the full employment budget is simply a projection of what the tax receipts and expenditures of the government would have been if the economy were employing all of its resources. Ward argues that reference to this budget shows that government spending has actually fallen under Prime Minister Thatcher. Thus, for Ward the reason for higher deficits is not increased government expenditures, but decreased government spending. He contends that this government policy fosters a recession in the economy—a recession which results in less tax revenues and causes the government to maintain high levels of social welfare spending.

Ward also examines the third issue raised by Friedman and Hayek, concerning Thatcher's experience with high levels of unemployment. Both Friedman and Hayek contend that high levels of unemployment are unavoidable and necessary if the British economy is to rid itself of widespread "overmanning." They believe that policies to rid the economy of this overmanning problem will inevitably foster a leaner, more efficient industrial base—that is, a more competitive British economy. Ward claims that a close examination of the facts reveals that the charge of overmanning is overstated. In fact, he finds that the performance of those industries that have reduced the level of employment has actually worsened in international trade markets.

WHO'S KIDDING WHOM?

Terry Ward, *Journal of Post-Keynesian Economics,*
Summer 1982

In 1956 unemployment in the UK stood at 250,000 or 1 percent of the labor force. Ten years later it was 350,000. By 1976 it had risen to 1.25 million or 5 percent. Toward the end of 1981 it was just under 3 million, or over 12 percent of the work force, and according to virtually all forecasters, it will go on rising. The figures, moreover, exclude unemployed school-leavers, elderly people forced into premature retirement, and the many married women discouraged from trying to find work. They also exclude almost half a million people temporarily employed on official government schemes and an equally large amount of concealed unemployment in services.

This job erosion is a direct consequence of a slowdown in output growth. Between 1956 and 1966 GDP* grew on average by slightly under 3 percent a year. Over the next ten years GDP growth averaged just over 2 percent a year. Between 1979 and mid-1981 GDP has fallen by considerably more than over *any* equivalent period since the war. Manufacturing output has declined by 16 percent; this exceeds the fall in the worst years of the Great Depression, 1929 to 1931 (11 percent). Manufacturing production in 1981 is no higher than it was in the mid-1960s, and in some major industries it is back to the level of the 1950s.

Successive governments have not only failed to come to grips with the central problem, i.e., an increasing deterioration in international competitiveness; they have reinforced its effect by pursuing restrictive fiscal and monetary policies in their preoccupation with finance and inflation. Under the Thatcher administration these policies have been applied with especial vigor. As a consequence, the exchange rate for sterling was pushed up, making British industries even less competitive than before. The opportunity provided by North Sea oil for the pursuit of expansionary policies designed to strengthen the productive base of the economy was squandered. Oil resources have

*Gross Domestic Product is comparable to Gross National Product in the U.S.—Eds.

instead served to cushion living standards in the face of a massive contraction of industrial output.

The main purpose of this article is to examine the claim that the debacle is an inescapable short-term price for permanently reduced inflation and sustained economic growth in the long term. This examination may have some relevance for the U.S. economy and its current malaise under President Reagan, who has adopted a similar policy with only a twenty-month lag.

The Thatcher Government's Economic Philosophy

The Thatcher administration, in power since 1979, differs from all previous postwar governments in its priorities and in its views about how the British economy works.

Above all, it has set its sights on the control of inflation as the overriding objective of policy. While recognizing that reducing inflation is likely to mean temporary unemployment, the government sees this as a necessary condition for restoring high employment in the long term. Indeed, unemployment is regarded as being *caused* by inflation—by economic efficiency being impaired, by investment being discouraged, and above all, by people pricing themselves out of work. As a corollary, the unemployment now observable in the UK can be dismissed as almost wholly "voluntary," on the surmise that nearly everyone could find a job if only they were prepared to accept a "realistic" wage for their work:

> Pay settlements must be based upon what companies can afford while remaining competitive. . . . The more pay settlements can be moderated, the lower the transitional costs of the fight against inflation in terms of bankruptcies, lost production and reduced employment. (Howe, 1980)

Inflation, the government believes, can only be reduced through a progressive reduction in the growth of the money supply, while it proposes to foster economic regeneration by releasing the vital energies of the British people through the incentives of lower taxation and interest rates.

Reductions in government expenditure assume critical importance for both strands of this policy. Thus, it is argued, government deficits, unless accompanied by bulges in the money supply and hence increased inflation, drive up interest rates and "crowd out" private sector borrowing for investment.

> Government borrowing has made a major contribution to the excessive growth of the money supply in recent years. The consequence of excessive borrowing has been high nominal interest rates and, in capital markets, the crowding out of business by the State. (Howe, 1980)

The only way to keep monetary growth, taxes, and interest rates down is, therefore, to cut government expenditure.

The Defects of the Thatcher Philosophy

This analysis generates a number of homilies about the importance (or even morality) of covering public expenditure by taxation, which appear to be entirely reasonable. Nevertheless, the assessment is seriously defective from beginning to end.

Money and Inflation

It used to be a confident assertion of monetarists that changes in the money supply were reflected some eighteen months to two years later in the inflation rate. In the words of Milton Friedman:

> There is perhaps no empirical regularity among economic phenomena that is based on so much evidence for so wide a range of circumstances as the connection between substantial changes in the stock of money and in the level of prices. (quoted by Tylecote, 1981 p. 119)

Unfortunately, any dubious statistical relationship which could be traced between the chosen measure of money (M3) and inflation has broken down in the UK. It is not possible to explain either the acceleration in inflation, to over 20 percent in the first year of Conservative government, or the subsequent deceleration in terms of the behavior of the money stock. The government has been put in the embarrassing position of claiming credit for the recent fall in inflation but having to explain why the growth of M3 in 1980 of almost 23 percent (from February to December 1980), as against a target of 7 to 11 percent, should not fairly soon cause a sharp resurgence of inflation!

In response to this breakdown there are two characteristic defenses. First, many who jumped on the M3 bandwagon originally now argue that M3 is the *wrong* indicator of monetary growth to use; they now advocate a range of different measures. Since the various measures of money can move very differently, the difficulty is that in the absence of specific guidance *before* the event, there is no way of reliably interpreting any particular configuration of changes.

The second line of argument is that whatever the money supply figures show, we know that monetary policy has been tight from other indicators such as high interest rates and a high exchange rate. This (entirely acceptable) proposition, however, betrays the hollowness in the monetarist case. The essential monetarist claim was precisely that monetary *aggregates* should be controlled in lieu of interest rates, the traditional Keynesian criterion for monetary policy. The new retreat, therefore, restores to policy-makers the freedom to *ignore* monetary aggregates and to focus directly on interest rates and the exchange rate.

A further defense is that the speed of response of inflation to monetary growth is heavily influenced by *expectations*; and since these are unstable, we *cannot* expect to observe any consistent relationship between money and

prices. This argument stands in stark contrast to earlier monetarist propositions which emphasized, above all, undiluted empirical support.

If governments accept this latter-day version of monetarism, the core of
economic policy rests on a theology for which there cannot *in principle* be any
supporting evidence.

Interest Rates and Government Borrowing

Increases in public expenditure have no effect on total output unless the
economy is fully employed. If there are idle resources, an increase in public
expenditure will increase total output, both directly and indirectly through
multiplier effects. Higher levels of income and output will be associated with
higher savings, and higher demand for financial assets of all kinds including
money.

The rate of interest need rise only if the stock of money is deliberately held
down. If, as the evidence suggests, the stock of money does not directly affect
inflation, there is no reason why the government should seek to prevent a rise
in the quantity of money; with idle resources available, higher public
expenditure, far from reducing private investment, will induce an increase.

The government can finance increased borrowing and reduce interest rates
simultaneously by selling as much or as little gilt-edged stock as the market
demands at the new, lower interest rates. This may imply growth of the stock of
money, but if so the reason will be that the private sector's demand for money
has increased. Indeed, the government cannot expand the stock of money in
excess of private sector demand for it (see Kaldor, 1980).

There is a limit to the fiscal stimulus which can safely be given when the
economy is underemployed, but the limit has nothing to do with the money
supply. It is set by the risk that the exchange rate might fall in an uncontrollable
way if the fiscal stimulus caused spending on imports to exceed export
earnings, or if investors switched their sterling funds to other currencies.

The Supply Side

The other component of the government's philosophy is the proposition
that sustained recovery can occur not only without any fiscal or monetary
stimulus to demand, but even under the restrictive policies thought necessary
to control inflation. It is open to a British entrepreneur in 1981 to produce the
right thing in the right place at the right price, and if he does so he will prosper
and create jobs in the process.

What makes this proposition implausible is that as a direct result of
macroeconomic policies, most businesses face depression of home markets
and a high exchange rate, making competition exceptionally difficult. Under
these conditions, profits have shrunk to their lowest ever level; for many the
test of managerial ability is one of mere survival. Under 1981 market
conditions the dynamic sectors in Britain are likely to be too small to carry out

the task of reemploying much of the labor and equipment put out of action by contraction of other businesses.

The notion that present unemployment is largely "voluntary" because it is caused by people refusing to accept the level of wages which businesses can afford to pay is a grotesque representation of the current position. Labor costs in the UK cannot be considered in isolation but have to be related to those in other countries measured at the prevailing rate of exchange. The question is whether it is reasonable to expect wage levels to adjust to compensate for any exchange rate appreciation, no matter how large. The movement in sterling has been so perverse in relation to relative rates of inflation that massive reductions in real wages would be necessary to offset the deterioration in the cost competitiveness of UK producers. Even if money wages were to be frozen, it would take many years before most British industries regained the loss in cost competitiveness since 1979.

Recent Developments in More Detail

Is the Thatcher policy working, irrespective of our criticisms?

Fiscal Policy

A progressive reduction in the scale of public sector borrowing (PSBR) achieved through cuts in public expenditure is a central element of the Thatcher government's economic strategy, as indeed it was of the previous Labour government's policy. The failure so far to hit the PSBR targets set at the beginning of each financial year, or to substantially reduce the PSBR and public expenditure in relation to GDP, has evoked criticism from many government supporters, who have argued that such fiscal laxity has been a major cause of high interest rates and, therefore, of a high exchange rate. As a result, the argument goes, private industry has been hit unduly hard by the tight monetary policy, a consequence which could have been avoided if only the government had been more resolute in cutting back public expenditure. At the same time, the fact that there has not been a significant reduction in either the PSBR or public expenditure has been used to refute the contention that tight fiscal policy has been a primary cause of the recession.

There is no doubt that the planned level of PSBR has been reduced substantially over the past five years, and as shown in Table 1, this has entailed not only sales of government assets and a cutback in lending (both of which have minimal direct effects on aggregate demand) but more importantly an intended reduction in the financial, or budget, deficit. It is the latter with which we are concerned here. Up until 1980-81 the targets for the budget deficit were more or less achieved, with the actual deficit being reduced from around 8 percent in 1975-76 to 4 percent in 1979-80. In 1980-81, however, the budget deficit exceeded what was planned by over 2 percent of GDP. The intention behind the tax increases and other measures implemented in the March 1981 budget was to rectify this overexpansion in 1981-82.

The figures in Table 1 make no allowance for the effects of changes in income on government spending and revenue and are thus a misleading guide to changes in fiscal policy. To measure such changes, we need to examine the movement not in the actual budget deficit but in the deficit purged of any changes caused by variations in income and expenditure from a trend growth path.

Table 1

PSBR TARGETS AND BUDGET DEFICITS
(percent of GDP at market prices)

	PSBR	Planned asset transactions	Target budget deficit	Actual budget deficit
1976-77	9.4	1.1	8.3	5.7
1977-78	5.9	0.6	5.3	4.3
1978-79	5.3	0.8	4.5	4.9
1979-80	4.2	0.6	3.6	3.9
1980-81	3.8	0.7	3.1	5.3
1981-82	4.4	1.2	3.2	-

Sources: Targets as given in the beginning of the financial year.
Outturns from Financial Statistics (outturn for 1980-81 from UK Treasury, 1981b).

The figures in Table 2 show both the target and the actual budget deficit adjusted for the shortfall in GDP from a nonrecessionary trend (taken as a growth rate of 3 percent a year from 1974) and are equivalent to estimates of a full-employment budget surplus. Since 1976 the target measured in this way

Table 2

BUDGET DEFICITS ADJUSTED FOR RECESSION
(percent of GDP at market prices)

	Expected GDP shortfall	Implicit demand-adjusted target for budget deficit	Actual demand-adjusted budget deficit	Actual GDP shortfall
1976-77	4.8	5.9	3.7	4.0
1977-78	8.9	0.9	1.7	5.2
1978-79	8.2	0.4	2.4	5.0
1979-80	7.4	-0.1	0.6	6.6
1980-81	12.6	-3.2	-1.0	12.6
1981-82	15.7	-4.7	-	-

Sources: Expected GDP and target budget deficit from Financial Statement at the beginning of the financial year. Actual GDP and budget deficit from Financial Statistics and Economic Trends (1980-81 figures from UK Treasury, 1981b).

Note: GDP shortfalls measured relative to a 3 percent per year real growth path starting from actual GDP in 1974. Demand-adjusted budget deficits calculated as target or actual deficits less 50 percent of the expected or actual GDP shortfall.

has been reduced by over 10 percent of GDP. Despite a government forecast for 1981-82 of GDP no less than 15 percent below trend, fiscal policy is now so tight that there would be a budget surplus of 5 percent of GDP if output were on trend. This represents a more deflationary stance than at any time in the UK since the war.

Although the adjusted budget targets have not been entirely fulfilled, the fiscal stance on the measure used in Table 2 was tightened by nearly 5 percent of GDP between 1976-77 and 1980-81 and promises to be tightened by a further 3.5 percent in 1981-82 through increased tax rates and public expenditure cuts. This is sufficient to explain a major part of the slowdown and subsequent contraction in domestic output which has occurred over this period. The fact that the actual budget deficit has not been significantly reduced is entirely the consequence of the recession engineered by policies aimed at such a reduction. The phenomenon illustrates the self-defeating nature of the government's strategy. . . .

Employment and Productivity

Between 1970 and 1979 manufacturing employment fell by 14 percent, a reduction of over one million in the number of jobs. Between 1979 and the second quarter of 1981, however, the rate of job loss accelerated sharply, with employment declining by 13 percent, nearly as much as over the preceding nine years. This has been taken as indicating a significant change in behavior, with companies allegedly reducing the degree of overmanning. In fact, the reduction in employment during 1980 has been more or less in line with the fall in manufacturing output.

On the basis of past experience, labor-shedding does not seem to be a necessary first step to a strengthening of industrial performance. A comparison of different industries shows that those which reduced labor significantly during the recession of the early 1980s in fact performed *worse* in international trade in subsequent years than those which expanded employment. Redundancies and plant closures appear to achieve no more and no less than a contraction of the industry in question. There is no presumption that they foreshadow any improvement in competitiveness, as government spokesmen are now alleging.

More significant for future competitiveness is the fact that investment in new plant and machinery by manufacturers has fallen by over 20 percent between the fourth quarter of 1979 and the second quarter of 1981. According to surveys of intentions, it will continue to fall during 1981 and 1982.

Conclusions

The above review suggests that there is little or no substance in the Thatcher government's contention that its policies have caused a fundamental change in economic behavior or created the conditions for sustained growth with low inflation. What has happened so far is entirely consistent with Keynesian analysis, but it is difficult to explain in terms of the monetarist propositions enunciated by the government. The response to fiscal and monetary restriction, coupled with a grossly overvalued exchange rate, has taken the form almost wholly of reductions in real output rather than lower inflation. As would have been predicted on past behavior, profits, investment, productivity, and trade performance have all declined significantly under these conditions.

So long as policy continues in the same vein, there is no presumption that sustained recovery will occur at any stage. To generate recovery requires a reversal of most of the Thatcher policies. In particular, fiscal and monetary policies need to be greatly relaxed to stimulate expansion and reduce the exchange rate to a level at which British goods are competitive on world markets. The substantial balance of payments surplus at present being earned provides scope for a significantly higher level of economic activity. The starting point is so appallingly bad and the industrial base has been so weakened, however, that a package of conventional measures of this kind may well be incapable of securing a high enough growth rate over a sustained period to bring unemployment down to acceptable levels. It is always possible to hypothesize a large enough devaluation to resolve the balance-of-payments problems which would otherwise become acute with rapid growth. It is less easy to formulate plausible ways of overcoming the inflationary repercussions of such a policy. However an incomes policy is dressed up, the problem remains one of getting agreement on significant reductions in real wages over a number of years. So far, various forms of wage restraint in the UK have been effective only for two or three years at most and have been followed by pay explosions.

These difficulties suggest the need for a wider examination of economic policies, including measures such as controls on trade and exchange, with the aim of easing the pressure on real wages and promoting industrial re-generation. Once the UK has purged itself of Thatcherism, the equally important task of implementing a strategy for recovery remains.   focus

The Case of the Third World

Development economist Kenneth Jameson, in the article that follows, looks at the success of supply-side economics in the developing world. He believes supply-side economics can be credited with producing high growth rates for these developing countries. However, his essay also focuses upon a major negative consequence of supply-side economics as applied in the Third World. He writes: "The increase in supply . . . came only at the expense of the poor and powerless, as income was redistributed in favor of the rich." In other words, the rich got richer and the poor got poorer. In essence, Jameson says that if economic development is defined in terms of Gross National Product, supply-side economics has been successful in helping developing countries increase the overall availability of goods and services. However, if development is defined more broadly to include such things as improving the level of welfare for *all members of society*, then the success of supply-side economics is not so certain. Indeed, one could even question whether supply-side economics has been successful at all in these terms. As Jameson sees it, the lesson for the U.S. experiment with supply-side economics is clear: Questions of income distribution should not be ignored when measuring the success of supply-side economics.

LET'S NOT FORGET ABOUT INCOME DISTRIBUTION

Kenneth P. Jameson, *Challenge,*
November/December 1980

It is certainly far from common for an eminent thinker in economics, or in any other discipline, to become a major critic of his own views. More typical is a tenacious defense by the author of all aspects of his work, with a realistic assessment forthcoming only years after the author has disappeared from the scene. It is the more noteworthy, therefore, that in recent years two well-known and respected economists have joined the ranks of their own critics.

The first is the Pakistani development economist, Mahbub ul Haq, now with the World Bank, who in the preface to his recent book, describes it as "an evolution of ideas over time (in which) I have tried to relate them as honestly as I could, including my own mistakes and rediscoveries."

A more recent metamorphosis occurred with Michael Evans' article in *Challenge* (January/February, 1980). It began with some chest-thumping for having built two of the "big three" macroeconomic models, then turned to *mea culpas* for having omitted supply-side phenomena, and finally ended with a good deal of browbeating of other economists in an effort to persuade them to follow this new tack.

The appearance of two such conversion experiences in such a relatively short period is remarkable in itself. Even more impressive, however, is the fact that Evans is sounding the supply-side call while Haq's evolution is away from the same and his apology is for having concentrated too much on the supply side as an approach to development. To be sure, there are some differences in what is meant by supply-side economics in the development context and in the area of U.S. public policy, but the similarities are great enough to cause puzzlement over the contrasting trajectories of the two economists.

Such an intellectual tangle deserves unravelling, and in the process some light may be shed on the intellectual fashion of the day, supply-side economics.

Development Thinking and the Supply Side

A survey of the writing on economic development in the postwar period shows clearly that the dominant concern has been the supply side. In other words, how can the economy's output be increased most effectively? Initially, conditions of labor surplus were seen as a potential source of growth in GNP. Sir Arthur Lewis' 1979 Nobel prize was given in part for his contributions to the analysis of the process by which the transfer of surplus labor into more productive employment would increase societal output. Much subsequent work has examined the many factors which can affect this transfer and its effect on supply. Theodore Schultz received his share of the Nobel prize partly for his critique of the idea of labor surplus. But his main contribution was to an understanding of the conditions of supply in the agricultural sector, with primary concentration on factors affecting efficiency and on the contribution of technical change to productivity.

Other sources of increased supply also received their due in the development literature. Human resource development through education and health was seen as a major contributor to growth of output. Entrepreneurship and its nurturance were areas of major concern, as was the question of the need for infrastructure to allow efficient production by business.

Implicit in all of these questions was a concern with the saving rate in the developing countries. In its crudest form, in the "stages of growth" literature, an increase in the saving rate was seen as the motive force for the takeoff into development—the sustained increase in per capita GNP. In all models, saving was given a central role as the source of the investment funds necessary for growth and for the increases in productivity in the economy. Questions of foreign aid and foreign investment were formulated in the same fashion.

Of course there was some concern with demand and its management, raising the issue of the role of government expenditures and monetary policy. The most prolific writing was in the Latin American debate between the monetarists and the structuralists. But primary consideration was given to increasing supply.

Haq's writings as Chief Economist of the National Planning Commission of Pakistan correspond directly to the overall concern of development thinkers. Growth in supply was the goal; increases in saving were fundamental. And in dealing with these questions, Haq pointed to a linkage between saving and income distribution which has been a central component of the resulting development debate. He made the argument that economic policy should favor entrepreneurs and those with high saving rates—that is, the wealthy— for this would increase saving, investment, and growth. Indeed, his eloquence in this regard is notable.

In a 1963 essay, Haq, the supply-side economist, minces no words in dismissing any policy emphasis on "distribution and welfare state considerations." He counters that "the best . . . form of social security is a rapid extension of productive employment opportunities to all through the creation of sufficient capital by some. There exists, therefore, a functional justification for inequality of income if this raises production for all and not consumption for a few. The road to eventual equalities may inevitably lie through initial inequalities."

With less overt emphasis on income distribution, this statement could have been penned by any self-respecting supply-side economist. For example, Evans writes, "Hence, the increase in taxes results in a decline in assets of the rich, which reduces the flow of funds to the banking system. . . . Eventually this reduces capital formation and housing construction." Elsewhere Evans criticizes other models for "their inability to link changes in saving and investment, and changes in investment to productivity and economic growth."

But Haq is immune to those critiques, and his earlier statements resonate with Evans'. Why then is he quoting them now in his book in order to subject them to specific rejection—and at the very time when the U.S. economics profession is rushing to embrace his earlier views?

One logical explanation—an incorrect one as it turns out—is that his suggested policies failed in Pakistan and in other third world countries, that supply did not respond as expected. Let us examine this possible explanation.

The Record of Growth in the Third World

A number of efforts have been made to summarize postwar development performance in the third world countries which followed the supply-side approach. They range from the studies for the World Bank by David Morawetz to those of Bill Warren and John Gurley done from a Marxist perspective. All of the studies agree that the policies adopted were successful in attaining the results desired: GNP grew, and at rates which were far higher than the historical experiences. In most cases the same can be said for GNP per capita. As Warren says: "the period . . . has witnessed titanic strides forward in the establishment, consolidation and growth of capitalism in the Third World, with corresponding advances in material welfare and the development of the productive forces."

No matter how the data are organized, postwar growth in output was impressive. Even with the OPEC countries excluded, from 1960 to 1974, GNP in the third world grew faster than in the advanced capitalist countries, though somewhat more slowly on a per capita basis. A similar comparison with Marxian socialist countries favors the third world as well. Specific third world countries such as the Republic of Korea, Singapore, Brazil, and Taiwan were the fastest-growing countries in the world in the same period. In virtually every country with time series data on growth rates, there was a marked acceleration from the pre-1950s to the 1950s and then again to the 1960s. Even Haq's Pakistan from 1960 to 1976 grew at a very respectable 3.2 percent annual rate in terms of GNP per capita.

This would seem to be proof positive of the effectiveness of supply-side economics. The goal of growth was achieved, a whole series of policies were developed which would differ from place to place but which were effective in attaining that goal. And most important, they dealt primarily with the supply side, leaving the demand side as a secondary consideration. This experience would seem to support similar efforts in the United States as urged by Evans and others. Why then would Haq reject this very success story and his role in it? To understand this we must turn to the "side effects" of such policies.

A Broader View of the Development Record

Increases in supply should be taken as a means to an end, in this case the end being "development" or an improvement in the level of human welfare in a society. While growth often took on many of the attributes of a fetish, most economists saw it as desirable for its supposed wider effect of increased access to goods such as food, health care, education, and improved performance in other areas such as life expectancy, infant mortality, or literacy.

Dissatisfaction with the supply-side approach to development originated in the realization, based on experience, that the translation of growth rates into these ends was not direct, that high growth rates did not of necessity enhance performance in these more central areas.

This led Haq to write in 1971: "It is time to stand economic theory on its head, since a rising growth rate is no guarantee against worsening poverty. . . . Divorce between production and distribution policies is false and dangerous: the distribution policies must be built into the very pattern and organization of production."

For Haq, the strategy of growth which had relied on the savings of the wealthy as the motor of growth was now unacceptable; the emphasis had to be on dealing with poverty and shifting the distribution in favor of the poor. The record of development showed the need for this reorientation.

Despite, or as part of, the rapid growth rates in the third world, the income distribution in a large percentage of the countries became more skewed toward the wealthy. While this had been foreseen, there were two reasons for concern over the pattern. The first was that the inequality showed no tendency to reverse itself. The usual assumption was that inequality would show an inverted "U" pattern, the Kuznets pattern, where there was an increase up to a certain level of GNP and then improvement. There is little evidence of such a reversal in third world countries. This undercuts some of the justification for such trends. In addition, recent evidence seemed to indicate that there was no close link between inequality and growth or, conversely, that growth could occur without major increases in the inequality of the income distribution.

Other aspects of third world performance caused additional doubt about this strategy. Substantial evidence drawn from Africa, and more extensively from Asia, indicates that the incidence of absolute poverty, generally measured by numbers or percentages of populations below some poverty level, increased *pari passu* with the growth in GNP. Although the evidence is less clear, unemployment and underemployment in these countries was also a continuing and probably a growing problem. Other indicators showed equally mixed results. Haq noted that the literacy rate in Pakistan actually fell from 18 percent to 15 percent during the 1950–1970 period. Malnutrition continued and in some cases grew. Even diseases such as malaria and cholera began a resurgence.

So at one level, Haq and many other development economists have rejected the single-minded pursuit of supply-side development because of the awareness of the costs which it entails. The increase in supply under the types of policies the early Haq advocated came only at the expense of the poor and the powerless, as income was redistributed in favor of the rich. The costs now seem too high, the type of "development" which occurs too skewed, the loss to the poor, by their being left behind or having their situation deteriorate, too great.

It should be pointed out that the rejection of the simple supply-side policies and their implications for income distribution does not result in an option for stagnation. As noted above, there are certain countries like Taiwan, Costa Rica, or Singapore which were able to attain relatively high growth rates without the detrimental aspects of maldistribution of income. *Post hoc* evaluation of the programs has isolated a number of factors—such as widespread access to productive resources and broad-based human resource development—which have been formulated as a "growth with equity strategy" of development. In recent years there has been a major reorientation among segments of the development community, Haq included, toward this new understanding of the process and problems of development.

The Lesson for U.S. Economists

As the American economics profession proceeds to be browbeaten into wholesale acceptance of supply-side economics, there are a number of questions which should be raised, some of which may receive some illumination from the development thinking chronicled above.

The first question is what is meant by supply-side economics in the United States. This is a matter of some controversy, as recent articles in the popular press by Herbert Stein and others would attest. Stein lists eleven propositions; Representative Kemp in response adds two more; Evans isolates ten supply-side effects from his model. While most seem to deal with the effect of tax rates on productivity and work effort, and to some degree with the final revenue impact of tax cuts, their sum total does not differ substantially from the supply-side approach of early development thinking. They talk of tax cuts which are targeted so as to maximize their effect. Put another way, the cuts should go to individuals who will increase their saving as a result, and this means the rich. In addition they should go to corporations in order to increase their rate of return and thereby their investment. Some taxes may be lowered for workers, but the impact on income will be small as this will result in "more modest demands for wage increases." So as taxes are cut for upper-income individuals in the interest of increasing their saving and their work effort, of necessity there will be some redistribution of income in favor of the wealthy.

Since in actual practice, the U.S. income tax is not notably progressive, the distributional effects are not likely to be major. There may be a much more significant impact on the expenditures side, however. The problem is to ascertain the position of supply-siders on government expenditures. At the risk of incorrectly identifying some of their arguments, let me suggest the following as the corollary propositions of supply-side economics for government expenditures. Most supply-siders would agree that tax cuts will lead to lower government revenues. The opposite argument, based on what is called "the Laffer curve"—that is, lowering taxes leads to growth in revenue—has few staunch partisans. Next, government spending has a tendency to crowd out more productive private expenditures, and so should be limited, perhaps through the requirement for a balanced budget. In addition, transfer payments have a negative effect on productivity and on the incentive to work. Thus they are prime candidates for reductions. This case is even stronger when there are international threats which require increases in military expenditures. When these strands are woven together, they lead very clearly to a policy of substantially lower government expenditures and transfer payments. While there is some variation among supply-side economists on these issues, I think most would agree with most of the points. Certainly, the supply-siders in Congress would identify with these views.

Given these propositions, the effect on income distribution of this set of policies becomes much clearer. If there has been any equalization in our society in terms of access to goods, it has come about as a result of transfer payments and certain particular government programs aimed specifically at certain groups of recipients. If these programs are cut out, the distribution effects will be much more profound. And they will resemble much more closely the types of policies implemented in the interest of development.

With this understanding, some lessons can be drawn from development. The first lesson is that such policies were successful in raising GNP in third world countries. They may be equally as successful in the United States. The second lesson, however, is that the question of income distribution cannot be assumed away. If "supply-side economics" is a euphemism for "change the distribution of income to favor the wealthy," this should be spelled out. Of course U.S. economists are hesitant to deal with these issues, and few would ever be so bold as the early Haq in arguing for inequality. But the suspicion must be that under all of the rhetoric, when the proposed policies and the probable manner in which they will be implemented are examined, it is highly likely that they will lead to greater inequality in the distribution of income—at least in the "short run."

In addition to deterioration in the relative situation of the poor, it is likely that there will be a growth in the absolute level of poverty, such as occurred in third world countries. The early development economists were willing to accept this "short-run" result, until its magnitude and permanence were realized. Supply-side economists in the United States have to confront these same issues and admit their centrality to the policy debate. This need is more acute since the skewing of the income distribution does not have any automatic tendency to reverse itself. There is little evidence of "trickle-down" or of the U-shaped income distribution curve. The same is likely to be true for high-income countries.

If this proves to be the case, the basis for such policies is difficult to find. It is not possible to justify such results by welfare criteria such as Pareto-optimality or even Rawls' difference principle. It becomes a political choice or one based upon one's own interests, hardly a satisfactory situation for rational policy-making.

There is of course one other possibility. That is for the economics discipline to avoid being stampeded into supply-side economics with the implications noted above. Perhaps the models that should be looked to are those of countries which grew rapidly but without the negative impact on distribution— the Taiwan-Costa Rica-Singapore syndrome.

Though they are all very small countries by comparison with the United States, there were a number of common factors in their experience which may be relevant. First, they were not embarrassed by government involvement in all aspects of the economy; indeed there is generally an explicit or implicit type of planning, and it is not felt that the private sector will be able to do it alone. Perhaps a successful and conscious effort in this direction could have a beneficial impact on investment by removing some of the uncertainty. It would certainly be preferable to the "after-the-fact" planning we see with the Chrysler loan guarantee.

Second, these countries consciously ensured that the poor of their societies would be incorporated directly into their plans. For the most part this meant ensuring that small farmers would receive prices that would allow them to live, and that they would have access to land. In our society it might imply a broad range of policy options, including much more active support of worker ownership and self-management, community projects and enterprises, and programs to aid small business. If for some reason, direct access to productive assets were not possible, then assurance would have to be given that minimal needs for housing, food, and other basic necessities would have to be met. The benefits of such an approach, which is directly contrary to tendencies in our domestic policy, have been formalized in a "basic human needs" approach to development.

Finally, these countries adopted a variety of techniques of production, not relying solely on the large-scale and capital-intensive modes. In this regard, efforts at community-based production and decentralization of energy generation may be useful.

Rather than simply repeating the errors of these countries, with a forced metamorphosis later, it should be possible in the United States to find a new approach to growth. It would have to take into specific consideration questions of poverty and of income distribution, and it would have to move beyond the chimera of making the rich richer in order to make the poor richer—in the long run.   focus

Some Concluding Thoughts

In concluding this chapter, it is tempting to make predictions about the future of supply-side economics in the U.S. by drawing heavily on the British model. Such a temptation must be resisted, however, since it is full of risks. Basic conditions in the U.K. and the U.S.—economic, political and social—are very different. The same can be said about the specific economic policies that have been enacted here and in England. Nevertheless, keeping these fundamental differences in mind, one conclusion seems safe to make: In neither England nor the developing countries, where supply-side theories have been enacted, have these conservative/supply-side policies been an instant macroeconomic cure-all for the economic ills facing those societies. Therefore, these policies are unlikely to be an instant macroeconomic panacea for the U.S.

AFTERWORD

The Preface of this book stated our intention: We hope to provide the tools to evaluate the phenomenon of supply-side economics. We believe that the essays in this book have accomplished this task. That is, they have examined and critiqued the major issues associated with this modern-day economic revolution from the perspective of both proponents and opponents. Such a balance, we believe, has enabled the reader to better understand and, thus, better judge the implications of supply-side economics.

In addition to providing a balanced perspective, the selections in this book have also highlighted an important component of the whole supply-side economics debate. That is, they have underscored the important fact that economics is not merely an academic pursuit, dealing with abstract theories. The policies which have been debated in this book will have an important impact on many people. The questions of full employment, stable prices and economic growth have direct and obvious implications for every one of us in this society. The questions of equity and efficiency thus become primary considerations in the establishment of economic policies. Often, questions of equity are in conflict with the requirements of efficiency, and the resolution of this conflict will determine the extent to which conservative/supply-side policies remain in effect. Its future is in your hands. As you discharge your responsibility as a citizen/voter, you will be passing judgment on the principles and theories of supply-side economics as it will be practiced in the future.

Index

Adams, John, 172
Adams, John Quincy, 188
Adenauer, Konrad, 64
Africa, 234-35
aggregate demand, and Keynesian economics, 3, 28; stimulation of, 25, 73
aggregate supply, role of, in fiscal policy, 25
Aid to Families with Dependent Children, 39-40, 101, 109, 119, 182, 193; and New Federalism, 194, 195, 196, 197, 198
Alger, Horatio, 16
Anderson, Martin, 109, 111, 114, 194
Anti-Federalists, 170, 171, 172, 175, 176, 177
Appalachian Regional Commission, 101
Auchter, Thorne, 83, 86, 87
auto industry, employment problems in, 104

Babbitt, Bruce, 195
balanced budget amendment, 145, 147
Bank of England, 205
Bank of the United States, 187
barter economy, and Laffer curve, 51
Beer, Samuel, 174, 175, 184, 185
Benderly, Jason, 153, 154
benefit-cost analysis, criticism of, 86, 87; of government regulation, 77-82. See also cost effectiveness
Bishop, Jane, 210
Bosworth, Barry, 119
Brazil, 233
British Pound Sterling, valuation of, 201, 205, 206, 223, 227, 230
Browning, Edgar K., 107
brown lung, see byssinosis
Brozen, Yale, 104, 105, 108
budget: balanced, 134, 139, 145-47; military spending in, 121; and Reagan economics, 48, 94-99; social services in, 203; and supply-side economics, 6; of Thatcher government, 227-29; types of, 132-34; unified, 132-33. See also budget deficits
budget deficits, consequences of, 140-41, 150, 151; and the FED, 148; and interest rates, 140; and Laffer curve, 58; minimizing importance of, 135-36; and Reagan economics, 13, 49, 96, 132, 135-36, 140, 149; and savings, 141, 142; supply-side view of, 50, 160, 167; Thatcher's attitude toward, 201, 203, 227-28
bureaucracy, and individualism, 17
byssinosis, and benefit-cost analysis, 83; medical surveillance of, 86; prevention of, 87

capital, and capitalism, 34; in 1980s, 60. See also capital formation, net
capital formation, net, and deficits, 143, 144; determining, 70, 141; in 1960s and 1970s, 60; and Reagan economics, 73
capitalism, British attitudes toward, 208, 211; conservative view of, 9-10; development of, 8; features of, 8-9, 34, 36, 64; government role in, 33-34; liberal view of, 10, 13; role of individualism in, 9; and supply-side economics, 5; in Third World, 233
"capital shortage," in Reaganomics, 74
Carleson, Robert B., 194
Carter, Jimmy, 177; administration of, 45, 65, 119, 120, 205; EPA under, 88, 89; current services budget of, 100; and FED, 148; and government spending, 92, 93; and military spending, 121, 129
Chile, 4
Churchill, Winston, 64
Civil War, 190
classical economics, 26, 29, 203-04; and supply-siders, 50. See also supply-side economics
Cloward, Richard A., 117
Coe, Richard, 109
Cogan, John, 101, 104, 108
Collins, Lora, 140, 144
Commager, Henry Steele, 185
Common Cause, 41
Comprehensive Employment and Training Act (CETA), 100-01, 119
Congress, effectiveness of, 180; supply-siders in, 236
Consciousness Revolution (Wuthnow), 14
conservative economics, philosophy of, 9, 37; and supply-side economics, 11. See also Reagan economics; supply-side economics
Constitution, and national idea, 187; and New Federalism, 180, 184, 185
consumer product testing, benefit-cost analysis of, 79-80
consumption, and national output, 141; tax bias for, 143, 144
Coolidge, Calvin, 35, 55
corporate repos, 163
cost, incremental, 79
Costa Rica, 235, 237
cost effectiveness, 86. See also benefit-cost analysis
cotton industry, health hazards in, 83-84, 85
Council of Economic Advisors, 76, 135, 136